Intercultural Organizational Communication

Lisbeth Clausen

Intercultural Organizational Communication

Five Corporate Cases in Japan

Copenhagen Business School Press

Intercultural Organizational Communication
Five Corporate Cases in Japan

© Copenhagen Business School Press
Printed in Denmark by Narayana Press, Gylling
Cover design by Daniel Sjöfors, Blå Huset, Sweden. Japanese cover-quote by
Karl-Heinz Toosbuy, see p. 205
1. edition 2006

ISBN 87-630-0160-8

Distribution:

Scandinavia
DJOEF/DBK, Mimersvej 4
DK-4600 Køge, Denmark
Phone: +45 3269 7788, fax: +45 3269 7789

North America
Copenhagen Business School Press
Books International Inc.
P.O. Box 605
Herndon, VA 20172-0605, USA
Phone: +1 703 661 1500, fax: +1 703 661 1501

Rest of the World
Marston Book Services, P.O. Box 269
Abingdon, Oxfordshire, OX14 4YN, UK
Phone: +44 (0) 1235 465500, fax: +44 (0) 1235 4656555
E-mail Direct Customers: direct.order@marston.co.uk
E-mail Booksellers: trade.order@marston.co.uk

Acknowledgements

This book addresses intercultural issues in business communication between corporate headquarters in Denmark and subsidiaries and alliance partners in Japan. For Danish companies, Japan is an important and interesting market, as it is a highly profitable one and the quality expectations of Japanese consumers mean that products accepted in Japan are quality-stamped worldwide. Experience with the Japanese market also provides an advantageous stepping stone with respect to the rapidly developing Chinese market. Nevertheless, cultural issues and the complexities of penetrating the Japanese market provide substantial challenges for Danish companies. This book presents and analyzes the cultural lessons learned from the perspective of both Danish headquarters and their Japanese subsidiaries and alliance partners.

The book is targeted bachelor, master and MBA students in intercultural communication and management. Although it is meant to serve as teaching material, I hope that business professionals will also find inspiration and interesting insights applicable to their own organizations concerning the management of intercultural communication between headquarters and subsidiary/alliances.

I would like to thank the Danish Social Science Research Council for financing the project on 'management, organization and competence' (LOK) in cooperation with the participating companies and the Department of Intercultural Communication and Management at Copenhagen Business School.

I would also like to pay tribute to the many individuals who have contributed to the development of this project. Without their professional and personal help, feedback and inspiration this book would not have been possible. First, I would like to extend my sincere appreciation to the people involved from each of the participating companies, as this book is built on their reflections.

Specifically, I would like to thank: Bo Bendixen and the Huis Ten Bosch managers Paul S. Takada, Ai Kawanami, Yuki Maeda, and

Hiroshi Iwashiya; from VisitDenmark, Flemming Bruhn, Tanja Ibsen Nørskov, Karim Grau Nielsen, and Harro Christensen; from the Scandinavian Tourist Board, Asia, Søren Leerskov, Shoko Itoh, Kjell Ellefsen, Tue Paarup, Kazumi Yamanashi, Anne Stromoy, Kazumi Yamanashi, Midori Okabe, Nagisa Imamura, Yoshiko Asakawa, and Yuko Sato; from Rosendahl A/S, Henrik Rosendahl, Martin Glisby, Lin Utzon, Hiroki Saito, and Kuniko Matsushima Rasmussen; with respect to Rosendahl's business relations in Japan, Marehiko Yamada, Yasuhiro Ueda, Natsuyo Iwama, Takahiro Murakami, and Shizuo Koyama; from ECCO A/S, Jens Christian Meier, Kirsten Moesgaard, Axel Carlsen, Søren Steffensen, Henrik Noer, and Michael Hauge Sørensen; from Achilles (ECCO Sales Japan), Shizuya Yamanaka, K. Tonooka, Teruaki Nagashima, Shiaki Yoshi, and Jens Aarup Mikkelsen; and from Bang & Olufsen, Anders Knutsen, Lars Myrup, Chiyuki Komuro, Yoko Okuno, Takatoshi Hashimoto, and Emiko Fukuda.

I would also like to thank the flowing experts and diplomats for their insights: Senior Advisor Shigehiko Koshiba, Lundbeck; Mikael Østerrøgild Nielsen, Oak Associates; Pernille Storm, the Royal Danish Embassy in Tokyo; Hans Peter Kay, European Trainee Program (ETP); Junkichi Suzuki and Kristine Ahrensbach from the Danish Agricultural Council.

I appreciate the helpful academic advice on book chapters from my colleagues Lise Skov, Esben Karmark, Dana Minbaeva, Annette Risberg, Can-Seng Ooi, Anne-Marie Søderberg, Hans Hugo Arndt and Vesa Peltokorpi.

I would like to recognize Annika Dilling for the initial inspiration to undertake a LOK project and for helping me to apply for funding. I thank Pernille Andersen, my research assistant, who coordinated all activities related to the project. She transcribed the majority of the interviews and performed the layout for the entire book. I could not have completed the project without her professionalism and organizational skills.

I am also indebted to the following people for their assistance: Anne Mette Hou and Winnie Pejtersen for their support; Yoko Iijima and Aya Bisgaard for transcribing the Japanese interviews and translating them into English; Eugene Lyon Pottenger for proof-reading and excellent language work; Bente Faurby for IT support; and Hanne Thorninger Ipsen and Ole Wiberg from CBS Press for inspiring meetings.

Finally, I thank my husband Knud Munk for daily encouragement and continuous support and I kiss my daughters Sofia and Amanda to whom I owe much inspiration – and time.

Copenhagen, January 2006
Lisbeth Clausen

Note: ECCO Shoes A/S, Rosendahl A/S and Bang & Olufsen A/S are all public companies, but for brevity are referred to in the book without the A/S. The people interviewed hold different managerial positions in their companies; however, in this book they are all referred to as 'global managers'. All Japanese names follow the Western tradition with surnames last.

Table of Contents

Preface

Interview with His Excellency Gotaro Ogawa, the Japanese Ambassador to Denmark, December 2005.

How does the recovery of the Japanese economy affect Danish business?
At long last the Japanese economy seems to be recovering, and now after some 15 years analysts in the government and the private sector agree that this recovery is real and sustainable. International financial institutions and economic organizations also consider Japan to be in the middle of recovery. I am therefore quite confident that our economy will grow, not at a very high rate but rather steadily for some years at least. Companies are making profits and consumer spending is increasing. So there are many strong indicators which predict a future sustainable recovery. Many Danish companies have the impression that the Japanese market is challenging, but the ones who have made an effort have been successful. I can tell you that the Japanese market might be challenging, but it is also a very rewarding market of 127 million people with a strong purchasing power.

How are Danish businesses doing in Japan and what are their future prospects?
I have talked with Danish CEOs and managers and I think that Danish business people are doing quite well in Japan compared to other nationalities. My first impression is that Danish companies have their own well-defined special sectors and niche industries. Secondly, my impression from talking to Danish business people is that they consider human relationships to be a very important factor in doing business. Danish business people often seem to be successful at establishing good relationships with Japanese counterparts based on mutual confidence. In order to do this, Danish business people have a lot of contact with their counterpart and make a significant effort to understand them. The third point, perhaps, is that Denmark has a rather

good system for supporting business activities abroad. The Royal Family plays an important role, as we have seen with the visit of the Danish Queen and Prince Consort to Japan in November 2004, and on many other occasions of course. Also, you have a trade council in the foreign ministry, and a section at the Danish Embassy in Japan that facilitates Danish business activities. I think the combination of these factors means that the future prospects for Danish business in Japan are quite promising.

To follow up on your first point, which sectors do you think offer the greatest opportunities for Danish companies?
The design and welfare sectors, for instance, may present opportunities for Danish companies. Danish design is well-known and Japanese consumers are quite receptive to it. When advertising, it is good to stress being Danish. At the same time, the tastes of the younger generation are changing rapidly and it is important to find out what young consumers want. Another target market may be senior citizens who have retired and who are seeking a comfortable and stylish retirement. They also have substantial purchasing power. Novelty, and product specificity or differentiation are important factors in attracting Japanese consumers. Finally, Japan is trying to cope with the growing need for social welfare and elder care, and there is room for cooperation to take advantage of Danish experience and know-how in this area. Of course, further market research is of great importance.

Concerning your second point about human relations and business, how are Danish businesses doing with respect to cultural difference?
In fact, some aspects of the Danish and Japanese mentalities go quite well together in the sense that Danes try to respect the feelings of others and try to promote harmony. These considerations are very important when doing business in Japan, and many Danish business people are successful in this regard. They listen and show respect for their Japanese counterparts' arguments and ideas and also incorporate them into company policy. They also participate in the Japanese custom of networking. They talk business at the office, but they take the trouble to have dinner and drinks together to discuss business in an informal setting – which is also the Japanese style. Some Danes even invite their business associates to their homes and get close in this way. Establishing relationships is very rewarding when dealing with Japan. It enables long lasting confidence and mutual trust. To maintain

these relationships, it is also important not to do something that will cause your business partner to question this trust.

What do you mean by mental similarities?
It is my feeling living in Denmark that Danish people are open, casual and frank. They are also pragmatic, so it is very easy to discuss matters of substance. In Japan, we are rather formal, you know, and especially at first meetings we have to say something formal. But Danes are more direct and talk with confidence, which are very good points. However, compared to other countries within Europe, Danes are a little bit more reserved. They are not aggressive, which makes it easier for the Japanese to feel comfortable and speak freely. Having said that, it is also important that Danish business people consider the Japanese way of doing business, which includes such things as respecting hierarchy. If they respect this way of doing things, I think they can go far in business.

Another similarity, I believe, is connected to the Law of Jante [the Law of Jante is described in full in Chapter Two, footnote number ten]. I know many Danes are not happy with this interpretation, and Prime Minister Anders Fogh Rasmussen has said that we should overcome it, but in relation to Japan its influence becomes a positive factor. I see some characteristics in the Danish people that may come from this Jante's Law and which facilitates human relationships with the Japanese. Because of this, we feel comfortable and very much at ease being with Danes. If a partner from another country takes a very high handed, aggressive and very assertive attitude, the Japanese tend to be careful and may not say what they want to say. With the Danish attitude, we can talk more freely. We share the concept that we should be humble and not think that we are the best, as we are influenced by Confucian ethics that teach us to be humble, to be reserved, to respect others and so forth.

Your third point concerns the importance of Royal support for Danish business. How is this looked upon in Japan?
The good relations that exist between the Japanese Imperial Family and the Danish Royal Family create a feeling of closeness between the Danes and the Japanese. The visit to Japan in 2004 by the Danish Queen drew a lot of attention among the Japanese. Members of the Japanese Imperial Family do not play a role in business, but when the Danish Royal Family does, I think it makes a strong and favorable impression on the Japanese public.

As a final comment, what would your advice be to Danish companies that wish to establish themselves in Japan?

In Japan, there are many small and medium sized companies, of course, and the chances are good that Danish companies can find good business partners. But it is not always easy to find an appropriate partner. One way is to seek assistance from the Danish Embassy, and JETRO (Japan External Trade Organization) also has a number of good systems to match Japanese companies with foreign counterparts. JETRO has a lot of information, as well as the channels to distribute the information to potential Japanese partners.

Thank you for your cultural insights.

Chapter One

INTRODUCTION: DANISH BUSINESS IN JAPAN

Global Challenges in Communication

Ongoing changes in modern economies are influencing the basis on which corporations can build sustainable competitive advantages. Fundamental advances in information and communication technologies, as well as the imperative of innovation due to stronger competition, are making communication across boarders ever more important. International managers and researchers alike have looked for new ways to answer questions about the challenges of managing the complexity of intercultural communication when coping with overseas markets and alliance partners. Within this framework, if we consider the case of Denmark and Japan, the Japanese market is the tenth most important in terms of exports for Danish companies (Confederation of Danish Industries). Beyond its size, Japan is also a lucrative market on a per capita basis. However, the Japanese market poses a number of significant challenges to foreign companies due to its complex systems of business networking and its demanding, highly quality-conscious consumers. Danish companies which already face many general communication challenges in the competitive new economy are therefore doubly challenged when it comes to dealing with Japan. Within this setting, strategies to enhance entry mode, organizational structure, and intercultural communication with Japanese alliance partners and subsidiaries become critical in the pursuit of competitive advantage. The focus of this project is to explore how Danish companies cope with these cultural differences in facilitating communication and information exchange within companies and between headquarters and subsidiaries/alliance partners. This analysis is the first step in examining how these companies successfully facilitate the diffusion of knowledge that can be shared, combined and recombined within the company's global operations. Of particular importance will be the identification of processes that either inhibit or promote the incorporation of locally developed subsidiary/alliance partner knowledge and innovations into overall company strategy. Each company has its own set of ideas, strategic goals and communication practices. Common to all is the fact that they must try to overcome the asymmetrical amount of knowledge that exists either internally within the organization in Denmark and Japan – or between the organization and the subsidiary/alliance partner.

Does Culture Matter?

A large body of literature has examined the cultural uniqueness of Japan with respect to its markets, business and consumer practices and cultural factors in personal communication. It is generally asserted in intercultural communication studies (Samovar & Porter, 1997) that people from Western and Asian cultures have the greatest chance of misunderstanding each other. However, many of these studies have focused on US – Japan relations and therefore highlight differences between two very different countries and cultures (Ito, 2000). The present study provides insight into the complexity of bi-cultural communication between Denmark and Japan. It highlights not only cultural differences, but also cultural similarities that are in fact found to enhance communication.

Leading researchers in comparative management studies (Hofstede, 1980; Hampden-Turner & Trompenaars, 1993; Hall, 1959) have investigated how elements of national culture dominate the way people act, think and feel. Hofstede, for instance, argues that people are 'mentally programmed' by their national culture and that their mindsets determine how they act in intercultural encounters. According to this logic, these national values and characteristics can be used to determine likely future behavior. Countering this position, other researchers see culture as a collective and relational construct that is continuously being redefined in new contextual settings (Søderberg & Holden, 2002). Rather than being static, culture is therefore understood to be 'negotiated' and 'emerging' (Brannen & Salk, 2000). In particular, this perspective enables the study of processes and change. Rather than merely looking at national characteristics and values (which are admittedly important within limits), I see communication between individuals in organizations as complex and dynamic. Intercultural communication in this project is presented as being influenced by global, national, organizational, professional and individual factors. A multilevel model for analysis is developed and presented in Chapter Two. Also as part of this project, I show that the 'sophisticated' stereotypes (Osland & Bird, 2000) developed by the researchers above do no suffice, and I go behind and beyond these stereotypes to explore and describe cultural encounters in-depth and at length through the stories told by the people who experience these encounters.

It will become clear through the presentation of this study that cultural differences do matter in international business encounters and that communication and culture must be viewed as complex and dynamic processes.

The Aim of the Project and Questions Asked

The aim of the project is to generate knowledge of Danish business practices in relation to Japan through dialogue with employees from the companies involved. I investigate the professional practices, values and perceptions embedded within companies and the communication of these within the organization or between the Danish headquarters and the Japanese partner/subsidiary. The points of departure are challenges as seen from a cultural and communications perspective. The issues in focus are (see communication displays 2.1 and 2.2):

- Communication practices between companies and subsidiaries/ alliances (encoding and decoding).
- The communication of strategies in relation to distribution/ branding/retail consumers/product development (messages).
- The organization of communication (channels).
- Organizational learning between headquarters and subsidiaries/ alliances (feedback).
- The influence of culture on the above processes (noise).
- The development of intercultural management competencies and methods of dealing with business practices 'uniquely' Danish or Japanese (sender-receiver, dialogical co-creation).

Overall, the interviews that I conducted showed that although most companies have global strategies for sales and marketing, the actual implementation of these strategies in Japan involves significant adaptation. A Japanese partnership or subsidiary clearly presents cultural challenges to the organization and the people involved with Japan – and vice versa.

Fifty Managers from Five Companies

The project involves five Danish companies. Fifty managers from these companies made time for in-depth interviews about communication within their organizations, cultural differences and communication hurdles, strategies for coping, and lessons learned in promoting cooperation between organizations in Denmark and a subsidiary or partner(s) in Japan. The research design and method are described in the appendix.

As it turns out, successful business practices and strategies for the Japanese market are a combination of hard work, insightful and innovative investigation of strategic choices, loyal networks and appropriate social interaction, good timing, sensitivity, and sometimes just plain luck. The five Danish companies have managed to communicate, socialize, develop strong commitments and act dynamically, all in a market that is both physically and culturally distant from Denmark. Finally, they have also all made efforts to both leverage existing Japanese consumer trends and to co-create some new ones in order to develop the full potential of the market.

In this chapter, I first introduce the state of Danish business in Japan. I then introduce the participating companies and their particular organization in Japan, including the business context and considerations involved in market entry. Next, I answer the question: what are the images created or leveraged in Japan? I then outline the overall market potential based on input from each of the companies. Finally, in the last section, I show how managers become accustomed to a new culture, using the example of an American expatriate in Japan who relates his own learning processes. At the end of the chapter, I introduce each of the subsequent chapters of the book.

Danish Business in Japan

Japan is the world's second largest consumer market after the United States with 127 million high-income potential customers. Obviously, Japan has a lot to offer and is a potentially lucrative market for companies not yet doing business there. At the same time, however, the Japanese market also poses significant challenges to foreign companies seeking to tap this potential.

The foreign chambers of commerce in Japan analyzed the present outlook of foreign companies currently doing business in the market. The report states that ninety-nine percent of the companies surveyed view Japan as 'a land of opportunity'. Breaking this figure down, seventy-two percent expect continued growth during the next year, twenty-seven percent expect to maintain their present level of activity, and only one percent of the companies expect declining results. Notably, not a single company planned to withdraw form the market (Market Profile, 2004).

For the Confederation of Danish Industries, Japan is the tenth most important export market. Eighty Danish companies have subsidiaries in Japan and even more sell through agents. Danish food items, health products, transportation services and consumer goods are available in the Japanese market, and most large Danish companies have an established presence in the country. The food sector is represented by Danish Crown, Arla Foods, Danisco and Royal Greenland. The medico companies are Novo Nordic, Novozymes, LEO Pharma, Lundbeck, Coloplast, Widex, Oticon and Radiometer. Industrial machinery and equipment companies include Grundfoss, Foss Electric, JAI and MAN Diesel and the windmill producers NEG Micon and Vestas. The consumer goods industry has such representatives as Royal Scandinavia, Bang & Olufsen, Lego, Fritz Hansen, ECCO, Louis Poulsen Lighting and BoConcept. Finally, the shipping industry is represented by Mahe, J. Lauritzen, Armada Shipping and Maersk Sealand. Overall, Danish products currently make up only 0.6 percent of the Japanese market, although Denmark supplies thirty percent of the total amount of pork imported into Japan, and this in turn accounts for half of all Danish exports to the country. Interestingly, Danish pork has paved the way for other Danish products, particularly within the food industry. This has been accomplished through the promotion of an image of safety, cleanliness, and environmental friendliness. While Danish imports from Japan were DKK 3.5 billion in 2004, exports totaled DKK 17.3 billion, making Denmark one of the few countries in Europe that can boast a trade surplus with Japan. Although these figures are not enormous, they are nonetheless considerable according to the Japanese Minister of Economy, Trade and Industry (METI) Shoichi Nakagawa.[1] Areas with promising future potential, according to estimates by the Danish Embassy in Tokyo, are convenience and health foods, design and home appliances and eldercare equipment (The Trade Council of Denmark, 2004: 50).

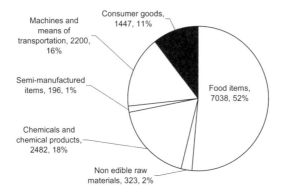

Display 1.1 Danish exports to Japan, in million DKK and percentage of total (Statistics Denmark, 2004)

Dealing with Cultural Challenges – A Case

Danish companies pursuing business in Japan are faced with both general communication challenges and those specific to the Japanese market. The following case illustrates how a Danish newcomer to the market tackled these culturally embedded issues. It is based on a presentation (Hatting Bakery, 2004) given at the Confederation of Danish Industries headquarters in Copenhagen as part of the preparations surrounding the promotional trip to Japan by the Royal Family and various business associations in November 2004.

Hatting Bakeries, part of the international Cerealia Food Group, started to export frozen bread products to Japan in 1996 after being discovered at a food fair in Japan. In 2003, Cerealia Japan was established and Hatting Bakery formed a partnership with Mitsubishi, one of the largest trading companies in Japan. Together, the partnership soon reached sales of DKK 200 million. What was the formula for their success? According to Managing Director Bent Pultz Larsen, the most important step was to make the right connections. Also, the product was both timely and a good fit for the market, largely due to the fact that there were few competitors in the pre-made frozen bread segment, a segment which represented the core competence of Hatting Bakeries. Hatting Bakeries worked for almost a decade on establishing the business agreements, but the payback for the time and effort invested has been that their Japanese partners have been extremely loyal.

The biggest hurdle to forming these partnerships was that the Japanese have the world's highest quality norms, according to the managing director. At first, it was difficult for the bakery employees in Horsens, Jutland, to accept the scrutiny of their Japanese counterparts. However, as a result of the agreement, company pride has developed around the stringent quality testing that has been required. In a very real sense, Japanese 'quality control' has given Hatting Bakeries a competitive edge in global bread production, since a 'certification of quality' from Japan is respected worldwide, according to the managing director. Another important cultural difference that has influenced the process has been that that Danes are typically independent self-starters who assume personal responsibility for their work, while the Japanese practice group decision making and view such personal initiative as ego-centric. The Danes 'prioritize' their work (some issues are more or less important according to their own agenda), and this is often perceived as laziness by the Japanese, who pay attention to everything – in detail. Finally, according to the managing director, Danes make promises at the negotiating table but often forget the smaller details (or reinterpret them to suit their agenda). In Japan, keeping promises even down to the finest detail is expected, and to not do so is a sign of general untrustworthiness. Despite this array of challenges, the most difficult issue for Hatting Bakeries has been the scrutiny to which their products and process have been subjected, in particular because they considered them already to be of high-quality. The key to success, in retrospect, has been not just to maintain an existing level of quality, but to consistently deliver more than promised. When this has not been possible, it has been critical to attend to problems within twenty-four hours and have a resolution ready at hand. Finally, openness to new ideas and a focus on new product innovation have been a winning combination. As seen above, cultural issues present continuous challenges to Danish companies. Against this, the political situation in Japan remains rather stable.

Good News from the Land of the Rising Sun

Japanese politics have been stable under the leadership of Prime Minister Koizumi, who was re-elected in October 2005. His government supports free enterprise and, although economic reform has been slow due to resistance even from within Koizumi's own

Liberal Democratic Party, efforts have been made to increase Japan's inward FDI. The closed corporate system of cross-ownership (keiretsu) between Japanese companies, often centered on a bank together with a large trading and manufacturing conglomerate, has been discouraged for more than a decade. Nevertheless, strong informal tries and agreements still hold between trading houses, wholesalers and retailers, and this complicates market entry for foreign companies.

While trade barriers have been cut and market entry is now easier, approval of foreign patents is still an extremely slow process. However, free-trade policies are expected to lead to bilateral free-trade agreements with South East Asia and Latin America, and the WTO Doha agreements in 2004 included negotiations with Malaysia, Thailand, Philippines and South Korea. Nonetheless, trade restrictions and quota systems still have implications for some of the companies participating in the study.

One very bright spot is the fact that the bad-debt crisis that had paralyzed banks and private companies is now under control, according to the chief Japan analyst at Merrill Lynch Japan, Jesper Koll. Banks and private companies have reduced their debt dramatically and this has freed resources for new investments that in turn should support economic growth (speech, 17 November 2004).

While China is predicted to catch up in ten to fifteen years in terms of GNP, Japan will still be a world economic power with a very important internal market. It is estimated by the Trade Council of Denmark that the growth in China is seen by the present Japanese government "as a win-win situation if both parties play their cards right" (the Trade Council of Denmark, 2004: 45-48). Within this context, as we will hear from the companies involved in this project, regional strategy in Asia involves both Japan and China.

Five Danish Companies – Consumer Products

The companies presented in this project are all in the consumer products/experience industry and range in size from very small (a few employees) to quite large by Danish standards (over 9000 employees).

The brands are well-known in Denmark, and four of the companies (Bo Bendixen, Rosendahl, Bang & Olufsen and ECCO) have flagship stores in the upscale shopping district of central Copenhagen. The companies are well-established in the Danish home market, and they have been represented in Japan for periods ranging from 7-24 years. The following is an introduction to the companies, their products, and their organizational setup in Japan. As we will see, Japan is important to these companies not only for its own market potential, but also for its role in the development of corporate strategies for the Asia Pacific Region. This introduction briefly describes the challenges faced by each company in Japan, with individual cases described fully in the subsequent chapters.

Bo Bendixen Graphic Design

Bo Bendixen Graphic Design started doing business in Japan in 1991. The company designs and sells postcards and other souvenir items, and Bo Bendixen is both chief designer and the owner of the company. His postcards were discovered in the Netherlands by one of the directors of a new Japanese theme park, the Dutch village Huis Ten Bosch. If you are a small to medium size business, being discovered is without a doubt the most favorable mode of entry to the Japanese market. In forming the partnership, Bo Bendixen signed an exclusive licensing agreement with Huis Ten Bosch. However, Huis Ten Bosch, like other theme parks, has faced difficult times economically and was recently taken over by Nomura Principal Finance, a financial holding company. Nonetheless, Bo Bendixen's products are among the few that still generate considerable revenue for the park. Because of this, Bo Bendixen's store in the park has doubled in size, despite the economic downturn.

Overall, the experience has been culturally challenging for both parties, and the case chapter highlights a number of cultural differences at several levels. Despite the challenges, however, Bo Bendixen is an exemplary success story of a small Danish company that has made it big in Japan. Although the initial plan was to expand further into Asia, this is currently on hold for a number of reasons that will be discussed in detail in the case chapter.

Display 1.2 Bo Bendixen's logo

Rosendahl Interior Design Products and Kitchen Utensils

Rosendahl is a family owned business producing interior design goods and kitchen utensils. The company entered the Japanese market in 1998 with very limited sales. However, through agents and importers, Rosendahl products are now displayed in the most prestigious department stores in Japan and the country is the company's second largest export market. One of the reasons for this success is a wining combination of market knowledge, linguistic and cultural competencies, and entrepreneurial spirit. In particular, the Rosendahl case will highlight the very thorough and well-planned strategy which leveraged the Danish Royal Family and business delegation visit to Japan in November 2004. This strategy had two main objectives: to build closer relationships with Rosendahl's partners and to upgrade the brand's image by promoting an exclusive line of porcelain in conjunction with the H.C. Andersen bicentennial. Rosendahl was successful in achieving both of these objectives.

The case chapter focuses on how Rosendahl has innovatively reshuffled cultural dos and don'ts in working with Japan – and in doing so has created a new and successful organizational setup that has fostered closer ties to their business partners. Rosendahl coordinates its business transactions with Japan from their headquarters in Denmark. China is seen as an up and coming opportunity.

Display 1.3 Rosendahl's logo

	Market Entry	Products	Ownership	Organizational setup in Japan	Importance of Japanese market	Coordination of Asian activities
Bo Bendixen	1991	Designs, posters, postcards, t-shirts	Bo Bendixen owner	License partner (exclusive)	Most important international market	Headquarters, Denmark
Rosendahl	1998	Interior design items and kitchen utensils, H.C. Andersen porcelain	Rosendahl family owner	Several importer and agent partners	Second largest export market	Headquarters, Denmark
Scandinavian Tourist Board	1986	Tourism promotion and research for Scandinavian partners	The national tourist offices of Sweden, Norway & Denmark	Subsidiary (A/S)	Tenth largest market	Tokyo office
Bang & Olufsen	1982	Audio – visual design products	Bang & Olufsen Group A/S	Subsidiary (K.K.)	13th largest market in sales (5 percent of total sales)	Singapore office
ECCO	1982	Casual leather and golf shoes	Family owned	License partner (exclusive)	Third largest market in sales	Hong Kong Office

Display 1.4 Five Danish companies in Japan, key details

25

Scandinavian Tourist Board – Tourism Promotion in Asia

The former Danish Tourist Board, now called VisitDenmark, started promotion in Japan in 1970, and the joint Scandinavian Tourist Board (STB) was established in Tokyo in 1986. The office promotes Norwegian, Swedish and Danish tourist destinations and tourism related organizations to consumers and, most importantly, to the travel trade. It is an independent company registered in Denmark and jointly owned by the Swedish Tourism and Travel Council, Innovation Norway and VisitDenmark. Private businesses and public organizations from the tourism industry in all three countries are partners in the promotion of tourism projects. This partnership between government and private tourism businesses has been particularly successful in Japan, measured by the involvement and financial investment of the Danish tourism industry. Business activities are approved by the Scandinavian board members from all three countries. Currently, there are 80,000-100,000 Japanese bed-nights in Denmark annually, and while this number is modest in comparison with tourists from other countries, the Japanese spend a relatively larger amount of money during their stays, thus making investments in developing the market worthwhile.

The company case demonstrates how Japan differs from other tourism markets and how the Tokyo office is a cultural cocktail of the best of Scandinavian and Japanese management practices. The Scandinavian Tourist Board is a regional office in the sense that all other tourism promotion activities in China, the Philippines and Korea are coordinated from the Tokyo office.

Display 1.5 Logo of Scandinavian Tourist Board, Asia

Bang & Olufsen Audio – Visual Equipment

Bang & Olufsen first entered Japan in 1982 and has used two different organizational setups: wholly owned subsidiaries and an importing arrangement. The company sells high-end audio visual and communication equipment known for its stylish and functional design and Japan is currently their thirteenth largest market. When Bang & Olufsen decided to close their first subsidiary in 1993, they left their business in the hands of an industry partner. In 2000, Bang & Olufsen reestablished a subsidiary in Japan, and this presented them with a new opportunity to focus on strengthening customer relationships.

The case chapter deals with the changes in company culture as Bang & Olufsen's presence in Japan transitioned from a wholly-owned subsidiary to an importer and back to a wholly-owned subsidiary. With respect to Asia, Bang & Olufsen opened an Asia Pacific Regional office in Singapore in 2003 to support retail and franchise marketing and training in Asia. According to Lars Myrup, the president of Bang & Olufsen Japan, the company will structurally and strategically focus much more on Asia in the coming years.

BANG & OLUFSEN

Display 1.6 Bang & Olufsen's logo

ECCO Shoes

ECCO Shoes have been represented in Japan since 1982 by the Japanese shoe manufacturer Achilles, and the market is now their third largest in sales behind the United States and Germany. ECCO is the fifth largest brown (casual and leather) shoe brand in the world. In 2003, ECCO renewed their licensing agreement with Achilles for another ten years. The coordination of production, logistics, design and development, branding, and sales and marketing is monitored from headquarters in the two towns Bredebro and Tønder in Jutland, the western part of Denmark.

However, in line with their goal to create a global brand, ECCO would like to have even more influence on activities in Japan, and the case chapter analyzes how ECCO is working to implement its global brand strategies within the Japanese market. As part of this process, organizing and ensuring the effectiveness of intercultural communication arise as central challenges.

In 2002, an Asia Pacific office was established in Hong Kong as an operational platform for the region. The Hong Kong office develops the annual business plan for the region and mediates communication between headquarters and Japan. In this sense, Japan is an important market both in its own right and as part of ECCO's strategy for growth in Asia. Recently, ECCO established a factory in China that is already producing several million shoes annually.

Display 1.7 ECCO's logo

Without a doubt, all of the participating companies see the Asian region as increasingly important, and some have established regional offices to coordinate their activities. Nevertheless, there has been a uniform strategy of successfully entering and establishing a platform of operations in Japan before moving on to tackle other countries, such as China which now is seen as particularly promising. As part of this process, the focus of this book is the exploration of how these five companies have successfully navigated cultural challenges in order to promote effective intercultural communication between their Danish headquarters and their Japanese subsidiaries or alliance partners.

Images of Denmark in Japan

How do the Japanese perceive Denmark and Danish products? The following introduces some of the promotion that has taken place with respect to Denmark and Danish products, certain core images that the Japanese have of Denmark, and a few of the more important trends within the Japanese market that, as we shall see, have been leveraged by some of the companies in this study.

The Royal Family and Business Delegation Visit

The largest Danish business promotional activity ever in Japan was the Royal, state and business delegation visit 15-19 November 2004. The state visit was coordinated by the Danish Foreign Ministry, the Trade Council of Denmark, the Royal Danish Embassy in Tokyo and the Danish agency Export Promotion Denmark (EES). It lasted four days and featured fifty-two Danish companies of all sizes plus nine organizations representing diplomatic, ministerial, and business councils. Given the Japanese preoccupation with royalty, the participation of the Danish Royal Family gave a very special boost to the proceedings, and by association allowed many of the Danish companies to strengthen their image with both their Japanese business partners and the public at large.

Most activities took place at the Grand Hyatt Hotel in Roppongi in Tokyo. On 17 November, the windmill company Vestas and Aalborg Industries conducted exhibitions and workshops for their business partners, while Royal Copenhagen, Louis Poulsen Lighting, Fritz Hansen and Bang & Olufsen presented a joint exhibition in the Mori Hall at the hotel. Nearby, Prince Henrik met Seiichi Takaki, the president of the Andersen Bakery Group, which owns 54 Little Mermaid and 457 Andersen bakeries in Japan. The designer Charlotte Sparre, who had exclusive rights to produce H.C. Andersen merchandise, made a joint exhibition of products together with Skagen Design and Rosendahl. A formal lunch was arranged by the Danish Queen Margrethe and Prince Henrik for 400 guests. Later that evening, the Japanese Emperor and Empress hosted a dinner reception at the Royal Palace for the Royal Family, members of the Danish delegation and prominent members of the Japanese business and political communities. In particular, the presence of the Danish Royal Family was seen as a special honor.

Most of the delegation companies took advantage of the opportunity to invite their business partners to Queen Margrethe's lunch, as well as to the very special dinner reception hosted by the Japanese Emperor at the Imperial Palace in Tokyo. Since the Japanese have a much more formal relationship with their Royal Family, this was a rare and extraordinary opportunity.

Clearly the involvement of the Danish Royal Family provided an invaluable boost to the businesses represented. In particular, the presence of Royalty helped to give an 'official stamp of approval' to the companies involved, according to Birger Riis-Jørgensen, president of the Trade Council of Denmark (Trade Council of Denmark homepage). Although the effect may not have been immediately visible, it was of great importance in establishing and strengthening future relationships, something of the utmost importance in Japan. Especially for small and medium sized companies, this was a unique opportunity to create momentum.

Display 1.8 The Danish Royal Couple with the Japanese Emperor and Empress in Tokyo, November 2004 (Photo: Reuters/Scanpix)

The Hans Christian Andersen Bicentennial Celebration

The H.C. Andersen Foundation was established a few years ago in preparation for the celebration of the bicentennial of the author's birth. Lars Seeberg, the former general director went to Japan as part of the entourage of business people, politicians, academics and journalists accompanying the Danish Queen on 17 November 2004. As part of the overall events, nine H.C. Andersen ambassadors were appointed by the Danish Ambassador in Japan at the time, Poul Hoiness. The ambassadors appointed were: designer Jun Ashida, actress Masumi Okada, singers Sachiko Yasuda and Saori Yuki, Danish consul and president for Andersen Bakeries, Seiichi Takaki, tennis player Shuzo Matsuoka, TV-host Matthew Minami, singer Ryoko Tsunoda and football player Yoshikatsu Kawaguchi (goal-keeper for the Danish football club FC Nordsjælland in 2004).

Involved with the appointment of ambassadors was also Shigehiko Koshiba, nicknamed 'Mr. Porcelain', who has been an advisor and promoter of Danish design in Japan since 1965. Shigehiko Koshiba is the former chairman of Royal Copenhagen and executive vice president of the company's Asia Pacific region. Among his successful engagements he has established businesses for Royal Copenhagen and

George Jensen in Asia, and he is presently a senior advisor for several Danish design companies. Not surprisingly, Shigehiko Koshiba is well connected, and many of his friends and business associates hold important positions among the Japanese business elite. Thanks to this network of business relationships, his endorsement has instantly secured substantial business for any company under his care. Shigehiko Koshiba praised Rosendahl's initiative in promoting H.C. Andersen via the commercial means of the H.C. Andersen porcelain series. However, he thought the Andersen Foundation should have started their preparations many years in advance to effectively promote the Danish writer. According to Koshiba:

> *Danes are overconfident with respect to H.C. Andersen. They think that everybody knows the H.C. Andersen fairy tales, but the Japanese youngsters only remember the titles. Japan has one of the world's leading animation industries and the Japanese are keen animation buffs. If the H.C. Andersen foundation had made an animated movie like 'Finding Nemo'* [a Disney/Pixar blockbuster]*, the Japanese would have more readily become reacquainted with the H.C. Andersen fairy tales. The H.C. Andersen foundation should have been in continuous planning for ten years to make the H.C. Andersen event a success.*

Despite the above criticism, the celebration of the H.C. Andersen bicentennial (2 April 2005) ended with a great deal of activity after all. At the mass communication level, the national Japanese broadcaster NHK agreed to produce a thirty-nine-episode animated series of Hans Christian Andersen's The Snow Queen. The Snow Queen is to be aired between early 2005 and January 2006 as arranged by Hans Peter Kay, Commercial Attaché, Royal Danish Embassy Tokyo (Interview, 21 September 2004).

H.C. Andersen's birth city Odense has a Japanese sister city, Funabashi, a suburb to Tokyo. Here Hans Christian Andersen has his own park with miniatures of houses from the Funen Village and landscapes that illustrate the writer's fairy tales. The park contains complete replicas of Danish houses, farms and windmills as well as the H.C. Andersen house in Odense. Among other highlights, Crown Princess Mary visited the park to open an exhibition of the Tinderbox. Later, Thumbelina was staged at the park, as well as at various locations throughout Japan. The choice of Thumbelina reflected the fact that nature is an integral part of Japanese culture. Nature was also a central theme for Hans Christian Andersen, according to chairperson of the Tinderbox Foundation, Conny Stolberg-Rohr (Phone interview, 22 November 2005). The Scandinavian Tourist Board in Tokyo also offered various H.C. Andersen event tours to Denmark. Meanwhile they also concluded a business agreement on their invention of 'the Green Santa Claus'. The following section explains how.

Display 1.9 The H.C. Andersen Ambassadors (Photo: Reuters/Scanpix)

A Green Santa Claus – The Business of Image Creation

For several years the Scandinavian Tourist Board[2] and the Finish tourism organization in Japan have been competing with each other in a friendly way over the rights to Santa Claus. However, the battle may have definitively swung in Scandinavian Tourist Board's favor as a 'Green Santa Claus' from Denmark has once again received substantial media attention in Japan. The idea for a Green Santa Claus was developed by the Scandinavian Tourist Board to promote technical visits and environmental tours in Denmark. For a number of years, Japanese government officials, as well as business people, have visited Denmark in large numbers to conduct technical visits of Danish companies that are highly advanced in environmental protection. Technical visits have also focused on elder care. As an idea to promote these tours, a Green Santa Claus has made an appearance in Japan for the last three years. He has greeted both children and Japanese politicians (Børsen, 4 May 2005), and his message has been that

Denmark is an environmentally conscientious country. The promotion of the Green Santa Claus has now resulted in a licensing arrangement between the Scandinavian Tourist Board in Japan and Panasonic, a subsidiary of Matsushita Electric Industrial Ltd. Panasonic would like to boost its image as an environmentally friendly company, and the Green Santa Claus mascot is now going to be used in Panasonic promotional material (Ibid). As a part of this campaign Panasonic has promised to highlight that Denmark is a model country with respect to environmental protection. Panasonic is planning to spend DKK 110 million on the campaign, which is expected to have a positive and wide-ranging impact on Denmark's environmental reputation within Japan (Børsen, 4 May 2005).

The above exemplifies the creative reinvention of a well known icon, namely Santa Claus. A question remains, however. Would a green Santa Claus be universally adopted by both children and politicians of other countries, or is there something unique going on in Japan?

The Cute 'Cult' – A Japanese Phenomenon

Among the Japanese, an extreme fondness for all things cute is in no way limited to young girls. Japanese images of all kinds are saturated with 'cuteness', from mega hits for the young, such as Hello Kitty (pink) and Doraemon (pastel blue), to a Green Santa Claus courted by leading politicians. Mass media images and material objects for consumers of all ages build on and replicate this affinity for all that is cute. Cute culture is to Japan what Disney without age limits would be to the United States, and two explanations are typically advanced to explain this situation. One is that Japanese society is so restricted, stressful and serious that 'cute' provides a space for being infantile and carefree far from the harsh reality and responsibilities of adult life. Essentially, it provides a mental break from the stressful Japanese lifestyle. Secondly, the consumerist behavior of the Japanese provides a fertile environment for the instantly gratifying, materialistic experience of purchasing. Japan is a hyper-advanced consumer society where the hobby of many is to go shopping. While 'cute' culture was not created by the marketers, it did not take them very long to discover and capitalize on the cute style that had emerged in *manga* cartoons and young people's handwriting (Kinsella, 1995). In Denmark, dolls and cute bears are popular, but mainly among children and young girls. In Japan, you see men with cute dolls attached to their mobile phones and news anchors who explain the news with dolls of politicians, not to mention the news headlines that are often animated with cute figures to introduce and soften 'hard' news (Clausen, 2003).

As we shall see in the case chapters, the Scandinavian Tourist Board has successfully tapped into this 'cult' of cute with the promotion of their Viking mascot, as has Bo Bendixen with the very nature of his design.

Simplicity, Zen and 'Slow Life'

Simplicity is the one word that best explains Japanese aesthetics. From a design point of view, the Japanese appreciation of simplicity is grounded in Japanese lifestyle and the philosophy of Zen Buddhism. Although growing out of a different tradition, the simplicity and clean lines of Danish design resonate remarkably well with the Japanese aesthetic. While this was commented upon by several employees of the subsidiaries and partners interviewed, the cultural transference is most relevant for Bang & Olufsen and Rosendahl, companies whose products could easily be labeled 'very Zen'.

Finally, 'slow life' is a recurring image of Scandinavia and Denmark for some Japanese. It conjures up wonderful associations for busy Japanese cosmopolitans whose lives resemble the exact opposite. This particular Japanese attraction to Scandinavia was mentioned by employees from the Scandinavian Tourist Board, Rosendahl and ECCO. In fact, the notion of 'slow life' is strongly associated with 'simplicity' and a vision of a simple Scandinavian way of life that appeals greatly to the Japanese.

Having introduced some of the trends in Japan that influence image and brand creation, the individual case chapters will focus on how the companies involved have organized their business in order to fully leverage these trends in creating and promoting their brand values.

The Potential of the Japanese Market

The Danish companies involved in this study perceive doing business in Japan as desirable for a number of reasons connected to brand opportunity, including the possibility for high profit margins and quality conscious consumers with significant disposable income. Each of these is described further below.

Japan – A World Brand Centre

As products can be produced cheaply anywhere in the world, 'branding' is the most important marketing tool for consumer goods.

Any company is able to source and make inexpensive products, so it is the image and the added value of the brand that is important. This is especially true in Japan which has developed into a consumer society with an obsession for quality and brand names. Within this context, as a company there is no middle road – you either make it as a brand or you gradually fade out of the market (Merrill Lynch, chief Japan analyst, Jesper Koll, 17 November, Japan). It may seem paradoxical that the Japanese brand 'no brand name' (Mujirushi) has become very popular. Ironically, in its own way it illustrates the Japanese fondness for brands. According to Lars Myrup, president of Bang & Olufsen Japan:

> *On a regular world map, Europe and the United States are giants compared to Japan, but on a world map according to the proportion of wealth, Japan suddenly becomes a huge island on the right side of the map. Visually, Japan, a little long narrow island, by economic measures suddenly becomes an extremely important nation. In the 1980s and early 1990s, Japan was on the front covers on all the business magazines. In the new millennium, China and South East Asia have taken the lead on the covers of business magazines.*

Top managers in international companies focus on cover page stories and articles, he continues. Nevertheless, according to Lars Myrup, Japan still accounts for seventy-five percent of Asian GDP and is therefore an incredibly important economy. In particular, with so much wealth among its consumers, it is considered an oasis for luxury products. Most foreign companies, he says, sell their luxury brands at a premium. Beyond the fact that Japanese can afford these brands, they happen to appreciate and prefer Western ones. A Japanese car park today, for instance, is dominated by upscale models of European cars, such as Porsche, BMW, Mercedes and Volvo. In the fashion industry, including jewelry and watches, foreign brands are particularly successful and appreciated by the Japanese. Many of the big fashion houses earn more than fifty percent of their global sales revenue from Japan, says Lars Myrup. The Japanese also appreciate high quality. They have high disposable income and they are ready to pay for good quality and good service. A CEO of a luxury brand who wants to be comfortable with his strategy sells thirty percent in the Americas, thirty percent in Europe and thirty percent in Asia. While the percentage sold in Japan may be dropping because it already accounts for so much of the global revenue for fashion, car and luxury companies, in his view Asia is going to continue to play a massive role for premium brands.

Different in the Same Way

"The Japanese tend to express their status in society through consumption", according to Sociologist John Clammer (Financial Times Media, 9 November 2004). According to Martin Glisby, Asia manager at Rosendahl, ninety global companies are among the dominating brands. He points out that for instance, the Elvira Mate group, which includes Louis Vuitton, earns eighty-eight percent of their global turnover in Japan. Likewise, Tiffany and Company have stores all over the world, but forty-seven of these are in Japan, which is by far the largest number for any country. Japan is the biggest market for the Danish porcelain of Royal Scandinavia, which has a brand awareness in Japan of more than sixty percent. Clearly, Japan offers a great deal of potential for strong global brands. When asked why brand driven companies can tap into this exceptionally strong potential in Japan, Martin Glisby answers: "A social or cultural explanation for that can be the homogeneous society. This is a stereotypical explanation, but in a sense everybody wants to be different. At the same time, everyone would like to be different in the same way". In Japan, there are no niche players. If a niche brand or product catches on, it catches on big time. On the other hand, if it fails to catch on, it will die out within a few years. There is nothing in between. If a company can create a strong brand name in Japan, they will likely achieve global success (Johansson & Nonaka, 1996).

The above has described the business context for Danish companies operating in Japan. It has introduced the companies, current market trends and Danish image promotion in Japan. It has also underscored the importance of brand and image development for long-term success. In closing this chapter, I will try to provide a taste of what it is like to come to Japan as a manager from the outside in order to highlight the many different levels at which learning must take place when dealing with this complex culture.

Cultural Challenges and Levels of Learning

The following exemplifies a progression of different steps in learning and awareness that can take place when working in or with Japan. As related in Osland and Bird (2000: 68), an expatriate manager working in Tokyo describes his experience of a progression of understanding as a Westerner trying to pierce the veil of Japanese culture. Highlighting the complexity of reaching such an understanding, his experiences alternate between perceiving the Japanese as significantly different and not very different at all (paraphrasing Osland & Bird, 2000: 68; original Collins, 1987):

1. The initial Level on a Westerner's perception scale clearly indicates a 'difference' of great significance. The language is indecipherable and people hurry only to stand in lines everywhere. Difference is all one perceives when entering Japan.

2. Level Two is represented by the sudden awareness that the Japanese are not different at all. They have a dynamic industrial/trade/financial system. They serve Western foods at five star hotels. We are the same.

3. Level Three is the 'hey, wait a minute' stage. The Japanese come to all the meetings, smile politely, nod in agreement with everything said, but do the opposite of what is expected. And they do it all together. They really are different.

4. But are they? Level Four understanding recognizes the strong group dynamics, common education and training, and the general sense of loyalty to the family – which in their case is Japan itself. That is not so unusual; things are just organized on a larger scale than any social unit in the West. Nothing is fundamentally different.

5. Level Five can blow one's mind, however. Bank presidents skipping through streets dressed as dragons at festival time, single ladies placing garlands of flowers around huge, and remarkably graphic, stone phallic symbols; Ministry of Finance officials rearranging their bedrooms so as to sleep in a 'lucky' direction; it is all somewhat odd. At least, by Western standards. There is something different in the air.

And so on (cf. Osland & Bird, 2000: 68; original Collins, 1987).

Some Westerners, the long-time expatriates or 'old Japan hands', have gotten as far as Level 37 or 38 (Ibid). Since the 1980s when the above was experienced, the Japanese have continued to interact with Europeans and Americans and consequently have learned more about Western business etiquette, just as the Europeans and Americans have gained more knowledge about how to conduct business in Japan. In this sense, business practices are gradually becoming internationalized. As outlined in the Japanese Market Profile from the Royal Danish Embassy:

> *The Japanese do not expect foreigners to understand the proper Japanese ways of bowing and exchanging business cards. Visitors are advised to act naturally if they have not been prepared by colleagues. It is better to act in accordance with one's own national etiquette than make a clumsy attempt to model the Japanese* (Market Profile, 2004).

With the ubiquitous availability of such guidelines, this book is definitely not an attempt to describe 'how to do business' in Japan. While a variety of 'lessons learned' will be presented, the book is above all concerned with professional practices and the development of intercultural relations over time. It is a study of how to cope with cultural differences in the creation and implementation of global strategies in joint operations from the perspective of individuals in Denmark and Japan. This book thus offers an in-depth analysis of some of the dynamic personal and organizational attributes that were critical, within a intercultural context, to the creation of sustainable competitive advantage and success for five Danish companies entering and competing in the Japanese market.

Book Chapters – Introduction
This chapter presented the project and the business context in Japan. Chapter Two presents a theoretical framework for intercultural communication. It presents a model for analysis of cultural factors of influence at the global, national, organizational and individual levels of interaction in intercultural encounters. The theory addresses commonly held stereotypes and suggests how to get beyond these by developing the intercultural communication competencies of global managers to support successful operations in a bi-cultural context. Chapter Three presents Bo Bendixen and Japanese 'cute' culture. Chapter Four is about Royalty, Rosendahl and H.C. Andersen. Chapter Five is about the Scandinavian Tourist Board and the creation of a Viking Mascot. Chapter Six is about Bang & Olufsen and exclusive branding. Chapter Seven presents ECCO's long-term cooperation with the Japanese alliance partner, Achilles. And finally, Chapter Eight presents conclusions and lessons learned for the different levels of influence on

communication and intercultural encounters: a) global image adaptation in Japan, b) national cultural issues in market entry, c) organization of communication and corporate culture, d) professional and specific product knowledge, and finally e) intercultural competence development.

Bibliography

Brannen, Y. & Salk, E. J. (2000) "Partnering across Boarders: Negotiating Organizational Culture in a German-Japanese Joint Venture", *Human Relations*, volume 53 (4), pp. 451-487

Børsen, 4 May 2005, Section 1

Clausen, L. (2003) *"Global News Production"*, Copenhagen, Copenhagen Business School Press

Collins, R. J. (1987) *"Max Danger: The Adventures of an Expatriate in Tokyo"*, Rutland, VT, Charles E. Tuttle Co.

Confederation of Danish Industries: http://www.di.dk

Confederation of Danish Industries (2004) Japan, report published in relation to the Royal Danish State visit to Japan November 2004

Financial Times Media, 9 November 2004, pp. 11

Hall, E. T. (1959) *"The Silent Language"*, Greenwich, CT, Fawsett

Hampden-Turner, C. & Trompenaars, F. (1993) *"Riding the Waves of Culture. Understanding Culture and Diversity in Business"*, London, Nicholas Brealey Publishing

Hatting Bakery (2004) "Fra ide til success – Hatting Bageri i Japan", presentation at Danish Industry conference, 21 October 2004 [Hatting Bakery in Japan - From Idea to Success]

Hofstede, G. (1980) *"Culture's Consequences. International Differences in Work–Related Values"*, London, Sage

Ito, Y. (2000) "What Causes the Similarities and Differences among the Social Sciences in Different Cultures? Focusing on Japan and the West", *Asian Journal of Communication*, 10 (2), pp. 93-123

Johansson, J. K. and Nonaka, I. (1996) *"Relentless: The Japanese Way of Marketing"*, Butterworth Heinemann, Oxford, UK,

Kinsella, S. (1995) "Cuties in Japan" in *"Women Media and Consumption in Japan"*, Skov, L. & Moeran, B. (eds.), Curzon and Hawaii University Press

"Luxury Import Brand Market in Japan" (2005), Tokyo, Yano Research Institute

"Market Profile" (2004) The Royal Danish Embassy, Tokyo, January 2004 [Markedsprofil Japan]

Osland, J. S. & Bird, A. (2000) "Beyond Sophisticated Stereotyping: Cultural Sense Making in Context", *Academy of Management Executive*, volume 14, no. 1

Royal Danish Embassy, Tokyo (2001) "Etablering af Selskab i Japan", Andersen, Pernille [Establishing a Company in Japan]

Samovar, L. A. & Porter, R. E. (1997) *"Intercultural Communication: A Reader"* (Eighth Edition), Belmont, CA, Wadsworth Publishing Company

Søderberg, A. & Holden, N. (2002) "Rethinking Cross Cultural Management in a Globalizing Business World", *International Journal of Cross Cultural Management*, volume 2, no. 1, pp. 103-121

The Trade Council of Denmark (2004) "Japan", background material for the business event in connection with the Royal Danish state visit to Japan 15-19 November 2004, the Ministry of Foreign Affairs, the Royal Danish Embassy in Tokyo and EES

Trade Council of Denmark Homepage:
www1.eksportraadet.dk/view.asp.ID=7670

Chapter One: Endnotes

[1] Speech at the Opening Forum on Globalization, Strategies, and Synergies, 17 November 2004 in Tokyo, Japan. Part of the program of the Royal and Business Delegation visit.

[2] The Green Santa or Santa Claus project is sponsored solely by VisitDenmark.

Chapter Two

INTERCULTURAL COMMUNICATION IN ORGANIZATIONS: THEORY

Without any generalizations, meaningful intercultural business communication would become even more difficult than it is already. To concentrate only on the individual and approach every intercultural communication situation from ground zero would be exhausting and not very productive (Varner, 2000: 46).

For the most part, we do not first see, and then define; we define first and then see. *In the great blooming, buzzing confusion of the outer world, we pick out what our culture has already defined for us, and we tend to perceive that which we have picked out in the form stereotyped for us by our culture* (Lippmann, 1922: 81).

All business activity involves communicating. Within global businesses, activities such as leading, motivating, negotiating, decision-making, problem solving, and exchanging information and ideas are all based on the ability of managers and employees from one culture to communicate successfully with colleagues, clients, and suppliers from other cultures. Communicating effectively challenges managers even when working domestically with a culturally homogeneous workforce (Adler, 2002: 73-74). When colleagues speak another language and come from a different cultural background, communicating becomes considerably more difficult (Op. cit: 74-75). Judging by the high rate of expatriate failure, managers stationed abroad thus face even greater challenges in their efforts to develop adequate intercultural competencies for cross-cultural interaction (Peltokorpi, 2006).

Intercultural communication in the present project is viewed as a complex, multilayered, and dynamic process through which global managers exchange meaning. In this chapter, I will develop a framework for analyzing the dynamics and complexity of sense-making processes and the exchange of meaning between Danish and Japanese managers. In doing so, I draw upon Western and Eastern communication theory to create a model that employs the best of both approaches. In the subsequent chapters, this framework is then used to analyze strategic and operational communication between five Danish companies and their subsidiaries or alliance partners in the Japanese market. Before presenting the model, a literature review in this chapter highlights the characteristics of both Danish and Japanese management drawing on generalization studies as well as more in-depth research to introduce differences and similarities in Danish and Japanese national and corporate culture that may influence professional encounters across boarders.

From Global to Local

In their quest to join internationally competitive markets, companies create global strategies. These strategies then have to be adapted locally with a variety of implications. This study of communication between Danish companies and their subsidiaries and alliance partners in Japan suggests that managers who work in intercultural business settings have developed special competencies in intercultural communication. In particular, they have developed almost intuitive ways of reflecting on both cultures in their strategy formulation. Their position of understanding the business and cultural conventions, as well as the particular industry in the countries they deal with *and* the core competencies of their own companies is essential to communicating successfully. Knowledge of both their own and the receiving culture is critical to the process of interpreting and mediating global strategy with local partners, as well as communicating gathered intelligence back to headquarters.

The perceptions held by Danish managers and their business partners became apparent through personal interviews, and their statements form the basis for the company cases in each of the five subsequent chapters. It also became apparent through the interviews that global managers are, just like other professionals, influenced by several factors and actors. They deal with cultural issues that can be divided into several contextual levels for analysis. These include the global or international strategies of their companies, national cultural issues, industry culture, their own corporate culture, and professional or departmental culture. Last but not least, the individual level of knowledge and accumulated personal experience in intercultural encounters is an important factor of influence.

Standardization or Diversification

How do cultural differences affect organizations and people in organizations? Are organizations becoming more similar worldwide or are they maintaining their cultural uniqueness? These questions have puzzled global managers and researcher alike, and they serve as guides in analyzing the global strategic adaptations that companies in this project have made in Japan. If people around the world are becoming more similar through the influence of international business, global media and material consumption, then understanding cross-cultural differences should be less and less important. If, on the contrary, people are retaining or reinforcing their unique cultural identities, then understanding of cross-cultural differences in organizations will become increasingly important. The present study is an investigation in a bi-cultural setting of managers who work in Denmark and Japan. From the outside, business practices in these two countries may look similar, but closer analysis shows that the Danes and the Japanese largely continue to behave in their own culturally distinct fashions within nationally embedded organizations. Cultural perceptions may vary according to personality and professional experience, but any process of change takes time and depends significantly on an individual's motivation to adapt. Each of the five participating companies in this project has its own set of values, strategic goals and communication practices. Common to all of them is the fact that they try to overcome the inherent asymmetry between the national and the international through communication. This asymmetry arises from the disparate knowledge held by managers within organizations composed of headquarters in Denmark and subsidiaries or alliance partners in Japan.

Communication is Complex

Two communication models inspire the analysis of the perceptions held by global managers in this project, namely a Western model of transmission and an Eastern model of dialogue. The intention is to see how companies in practice can move away from thinking of communication as a way to inject information into an organization or alliance partner and instead pursue the ideal of integrated co-creation of meaning and strategy through dialogue.

Communication as Transmission – Western Logic

The transmission model in display 2.1 includes several components of communication: a source enables the production or encoding of a message; a channel is chosen; there may be noise (either real or perceived); a receiver(s) gets the message and decodes it. Subsequently, there is a response and feedback from the receiver to the sender. The context of the transmission of messages is also included, be it tangible or intangible.[1]

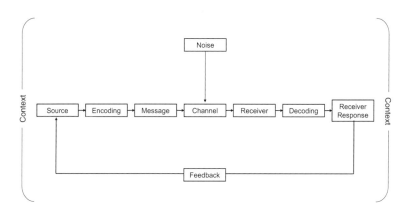

Display 2.1 The transmission model, including ten elements of communication (Jandt, 1998: 26)

As an example of communication from Denmark to Japan using the transmission model consider the following: an employee from corporate headquarters is the source; the message may be an idea or strategy (branding, marketing, sales, product development); the idea is turned into a message; a channel is chosen for communication (fax, phone, mail, intranet, face to face); and the recipient, a Japanese partner, decodes the message. Noise could include cultural issues such

46

as language, and context could include such elements as the physical setting of the receiver in Japan or the history of prior communication. Feedback on the message is then sent back to headquarters. Although it appeals to Western conception of linearity and clear (hierarchical) division of senders and receivers, it is important to recognize that the transmission model is far too simplistic to capture the reality of communication in all its complexity.

Models, that are more complex in terms of what is communicated, are presented by Leiniger (1997), among others. Specifically, Leiniger includes global mission, global management strategies, international communication approaches, and individual rhetorical strategies. With respect to increasing complexity in terms of factors that influence communication, Varner (2000) introduces a theoretical framework and a conceptual model which combines business strategy, intercultural strategy and communication strategy. Each strategic area encompasses a number of important factors.[2]

While these two models underscore the complexity of issues to consider when studying or participating in communication, they are nevertheless 'classic' communication models in the sense that they rely on the premise that communication is a linear process of information transmission from sender to receiver. From a linear perspective, the processes of communication relevant to this study would be from headquarters to subsidiary/alliance partner; from a small economy (Denmark) to a large economy (Japan); from (small to large) Danish companies to (small to giant) Japanese companies. According to the linear models, which to a great extent are applied by Western companies, this is the logical direction and order of communication and feedback. Nevertheless, in practice interaction is much more complex.

Yan (1997) has criticized the transmission model for being based on Western premises which places the sender in a dominant role. Any derived understanding of communication, in her view, thus becomes distorted and manipulated. Yan argues for a consensus approach inspired by Eastern philosophy as an alternative to the process models that have originated in Western scholarship. It particular, Eastern models usually place a great deal of importance on the context in which communication takes place, while Western models tend to focus on the explicit content of communication. In addition, Western models are more concerned with the results (effects) of communication, while Eastern models tend to focus on the process of communication. Within this study, the focus of analysis will be both on the content *and* the process and context. As a part of this more integrated approach, Yoshikawa's double swing model is introduced below to illustrate what I choose to call a model of 'co-created' communication.

Co-Creation of Meaning – East West Integration

The premise of communication in the model in display 2.2 is that communicators cooperate to create meaning. The model is in itself balanced as it encompasses both Western and Eastern thought.[3] As opposed to the linear transmission model in which communication is seen as a controllable process of meaning 'injection' from A to B, the double swing model points to a common sphere 'in-between'.

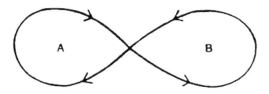

Display 2.2 Dialogic communication, the double swing model (Yoshikawa, 1987: 321)

Yoshikawa's model is the symbolic representation of his search for new ways of understanding interpersonal, intercultural, and international relations within which people of diverse cultures can reflect on their cultural differences as well as their similarities. The Möbius strip, or infinity symbol, signifies the idea of a twofold movement and the Buddhist concept of paradoxical relationships, as well as the multiple dualisms of yin and yang from Taoist teaching. But the model moves beyond duality to pictorially emphasize the act of meeting between two different beings. It does this without eliminating the otherness or uniqueness of each and without reducing the dynamic tension created as a result of meeting (Op. cit: 326). The model points to the creation of a commonly shared 'in-between' position.

> *The model is not to be constructed as a fixed entity or principle but in fact has much to do with the ways we perceive, think, and relate to whatever we encounter. It is essentially related to our basic attitude and life stance* (Yoshikawa, 1987: 327).

Yoshikawa's model can be applied to the whole spectrum of human existence – interaction between individual human beings, communication between countries, dialogue among different religions, and, as here, intercultural encounters of communication between organizations and between people. The assumptions behind the model (and the views on communication adopted for this project) are the following:

- The actors in Yoshikawa's simple communication model are not senders and receivers respectively, but are ongoing co-producers of the communication process.
- The processes of intercultural communication continue even when both parties (in face to face or virtual communication) leave the encounter.
- The awareness of self and other is created in the communication process through *reflection.*
- Difference and otherness, which are commonly perceived as problematic in intercultural communication, are viewed as positive factors and as essential ingredients for growth.
- The act of meeting occurs without eliminating the otherness or uniqueness of each culture and without reducing the dynamic tension created as a result of meeting.
- Dialogical communication processes do not create a homogenous world, but rather a diversified and pluralistic one.

While the linear process model views communication as a transmission of information from sender to receiver, communication in the double swing model is an ongoing dialogical[4] process of meaning creation. Communication through a dialogical process strengthens our consciousness of our own identity while at the same time strengthening our consciousness of the identity of others. This reflection on and mental negotiation of cultural knowledge are critical competencies in intercultural communication encounters. The strength of the double swing model is that Yoshikawa builds on the ideas of co-created meaning and instantaneous reciprocity as a part of a potentially never ending dialog. A weakness is the fact that he does not consider context (Jensen, 1998: 195), which is usually important in Eastern communication models.

In summary, Yoshikawa's model is an inspiration for the construction of the analytical model used in this study because of the assumptions that it makes about the nature of communication as a complex, pluralistic, dialogical, and reflective process. It is also general enough to encompass communication from the individual to the international level. Last but not least it represents an in-between mode of meaning creation which I shall return to below. First, let me define the notion of culture.

What is Culture?

"Culture is communication and communication is culture" (Hall, 1959: 186). While this statement reflects the importance of each of these subject areas, it leaves both culture and communication as all encompassing. For my purposes, I need to unpack them in order to understand their interrelationship and mutual dependence in greater detail so that I can adequately account for the effect of culture on communication in the analysis of the five case studies.

Organizational culture concerns the integration of symbols (logos), legends (stories about past successes and failures), heroes (influential managers or company leaders), shared experiences (projects) and values (business philosophies encompassing vision, mission and objectives). In this study it also concerns the intercultural dissemination of organizational culture.

Despite several decades of research on organizational culture, many cross-cultural studies (such as the generalization studies introduced below) are still inspired by the classic definitions of culture, whereby culture is understood as an internal system of assumptions, values and norms that are held by an organization or nation collectively and which are relatively stable. Organizationally, culture from this perspective is seen as a collection of values that can be instilled, modified, or acted upon in order to induce desired employee behavior and thereby ensure success. However, research does not support either this perspective or the assumption that a strong company culture automatically has a positive effect on the bottom line.

Within the literature, there are in general two ways of viewing culture: a) a functionalist view (such as the above) in which culture is something that you 'have' and 'belong to', and b) a social constructivist view in which culture is something that is mutually constructed among participants and depends on context. The meaning of being feminine or masculine from a functionalist perspective is a measurable, stable variable – an inherent characteristic. The meaning of feminine or masculine from a social constructivist perspective depends on the social context in which these characteristics are enacted.

Inspiration for a definition of culture building on a social constructivist perspective would be that culture is based on "shared or partly shared patterns of meaning and interpretation [which] . . . are produced, reproduced and continually changed by the people identifying with them and negotiating them" (Søderberg & Holden, 2002: 112). In other words, people identify and affiliate with a multiplicity of different values, the meanings of which are continually being negotiated. This is the viewpoint taken in this project, whereby culture is seen as being embedded in relationships, rather than in pre-determined structures, and the co-creation of meaning is seen as an ever-evolving process.

'Negotiated' Culture

The concept of 'emerging culture' or 'negotiated culture' is used in the present project to explain the dynamics of intercultural encounters and the processes of globalization and change at the micro level. These concepts are developed in a study by Brannen and Salk of a German and Japanese merger and acquisition (2000: 451). They describe how managers enter intercultural situations with certain mindsets based on national and organizational cultural values, and how a new situation-specific company culture then emerges based on the influence of national, organizational, personal and above all task-related factors. Thus, for the analytical model used in this study, the role of individuals and their influence on communication are seen as contributing to the formation of new cultural norms and rules for interaction which then become part of a 'negotiated and emergent culture'.

Communication as Knowledge Sharing

In the knowledge management literature knowledge is defined as "a fluid mix of framed experience, values, contextual information, and expert insights that provides a framework for evaluating and incorporating new experiences and information. It originates in and is applied in the minds of knower's" (Davenport & Prusak, 1998: 5). It is appropriate to draw on knowledge management research for this project because communication may also be understood as knowledge sharing. Yet, cultural knowledge about norms and values is often tacit or implicit. "We can know more than we can tell" (Polanyi, 1966: 4). In other words, cultural practices and know-how are often drawn upon in given situations, yet they are difficult to recall or talk about because they have become natural practice – or tacit implicit knowledge. For instance, as you get accustomed to the ways of the Japanese, you may automatically bow slightly when you meet people without even being aware of it. Cultural knowledge is also person dependent since knowledge is 'sticky' (Szulanski, 2003) – cultural knowledge and personal relationships belong to people. It is therefore important that companies make room for international information sharing to incorporate particular country knowledge into general company information. This is particularly important concerning Japan, since in many important ways Japan is culturally unique. If cultural knowledge is not shared with head office colleagues it becomes a monopoly held by those managers who work with Asia. The effects of such 'knowledge monopolies' are clearly seen in certain company cases presented in this book.

The next section presents previous studies of national and organizational culture in relation to Denmark and Japan.

Barriers to Communication – Stereotypes

Cross-cultural management studies have been dominated by efforts which try to identify patterns and variables that described differences across cultures. Consequently, a great deal of cultural research, as well as cultural training, occurs within a framework of bi-polar cultural dimensions. Osland and Bird (2000) refer to these theoretical stereotypes as 'sophisticated' stereotypes. 'Sophisticated' stereotypes are generated through research and are theoretical concepts (this does not mean, however, that they are generalizations without value attribution, as researchers are also influenced by their cultural world-views). These 'generalization studies' are based on an essentialist or functionalist view on culture as described above where culture is defined as an inherent and stable variable. I shall return to the pitfalls of the generalization approach below.

I have outlined a few of the numerous sophisticated stereotypes used to distinguish the cultural values of nations around the world (see display 2.3). After first using these dimensions to search for insight into Danish and Japanese culture, I will then describe the dangers of using even such 'sophisticated' stereotypes.

Generalizing Studies	Denmark/West	Japan
Hall (1959) Dimensions of communication and culture	Low context	High context
Hofstede (1980, 1991) Dimensions of national culture	Feminine Low risk avoidance Individualist Egalitarian	Masculine High risk avoidance Collectivist Hierarchical
Hampden-Turner and Trompenaars (1993) Dimensions of culture	Universal Individual Affective Specific (low-context) Achieved status	Particular Collective Neutral Diffuse (high-context) Ascribed status

Display 2.3 'Sophisticated' stereotypes, inspired by Osland and Bird, 2000

High-Context – Low-Context

US anthropologist Edward T. Hall, the founder of the field intercultural communication (Rogers *et al.*, 2002), gained substantial knowledge about American and Japanese cultural differences by training United States military personnel in Japan during the 1960s. Hall's (1959) notions of low-context versus high-context have been used to describe how people ascribe meaning in communication. A low-context communication is one in which the mass of information is vested in the explicit code, which is typical for individualist cultures such as in Denmark. In low-context communication thoughts are put into words, while in high-context communication meaning is largely implicit. Thus, for high-context communication, little has to be said or written because most of the information is either in the physical environment or is assumed to be known by the people involved. In Japan, where communication is considered to be high-context, the context and situation, much more than the words themselves, influence the creation of meaning. Hall has presented a continuum of the importance of context ranging from that found in Germany and Switzerland (home to the most explicit people in the world) to that found in Japan at the other end of the scale (Americans are close to the middle, although they have become icons of low-context communication) (Holden, 2002). Danes are thus low-context communicators while Japanese are high-context communicators. Hall's definitions, at first glance, contribute considerable insight. However, the two categories may also divide communication styles within cultures, companies, families and gender and thus may lose their explanatory power to describe communication styles of whole nations.

Hofstede's Four Dimensions

Hofstede set out to study what he referred to as the 'mental programs' of IBM employees within subsidiaries from forty different countries.[5] He later added more countries to his survey. He used a typology of four pairs of bipolar dimensions to measure and to characterize national cultural values.[6] The scores for Denmark and Japan are as follows: Denmark is a country with few masculine values (ranked 50 on the masculinity index), while Japan is the most masculine country in the world (ranked 1). Danes thus have feminine values and Japanese have masculine values. The masculine versus feminine dimension measures and classifies the equality of gender roles and work goals. Hofstede concludes that in countries with highly feminine values employees 'work to live' and try to maximize 'life satisfaction', while in countries with highly masculine values employees 'live to work' and try to maximize 'job satisfaction' (1980: 285-286). Further, Danes are not worried about uncertainty (ranked 51 on the high uncertainty avoidance index), while the Japanese wish to avoid uncertainty (ranked 7). Danes thus are less risk and conflict avoiding than the Japanese. Danes are individualistic (ranked 9 on the collectivist index), while Japan is considered a collectivist culture (rank 22/23). Finally, Danes have low power distance (ranked 51 on the power distance index), while Japan has higher power distance (33). From this it may be concluded that Danes are egalitarian and Japanese hierarchical (Hofstede, 1980: 286; 151; 87; 215).

In sum, Danes have more feminine values while the Japanese have masculine values. Danes do not avoid uncertainty while their Japanese counterparts do. Danes are more individualist than the collectivist Japanese. And, finally, Danes are more egalitarian than the Japanese.

The above briefly characterizes Hofstede's findings concerning Denmark and Japan. The data used for his research was collected three decades ago but the dimensions are still used as a starting point for many cross-cultural studies today. Hofstede's quantitative approach has also met with a substantial amount of criticism (see McSweeney, 2002). While the above characteristics are not disconfirmed in the present study, I set out to provide more detailed cases of how values are in play in professional interaction in a bi-cultural setting. While national character may influence people in organizations, other factors are also important in understanding behavior in cross-cultural organizational analysis. I will return to the pitfalls of the generalization approach below in relation to the present study.

Trompenaars' Value Orientations

Trompenaars (Hampden-Turner & Trompenaars, 1993) has identified five dimensions of how people relate to each other in business based on questionnaires and quantitative methods. Overall, Trompenaars' research is viewed as targeting practitioners rather than academia. If you apply his statistical findings to Denmark and Japan, the two countries in most cases are positioned at opposite ends of his various bi-polar continuums.

Trompenaars' categories are universal versus particular (in Denmark it is important to follow universal rules, while rules that are particular to the situation are important in Japan); collectivism versus individualism (in Denmark the individual is more important than the group or family membership important in Japan); emotional versus neutral (Danish managers show more emotion than the Japanese); specific versus diffuse (Danish people are straight forward while the Japanese remain detached and indirect); and achieved status versus ascribed status (Danish managers advance because of merit, while Japanese managers advance due to years of employment, family and school connections and/or seniority) (Hampden-Turner & Trompenaars, 1993: 29).

Some of these generalizations may be used as an explanatory framework in the present study. However, there is a missing link. Even with the above knowledge about values we do not know how these cultural characteristics unfold when managers from the two cultures meet.

In the three approaches above, linked pairs of opposites have been used to make generalizations to describe cultural values. While these categories may be helpful as a starting point, since they fail to offer more than basic background knowledge on the potential impact of national culture, there are nevertheless several risks to using such an approach. These risks include the following: a) stereotypes oversimplify nations and cultures, b) national characteristics do not automatically describe characteristics in business contexts, c) national generalizations do not provide insights about intercultural business contexts, d) using generalizations as a starting point for research guides questionnaires and maintains stereotypes, e) a generalization approach does not unfold the potential synergies or new understandings that can emerge from intercultural encounters, f) generalization studies provide a static approach, often devoid of context, that fails to account for how perceptions and intercultural work environments may change over time, and h) generalization studies do not deal with the level of complexity inherent in communication that is the point of departure for the present project.[7]

The discussion so far has highlighted both how generalization studies have defined Danish/Western and Japanese organizational culture based on national characteristics and how these studies have missed the 'in-between' character of culture and its impact. The following section describes particular Scandinavian/Danish and Japanese management styles based on findings from both generalization and in-depth comparative studies.

Scandinavian and Japanese Organizational Culture: Differences and Similarities

A distinctive feature of Scandinavian management is the emphasis on the decision-making process itself. Decision-making processes in principle are open, and decision-making before meetings is considered unfair as participants should have reason to believe that they have a real possibility of influencing the outcome (Schramm-Nielsen *et al.*, 2004: 161). Decision-making processes are also lengthy because employees should be properly informed in order to understand the basis on which decisions are being made. Nevertheless, even if employees do not agree with a particular decision, or if the decision is unfavorable for them, it is more likely that they will participate in the implementation of the decision if they are familiar with its rationale (Ibid).

Perhaps one of the more surprising elements of management in Scandinavia from the viewpoint of non-Scandinavians is the character of interpersonal organizational behavior. Apart from the importance placed on cooperation and consensual decision described above, this behavior is marked by low power distance, egalitarianism, informality, direct communication, decency and conflict avoidance.

> *Whereas some of these characteristics may also apply to other cultures, it is their combination that makes Scandinavia different* (Op. cit: 165).

According to Schramm-Nielsen *et al.*, Danish managers make a point of playing down their authority to an extent where they seem almost scared by its exercise. Direct orders are rare, and managers pride themselves in being able to talk on an equal footing with everyone, including shop floor workers. The informal and non-hierarchical nature of meetings is important; anyone present can speak their mind, and the atmosphere is relaxed and calm, though disciplined. It is not acceptable to shout or lose one's temper; feelings are not considered a good basis for making work related decisions; and people go to great lengths not to hurt the sensibilities of others. In this way, Scandinavians in general go to lengths to avoid conflict. Problems of personal chemistry are preferably dealt with on a general level. Instead of saying directly to someone that you do not like the way he or she handles things, you may talk to their manager in order to put certain procedures on the agenda. In an earlier study, Schramm-Nielsen (2000: 203) concluded that employees are expected to make independent assessments of situations and issues, and one consequence of this is that management decision are not automatically accepted and acted upon by lower levels. Thus managers are required to explain, persuade, conduct meetings and cope with the questioning attitude of employees.

Despite the temptation to lump Scandinavia together, there are differences in management style within Scandinavia that are important in relation to working with Japan. From their merchant past, the Danes have retained a management style that is described as having an 'orientation towards negotiation' (Vaara *et al.*, 2004). One manager finds that "Danes negotiate in a Latin way . . . so negotiating with the Danes is never difficult, it just always begins anew" (Vaara *et al.*, 2004: 78).

In addition, for fellow Scandinavians the Danish way is often problematic for more fundamental reasons:

> *The big difference concerns management style, and the Danes are process oriented . . . opportunistic and obsessed with power. As you can see, this is problematic . . . . You do not know if they mean yes or no or maybe or . . .* (Vaara *et al.*, 2004: 79).

This last part of this statement, if taken out of its Scandinavian context, is close to a generally held stereotype of the Japanese who are also considered to be enigmatic in negations.

However, negotiation style is not the only similarity between the two business cultures. The Japanese are also known for seeking consensus, and just as this is often problematic for Westerners working with the Japanese, Scandinavian efforts at consensus building may be similarly problematic in international settings. The soft Danish approach can be downright un-business-like according to some scholars. In particular, Danish egalitarianism is seen as different and potentially problematic in cross-cultural business settings.

Danish management values stress consensus, conciliation and egalitarianism, in which confrontation is not relished and hierarchy disdained, in which control over people is loose rather than tight, and in which human development is not overridden by economic considerations (Holden, 2002: 128).

From an international perspective, Danish managers are overly humanistic in striving for consensus and egalitarianism. On the other hand, Holden (2002) praises Danish management when he argues that "it is no coincidence that cultural facilitators[8] are the product of the Scandinavian management system". He argues that it might be difficult for the facilitator concept to take root in the more 'muscular management cultures of the United States, the United Kingdom or Germany', or what he refers to as the "authoritarian, rigid, ethnocentric management cultures of Japan or Korea, for whom in any case cross-cultural communication is often a form of angst" (Ibid).

Another issue that conflicts with international work practices is the fact that Scandinavians value their free time. Most Danish people adhere to a thirty-seven hour work week (although there are exceptions to the rule[9]) and they very carefully separate business and private life. This is difficult to understand for the Japanese who come to work on days off if necessary although the forty hour work week is a legal right. As a point of similarity, the Japanese also separate business and private life and they very seldom invite coworkers to their homes. However, Japanese companies take on a familial role through cultural values and lifetime employment systems.

Finally, egalitarian principles make Danes reluctant to be assertive or stand out in front of their peers. This principle supposedly guides the Danish mentality, where hierarchy is considered a 'necessary evil' for the functioning of an organization, but not a goal in itself (Schramm-Nielsen, 2000). This egalitarianism and censure of the display of superiority also make for greater homogeneity. "This does not make the Danes like the Japanese where rejection of individualism is near total, but it does make them a little bit more like the Japanese than for instance the French or the Germans" (Lawrence & Wincent, 2000: 154). According to the same research, "Danes, a little more than the

Swedes and Norwegians, recognize the distinctiveness of Japanese culture and also the possibility of learning from it" (Sjøborg, 1985; cf. Lawrence & Wincent, 2000).This recognition of distinctiveness was found in the present study as a feeling of emotional proximity and mutual cultural appreciation potentially motivated by similarity in such values as modesty[10] and consensus seeking.

Nevertheless, the egalitarian values of Scandinavian managers are in stark contrast to the hierarchical system present in Japan. According to the Confucian hierarchy of values, gender, age, and the status of the speaker are more important than the message delivered. In a study of thirty Nordic expatriate managers (all male) in Japanese subsidiaries, Peltokorpi found that the Japanese use politeness strategies in their communication with their Scandinavian managers. The Japanese would rather agree with their foreign manager than cause him to lose face by disagreeing with him (Peltokorpi, 2006). These values are difficult to uncover and decipher for foreign managers in Japan, not least because they may lack the language skills that allow them to pierce the veil of cultural subtleties.

While issues of hierarchy and egalitarianism are viewed from two ends of the spectrum by Danish and Japanese managers, modesty and consensus seeking are found to be common traits that encourage mutual cooperation. In the following, I suggest how managers – in theory – may overcome communication barriers.

Overcoming the Barriers

The main way to overcome cultural barriers in communication is through the raising of awareness. Two observations may be helpful here. One is that professional communication is often made easier by shared technical understanding. The other is that, according to the notion of negotiated culture discussed above, intercultural cooperation can create a new common culture that is more than the marriage of the two parent cultures in that it contains new and unique cultural elements.

Can We Get Beyond Stereotypes?

As expressed by Lippmann in the opening quote, stereotypes are fundamental to the way we process information and make sense of experiences (1922: 81). However, we must learn to move beyond relying on the stereotypes our culture has provided for us to become successful communicators, particularly in intercultural settings.

Strategies to overcome our natural parochial tendencies exist, and with care we can avoid our ethnocentric thought patterns and behaviors. We can learn to see, understand, and transcend our cultural conditioning, and Adler (2002) suggests how. She argues that when working with other cultures, we can emphasize description rather than interpretation or evaluation. In the process of describing cultures rather than evaluating them we minimize self-fulfilling stereotypes and premature judgments. Effective cross-cultural communication presupposes the interplay of alternative realities and rejects the actual or potential domination of one reality over another (Adler, 2002: 99).

While the process of changing stereotypes is a very protracted one, changes in perception can happen through cross-cultural encounters over shorter periods of time as real-world experience is compared with existing perceptions. Perceptions can be altered or updated in the presence of new information, and this updating can in turn lead to deeper levels of understanding, as well as fundamental changes in understanding over time. As a case in point, the Japanese scholars of knowledge management Nonaka and Takeuchi (1995) in their early research described Japanese communication as *empathetic* and Western communication as *sympathetic*. After involvement with international scholars, Nonaka *et al.* (2000) later changed this claim to the more universal notion that people from both parts of the world were able to be both empathetic and sympathetic.[11]

Trumping Values

While 'sophisticated' stereotyping is helpful as a starting point, it does not convey the complexity found in cultures or organizations. People working across cultures are frequently surprised by cultural paradoxes that do not seem to fit the descriptions they have learned. People who are familiar with an array of values are able to foresee which ones are most important in a given situation and thereby to understand 'value trumping' (Osland & Bird, 2000: 65). In a specific context certain cultural values take precedence over others. In other words, if you are truly familiar with cultural values you also know which values are most important in a given situation. While it is important to understand cultural values, in certain situations business driven values may actually trump cultural ones. However, throughout the case studies presented in this book, it is evident that an understanding of cultural values allows managers and others to have an insight into situations that ultimately enables them to behave and communicate in the most appropriate and likely most successful way in a variety of business situations.

The More You Know . . .

Mental categories, such as scripts and schemata from cognitive psychology, explain how we process information. Beamer and Varner (2001) use schemata to show how we perceive other cultures through projections based on our own culture. "Individuals hold preconceived conceptions about the culture and project mental schemata of other cultures based upon their preconceptions" (Beamer, 1995: 158). In other words, rather than perceiving culture (B) on its own terms, we experience it through our own cultural filters to arrive at a projected understanding (B1). People from the other culture in turn perceive us (A) through their projected image (A1). In other words, we act based on our projections of the other culture, rather than on the culture itself. They argue that the more knowledge we acquire about another culture the closer our projection approaches the reality, and the better and more successful we become in our communication. While this is encouraging, it poses some questions. What kind of information should we seek and how much do we need to know to work successfully with a foreign culture? How can we gain an understanding of other people's projections of our own culture in order to better understand their communication? What sort of mutual learning processes and mind-sets will encourage the projections to converge over time? The simple answer to all three questions is that practice, learning by doing, motivation and ability are all important factors. People at higher levels of 'cultural intelligence' have a cognitively complex perception of their environment (Thomas & Inkson, 2004: 68). They describe people and events in terms of many different characteristics and are able to see the many links between these characteristics. They can see a coherent pattern in a cultural situation without knowing what the final picture might look like. Culturally intelligent individuals are able to see past stereotypes and a superficial understanding of culture based on predefined dimensions. Nevertheless, working with a different culture will result in high stress levels throughout the various stages of adjustment. A global mind-set, personal stability and professional confidence are therefore important cornerstones for successful cross-cultural interaction (Ferraro, 1990: 182).

Knowledge about how to act and how to handle situations properly in intercultural encounters may guide us to behave appropriately and thus be more effective in getting our messages across. Culture as studied in this project includes global, national, organizational, professional and individual factors. Getting it right from this perspective requires global managers to have a great deal of knowledge.

Structure of Analysis – Multi-Level Communication Model

I have developed a multi-level communication model to structure and explain the stories in the five subsequent empirical chapters. It enables analysis of communication between global managers at Danish headquarters and their Japanese subsidiaries and alliance partners. The step by step analysis is made in a centripetal motion from the global through the national and organizational to the professional level in order to account for the variety of cultural influences that will act on the individual communicators within organizations in Denmark and Japan. Subsequent ongoing cultural encounters result in new cultural spaces, ideas, mentalities, and strategies that are then incorporated into the overall framework for communication. This incorporation can proceed with positive or negative implications for future communication depending on whether mutual understanding has been enhanced or not. Simultaneously, the circulation of images and knowledge at the global level influences people individually and as employees within national organizations.

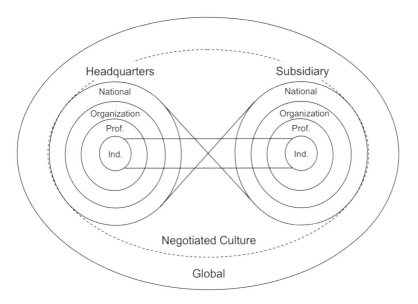

Display 2.4 The multi-level communication model, influences on managers in intercultural encounters: Global, national, organizational, professional, and individual levels

Global

Communication of global branding and marketing worldwide is a challenge for many companies. This level concerns the global or international corporate strategy and its local implementation. Companies work to develop their brand images and to find the right way to frame and present their products and concepts within markets, from the local (headquarters) to the global. Within the cases examined in this book, managers are dependent on their ability to successfully communicate their product offerings to the Japanese consumer in ways that tap into both the national psyche and market trends. To what extent, then, do Japanese retail and wholesale partners, not to mention consumers, accept these brand images and then adapt them to their own needs? In the best of cases, strategies are co-created. Global strategies and product knowledge are merged and adapted as much as possible to the local market. Meanwhile the cultural knowledge of the subsidiaries and alliance partners is transferred back to headquarters for future incorporation into the global strategy.

In Japan, as in all markets, the communication strategy therefore becomes a matter of targeting the Japanese mind-set as a collection of perceptions held by the desired segment of the consumer market. The closer the brand images get to commonly held perceptions and local trends the easier it is to communicate the message and to gain the 'mental market share' of both consumers and business alliances.

National

The national level concerns considerations of entry modes. It also concerns how companies learn and utilize information by communicating successes and failures back to headquarters. Further, it concerns how cultural issues influence strategy formation and the organization of business units in Japan, as well as ongoing issues of adaptation and conflict.

The key success factors as seen by all global managers are to get control of the brand and to build and attract the key competencies within brand and retail business development in Japan. This analytical level concerns communication related to the establishment of a presence in Japan, whether through a wholly owned subsidiary or some form of distribution alliance partner. Issues relating to business systems organization and national culture are of primary concern. For instance, when operating in Japan, the intermediary system used to organize distribution is a major constraint, and at the same time a channel of communication and an important source of information. Notably, this is where brand images are tested before they reach consumers. Yet, the communication of ideas can potentially be disturbed by national cultural knowledge barriers. Since ideas have to pass through the channels of intermediaries and alliance partners before reaching the eventual consumer, problems with interpretation can occur at each stage of the process.

In most cases, although the strategy is global, the legal, political, economic and socio-cultural values at the national level strongly influence business. The Japanese organizational setup of most companies differs not only because of different cultural perceptions as described above, but also because of different structural issues with respect to business systems that are particular to Japan. The number one criterion for success in Japan is to have local connections and networks. The industrial system is built on connections and access to human networks affects organizational setup and opportunities for cooperation.

Organization

This level concerns organizational culture and the organization of communication between employees in Denmark and Japan. An important factor in business success is an employee's knowledge about who knows what in the company, their social and professional networks and their access to information. Although it is fair to state that organizations do not communicate, people do, it is also important to reiterate Varner's observation (as cited in the beginning of the chapter) that "to concentrate only on the individual and approach every intercultural communication situation from ground zero would be exhausting and not very productive" (2000: 46). Company values can often help to bind employees together and create a common communication platform. Elements of company culture may include a carefully stated vision, mission and enunciation of corporate cultural values. When these are aligned (Hatch & Schultz, 2001), global managers on both sides are able to identity with a global corporate strategy that is the ultimate sign of successful internal and external communication.

The allocation of responsibility within the company is important for the enhancement of communication between individuals at headquarters and the subsidiary/alliance partner. The organization of communication influences information flow, just as perceptions of how issues should be communicated shape the outcome of intercultural encounters. Business philosophy and company culture, shared practices, feelings of identity and values are important as a common base for understanding. At this level, I describe how various degrees of shared culture exist. It was found that coherence in value-orientation and knowledge of headquarters' practices was most obvious in headquarters-subsidiary relationships, while the partner relationships were more connected to the brand values and the national cultural values. In addition, managers that had been stationed with alliance partners were aware of organizational values in both countries. In sum, this level describes the national and organizational cultural perceptions that influence communication, and how over time encounters enable new perception platforms for communication to emerge.

Professional

The professional level concerns functional departmental and product specific technical communication. Strategy, human resources, finance, marketing, communication, production, branding, and merchandising are some of the divisional knowledge fields that coexist within a company.

Organizational charts are included in some case chapters and they show how the companies divide their organizational members into professional (functional) areas of knowledge and responsibility. Managers need to communicate across professional knowledge borders even with people in the same organization. Communication bottlenecks may be found between designers and production or sales and marketing. Managers from specialized knowledge backgrounds must communicate with each other even within mono-cultural environments, and crossing cultural frontiers makes communication even more challenging. However, the opposite is also true, namely that functional specialists may be able to communicate via their professional knowledge to overcome language and cultural barriers.

Individual

While the above analytical levels concern professional knowledge and its influence on communication, the personal level is connected to the degree of internationalization of mindsets. The internationalization level is based on the linguistic ability, cultural knowledge and training and previous experience of the individual. Individuals have a level of personal experience based on their education, job responsibilities and years of exposure to international encounters. Their knowledge of national cultural issues and language ability will enhance or detract from business communication. Language skills are important, but as we shall see in the case studies, they are not sufficient. Experiences over time and professional business knowledge are equally important.

Conclusion: Communication and Change

A framework for the analysis of how managers from Denmark and Japan communicate was established in this chapter. For this project, communication is viewed as complex and dynamic and culture is considered to be 'negotiated'. That is, in the course of time, new practices and values emerge in intercultural encounters that are synergies of the parent cultures. They also involve new elements and thereby explain change. I argue that communication efforts from headquarters to subsidiary should ideally be approached as a form of co-created rather than transmitted meaning. The Western communication model presented here emphasizes transmission while the Eastern model of co-creation is drawn upon to explain communication as a dialogue between employees from headquarters and the subsidiary or alliance partner. The models additionally serve to explain some basic assumptions in the perception of communication held in the West/Denmark and in the East/Japan that influence and are influenced by organizational communication and culture. Intercultural (theory and) training has been based on stereotyping and generalizations about cultural differences. To move beyond stereotypes we need managers to tell their stories in their full length and complexity. The multi-level communication model is presented to enable an analysis of the complexity of the influences on managers in their interaction and communication between headquarters and subsidiaries in Japan. The companies participating in the project differ in size from one man to nine thousand people. Needless to say, the global managers who work in these companies meet different communication challenges. They are influenced differently by national, organizational, and professional factors in their communication and intercultural encounters. Moreover, their social, cultural and professional knowledge differ according to personal and professional experience. Finally, through their communication encounters, new cultural spaces consisting of new practices, rules and values emerge.

The five case stories are presented in the subsequent chapters. The analysis and conclusions based on the multi-level model are presented in Chapter Eight.

Bibliography

Adler, N. J. (2002a) 1997 Fourth Edition, *"The International Dimension of Organizational Behavior"*, Canada, North-Western

Adler, N. J. (2002b) *"From Boston to Beijing: Managing with a World View"*, Cincinnati, Southwestern

Beamer, L. (1995) "A Schemata Model for Intercultural Communication and Case Study: The Emperor and the Envoy", *Journal of Communication*, 32 April, pp. 141-161

Beamer, L. & Varner, I. (1995; 2001) *"Intercultural Communication in the Global Workplace"*, New York, McGraw-Hill companies, Inc.

Befu, H. (1980; 1987) *"The Group Model of Japanese Society and an Alternative"*, Rice University Studies (66), Houston, Texas

Blasco, M. & Gustafsson (2003) *"Intercultural Alternatives. Critical Perspectives on Intercultural Encounters in Theory and Practice"*, Copenhagen, Copenhagen Business School Press

Brannen, Y. & Salk, J. E. (2000) "Partnering across Boarders: Negotiating Organizational Culture in a German-Japanese Joint Venture", *Human Relations*, volume 53 (4), pp. 451-487

Collins, R. J. (1987) *"Max Danger: The Adventures of an Expatriate in Tokyo"*, Rutland, VT, Charles E. Tuttle Co.

Dale, P. (1986) *"The Myth of Japanese Uniqueness"*, Croom Helm

Davenport & Prusak (1998) *"Working Knowledge: How Organizations Manage What They Know"*, Boston, MA, Harvard Business School Press

Ferraro, G. P. (1990; 2002) *"The Cultural Dimension of International Business"*, Fifth Edition, New Jersey, Person. Prentice Hall

Gudykunst, W. B. & Kim, Y.Y. (1984) *"Communicating with Strangers: An Approach to Intercultural Communication"*, New York, Random House

Hall, E. T. (1959) *"The Silent Language"*, Greenwich, CT, Fawcett

Hampden-Turner, C. & Trompenaars, F. (1993) *"Riding the Waves of Culture. Understanding Culture and Diversity in Business"*, London, Nicholas Brealey Publishing

Hatch, M. J. & Schultz, M. (2001) "Are the Strategic Stars Aligned for Your Corporate Brand?", *Harvard Business Review*, February

Hofstede, G. (1980) *"Culture's Consequences: International Differences in Work–Related Values"*, London, Sage

Hofstede, G. (1991) *"Cultures and Organizations – Software of the Mind. Intercultural Cooperation and its Importance for Survival"*, New York, McGraw-Hill

Hofstede, G. (2001) Second Edition, *"Cultures Consequences. Comparing Values, Behaviours, Institutions, and Organizations across Nations"*, London, Sage Publications

Holden, N. J. (2002) *"Cross-Cultural Management: A Knowledge Management Perspective"*, London, Prentice Hall, Financial Times

Ito, Y. (2000) "What Causes the Similarities and Differences among the Social Sciences in Different Cultures? Focusing on Japan and the West", *Asian Journal of Communication*, 10 (2), pp. 93-123

Jandt, F. E. (1998) Second Edition, *"Intercultural Communication. An Introduction"*, Thousand Oaks, London, New Delhi, Sage Publications

Jensen, I. (1998) *"Interkulturel kommunikation i komplekse samfund"*, [Intercultural Communication in Complex Societies], Copenhagen, Roskilde Universitetsforlag

Krauss, E. S. (1984) *"Conflict in Japan"*, Honolulu, Hawaii University Press

Lawrence, P. & Wincent, E. (2000) *"Management in Western Europe"*, London, McMillan Press Ltd.

Laswell, H. (1948) *"The structure and function of communication and society: The communication of ideas"*, New York, Institute for Religious and Social Studies, pp. 203-243.

Leiniger, C. (1997) "The Alignment of Global Management Strategies, International Communication Approaches, and Individual Rhetoric, Rhetorical Choices", *Journal of Business and Technical Communication*, 11, pp. 261-280

Lippmann, W. (1922) *"Public Opinion"*, New York, McMillan

McSweeney, B. (2002) "Hofstede's Model of National Cultural Differences and Their Consequences: A Triumph of Faith – A Failure of Analysis", *Human Relations*, volume 55, no. 1, pp. 89-118

Moeran, B. (2001) "Hierarchies, Networks, Markets and Frames: Reconsidering Japanese Social Organisations", Working Paper presented at the Department for Intercultural Communication and Management, Copenhagen Business School

Nonaka, I. & Takeuchi H. (1995) *"The Knowledge Creating Company"*, Oxford University Press, Inc.

Nonaka, I., Von Krogh, G. & Ichijiro, K. (2000) *"Enabling Knowledge Creation"*, Oxford University Press, New York

Osland, J. S. & Bird, A. (2000) "Beyond Sophisticated Stereotyping: Cultural Sense Making in Context", *Academy of Management Executive*, 14 (1), pp. 65-79

Peltokorpi, V. (2006) "Knowledge Sharing in Cross-Cultural Settings: Nordic Expatriates in Japan", *International Journal of Knowledge and Learning*, 2 (4).

Polanyi, M. (1966) *"The Tacit Dimension"*, London, Routledge & Kegan Paul

Prud'homme, P. & Trompenaars, F. (2003) *"Managing Change. Across Corporate Cultures"*, West Sussex, Capstone Publishing

Rogers, E., Hart, M., William, B., & Yoshitaka, M. (2002) "Edward T. Hall and the History of Intercultural Communication: The United States and Japan", *Keio Communication Review*, no. 24

Schramm-Nielsen, J. (2000) "How to Interpret Uncertainty Avoidance Scores: a Comparative Study of Danish and French Firms", *Cross Cultural Management – An International Journal*, 7 (4)

Schramm-Nielsen, J., Lawrence, P. & Sivesind, K.H. (2004) *"Management in Scandinavia. Culture, Context and Change"*, Cheltenham, UK, Edward Elgar

Shannon, C. E. & Weaver, W. (1949) *"A Mathematical Model of Communication"*, Urbana, IL, University of Illinois Press

Sjøborg, E. R. (1985) *"Riding the tide: skandinavisk management mot år 2000"*, Oslo, Bedriftsøkonomens forlag [Riding the Tide: Scandinavian Management toward Year 2000]

Søderberg, A. & Holden, N. (2002) "Rethinking Cross Cultural Management in a Globalizing Business World", *International Journal of Cross Cultural Management*, volume 2, no. 1, pp. 103-121

Szulanski, G. (2003) *"Sticky Knowledge Barriers to Knowing in the Firm"*, London, Sage

Thomas, D. C. & Inkson, K. (2004) *"Cultural Intelligence. People Skills for Global Business"*, San Francisco, Berrett-Koehler Publishers

Vaara, E., Risberg, A., Søderberg, A. & Tienari, J. (2004) "Nation Talk. The Construction of National Stereotypes in a Merging Multinational" in *"Merging Across Borders: People, cultures and politics"*, Søderberg, A. & Vaara, E. (eds.), Copenhagen, Copenhagen Business School Press

Varner, I. (2000) "The Theoretical Foundation for Intercultural Business Communication: A Conceptual Model", *Association for Business Communication*, January

Yan, R. (1997) "Yin/Yang Principle and the Relevance of Externalism and Paralogic Rhetoric of Intercultural Communication", *Journal of Business and Technical Communication*, 11, pp. 297-320

Yoshikawa, M. (1987) "The Double-Swing Model of Intercultural Communication between the East and the West", in Kinkaid (eds.), *"Communication Theory: Eastern and Western Perspectives"*, London, Academic Press inc., Harcourt Brace Jovanovich College Publishers, pp. 319-329

Chapter Two: Endnotes

[1] The standard model of communication, known as the process model, was introduced by Shannon and Weaver in 'Mathematical Theory of Communication' in 1949. The signaling metaphor has been the most popular for developing other models and theories in communication since it provides a single, easily understandable specification of the main components of communication: source, message, channel, and receiver. A similar model for linear communication was developed at the same time by the American sociologist Laswell (1948) in his studies of propaganda. Laswell was concerned with the effect of communication and described the process starting with the original idea of the sender, with emphasis on the noticeable change in values and behavior of the receiver.

[2] The business strategy area includes the competitive position of the firm, the economic climate, the position of the product, the structure of the firm, the financial health of the firm, the rapidity of change, government regulation and law, HR practices, the size of the firm and corporate culture. The intercultural strategy includes the role of individual, formality and status, attitudes towards uncertainty, attitudes towards time, cultural sensitivity, willingness to take risks, high and low context, the role of gender, the role of hierarchy, race, and nationality. The communication strategy includes the discourse community, individual goals, the availability of technology, language, technical background, personal preference of channel, and awareness of audience and purpose of communication, the position in firm, appropriate richness, corporate goals, and the corporate communication policy.

[3] Gudykunst and Kim (1984) have presented a model which also includes several psychological and environmental influences on intercultural communication. The model here is inspired by Yoshikawa (1987) and his premises for communication.

[4] Yoshikawa (1987) is inspired by Enlightenment philosophy and Martin Buber's theory of dialogue. Buber and other Western colleagues, such as Bakhtin and Levinas, represent a strong 'Western' dialogical tradition (Jewish thinking, Continental philosophy, current American pragmatism) which is also beginning to gain ground in the intercultural paradigm (Blasco & Gustafsson, 2003).

[5] Hofstede (1980) based his findings on 116,000 internal company questionnaires administered in 1968 and 1972 (Op. cit: 11). Hofstede defines culture as the 'collective programming of the mind which distinguishes the members of one human group from another' (Op. cit: 25).

---

[6] Later, Hofstede added a fifth dimension inspired by 'Confucian work dynamism' (2001: 354), namely long-term and short-term oriented cultures.

[7] It is worth mentioning that Prud'homme and Trompenaars (2003) cited lessons learned by Japanese companies that merge and cooperate with foreign companies. Their findings (not included here) are contextual and company specific. Their 'reconciliation' approach resembles the 'negotiated culture' approach in the present project. They too show the impact of globalization on corporate culture and demonstrate how companies have learned to improve their global corporate culture by incorporating local cultural values.

[8] For example, 'cultural facilitators' travel to the Danish medical company Novo Nordisk's subsidiaries around the world to mediate information about corporate values and practices (Holden, 2002). In describing this as an advanced form of knowledge sharing and internal communication within global companies, Holden focuses less on the fact that these cultural facilitators also have a control function.

[9] Between eighty to ninety percent of Danish women work while forty percent of Japanese women work. This means that Danes have to share household chores and child rearing and companies have to respect private obligations. There are, however, many people particularly in management positions in the private and public sectors who work more than the labor market rules require.

[10] The author Aksel Sandemose (1899-1995 originally from Norway) promulgated what he called Janteloven, or the Law of Jante. Jante was the fictional name Sandemose gave a small town in Denmark where the law was enacted vigorously. The key values of the law were conformity, uniformity and envy. The commands were:
You should not believe that you are anything, that you are as much as us, that you are wiser than us, that you are better than we are, that you know more than we do, that you are more than we are or that you are good at anything. You should not laugh at us. You should not think that anybody likes you, or that you can teach us anything.

This supposedly explains Danish modesty. The Japanese by comparison have a saying that 'the needle that sticks out is hammered back' (deru kui wa utareru). These sayings highlight cultural factors leading to the modesty characteristic of individuals in both cultures. Nevertheless, the degree of modesty depends on the person and the context in which it is unfolded.

[11] Breaking away from generalizations poses a dilemma for researchers and practitioners. Among scholars who question the 'group model' of the nihonjinron theories are Harumi Befu (1980; 1987) and Peter Dale (1986). A model of conflict, as opposed to the traditional model of harmony, has also been introduced by Ellis Krauss (1984). However, it takes a 'Maoist leap' (Moeran, 2001) to part from the preconceived theoretical ideas that have hitherto determined the dominant way of thinking about Japanese society.

Chapter Three

BO BENDIXEN AND JAPANESE 'CUTE' CULTURE

Year	Event
1973	Bo Bendixen completes his studies at the Graphic College of Denmark in Copenhagen, and at the Academy of Fine Arts in Warsaw. He sets up his own design studio in Aarhus, Denmark.
1982	Bo Bendixen opens his fist gallery as well as a head office located in an old tobacco factory in the centre of the city of Aarhus, in Jutland, Denmark.
1991	Bo Bendixen's postcards are discovered in the Netherlands by a Japanese director of Huis Ten Bosch.
1992	Bo Bendixen signs an exclusive licensing contract with Huis Ten Bosch Park in Nagasaki.
1994	The first contract is signed with Japan's second largest newspaper, Asahi Shimbun.
2003	Huis Ten Bosch goes bankrupt. The new owner is Nomura Principal Finance.
2004	The Bo Bendixen store re-opens with twice the floor space in Huis Ten Bosch Park.

In 1991, Bo Bendixen made an international business break-through via his cooperation with the Dutch theme park Huis Ten Bosch[1] in Nagasaki, Japan. At the time, Bo Bendixen owned twelve stores in Denmark, but had only limited experience with extending his business internationally. His organization was not set up to deal with exports, and he was not used to dealing with foreigners. These factors made his business commitments in Japan a challenge. His business partner, Huis Ten Bosch, was a large, conservative Japanese company. However, while the organization in charge of the theme park was extensive, the sales and marketing people that Bo Bendixen dealt with in establishing the partnership also had limited international experience. In this setting, both sides were, and to a certain extent continue to be, challenged by cultural differences.

This chapter explores how Bo Bendixen and employees of Huis Ten Bosch perceive and handle national and organizational cultural differences which arise as part of both personal contact and phone and fax communication. It also underscores how experience over time creates news ways of communicating and understanding. The first part of the chapter presents the story of how the Japanese discovered Bo Bendixen, as well as that of their first cultural encounters. The next section shows how Bo Bendixen's 'cute' animal designs on postcards and t-shirts led to his success in Japan, while the subsequent part of the chapter explores the organization of communication and resulting perceptions of 'the other' from both Danish and Japanese perspectives. Finally, the last section concerns lessons learned and an assessment of future business opportunities as expressed by both Bo Bendixen and the Japanese staff of Huis Ten Bosch.

The chapter is based on interviews conducted with Bo Bendixen and Paul Takada, the businessman who discovered Bo Bendixen's postcards in the Netherlands, as well as the sales and marketing staff that Bo Bendixen has dealt with at Huis Ten Bosch for over fifteen years.

Danish Design Produced around the World
Bo Bendixen's product designs include Danish scenery, people, animals, flowers and national icons such as flags. His twelve stores in Denmark carry clothing and souvenir items with his logo and various designs. Although his logo promotes both Danish imagery and a promise of Scandinavian authenticity, his production is influenced by global trends. Like the other companies presented in this book, Bo Bendixen manufactures his design products around the world – including doormats in India and bathrobes in Turkey. A new swimwear collection is made through a Danish intermediary in Thailand and the Philippines, and several clothing collections are made in Asia (t-shirts are manufactured in Bangladesh and Mauritius). Additionally, the production sites change continuously. When Mauritius becomes too expensive, the production is transferred to Bangladesh, or to places that are even cheaper, he says. According to Bo Bendixen, it is an advantage to deal through Danish intermediaries because they are in direct contact with the producers and can guarantee

good quality. Bo Bendixen does not have the time to go abroad regularly to check up on the manufacturers. Consequently, it is much easier for him to deal through intermediaries with regard to issues such as colors and materials. Thus, even though the intermediary arrangement costs more, he considers it to be worth it as he is guaranteed that his designs will be delivered as expected.

Regarding the rest of his production network, Bo Bendixen manufactures certain products in Japan and Denmark. In particular, porcelain goods are produced in Japan, where even though the price is high, the quality is excellent. Other products, such as prints and embroidery on merchandise, are mainly completed in Denmark, which is also the site of production for posters, postcards, pens and key chains.

Characteristics of Bo Bendixen Products

When asked about the characteristics of his designs, Bo Bendixen says that he aims to convey a positive, happy message and to put people in a good mood. In his designs, he tries to capture some of the moments of pleasure that are part of the Scandinavian lifestyle and associated with Scandinavia's abundant natural beauty. He uses the following words to describe his work:

> *Originality, joy of life, happiness and creativity. Although creativity is such a worn out word, my designs have to touch and move people. People must not be indifferent! It is easy to make something that does not matter, but, this does not work for me. The product has to be of high-quality and the design has to be original. If something does not move you, it should be trashed. I have plenty of things that I should not have made, and they are currently taking up space in my warehouse. We may have to sell these products at a lower price. When I create a design, I may like it one day, but then after a month or two no longer find it to be interesting. It is very important to be critical. When you have printed 2000 t-shirts, it is no fun if they do not move you – or anyone else.*

'Move you' in this context can be understood to convey both inspiration and a motivation to buy. In other words, art and business are closely linked in the design process for Bo Bendixen. This may be a natural consequence of the fact that he is both a designer and a businessman.

Most often he challenges himself to draw something that is better and more joyful, he says. But it only works if it will sell. When asked whether he is generally happy when he makes these joyful designs, he answers:

Yes, otherwise I become happy in the process. That is also why I make the designs. I want to be in a good mood. In my position, I can decide for myself what I want to do, so I might as well draw something that makes me happy. I do not sit and laugh all day, but I love cozy things and sweet things. But it is difficult for me to talk about my own designs. I guess I often listen to what other people say about my things. I get them to put their experiences into words. My biggest satisfaction is to create something special and receive a compliment.

Bo Bendixen admits that his goals are ambitious. He wants to continue to make designs that are original, cheer people up, are different and have a positive message. Some measure of his success is that he has stayed true to this vision for more than three decades.

The Upstart in Japan – Background

In 1991, Bo Bendixen was contacted from the Netherlands by the Trading Company Europe-Japan Promotion with a request that he send some samples of his designs.

To start from the beginning, a Japanese businessman, Paul Takada, had been in Europe to contract certain Dutch designers for work related to Huis Ten Bosch, an enormous Dutch theme park located forty minutes by train from Nagasaki, on the Southern Japanese Island Kyushu. The park was planned to open in 1992 and Paul Takada was still looking for artists and ideas when he arrived in Amsterdam. Completely by chance, he encountered some of Bo Bendixen's colorful postcards on a wall in an office of the trading company. Paul Takada immediately knew that this was what he was looking for, and he asked the staff of Europe-Japan Promotion to contact the Danish artist.

Representatives from Europe-Japan Promotion visited Bo Bendixen in Denmark, after which he agreed to create some new trail designs for the theme park, although at the time he had no idea what kind of theme park it was. From the brochures they sent, it reminded him of Legoland, but the size of it was unbelievable. It was a city with eight kilometers of canals and big hotels, and many of the old-style buildings were copies of famous Dutch buildings. The Palais van Huis Ten Bosch was even built as a full-scale replica of the Palace of Queen Beatrice of the Netherlands.

Bo Bendixen made some sketches, although he did not really know what was expected of him. At first, he tried to adapt his designs to Japanese taste, as he very much wanted his designs to be well received. However, he finally decided that there was a reason why they had approached him: they obviously must have enjoyed what they saw. Still pondering whether he should try to do something that he thought they would like, he decided to stay true to his original vision.

Bo Bendixen came up with a number of different suggestions, and in the end he combined his most popular designs of dogs and cats with bridges and Dutch houses. They might as well have been scenes from Denmark – except for the windmills and tulips.

The Discovery – From a Japanese Perspective

Paul Takada was one of the directors of Huis Ten Bosch and a primary player in making connections between the Huis Ten Bosch park authorities and European designers. He left Huis Ten Bosch as director in 2003 when the park went bankrupt and most of the management was replaced by the new owner, the financial holding company Nomura Principal Finance, a subsidiary of Nomura Holdings.

Paul Takada now works as executive vice president of an advertising company in Nagasaki. When I met with him there we did not talk much about the crisis at the park, but rushed to talk about his background and his involvement in the establishment of the park. His English fluency and personal history were important assets in establishing connections between the Japanese management of the park and various service providers from the rest of the world, he said. The fact that he had a Christian name, Paul, led me to believe that he might have been an ancestor of the Japanese Christians who suffered for their religious beliefs in Japan, but he did not dwell on these historical issues.[2]

> *Let us make a long story short. When I was young, my boss used to be the honorary counselor to the Netherlands, but nobody around him could speak English. I was therefore selected when I was quite young to be a contact person for government and business people. One day Mr. Yoshikuni Kamichika, the founder of Huis Ten Bosch, came to see me. He wanted to start the*

Holland Village in Nagasaki, and because I had so many acquaintances and connections within Dutch society, I was asked to join the preparations for the Holland Village. The village was very successful, and about six years later we decided to make a bigger Dutch City. We built the amazing palace of Huis Ten Bosch itself, and the park was extended with exact copies of Dutch buildings and streets.

Paul Takada was the only person to travel to Europe to choose the products they were going to produce as original souvenir items for the park. Without knowing any designers beforehand, he went to the Netherlands. He met a number of people and was introduced to several graphic designers. He signed an agreement with the Dutch graphic designer Dick Bruna, who also designs cute animal and human characters, but he was not yet satisfied, and after a week of searching he was disappointed.

On the day he was to leave Amsterdam, he stopped at Europe-Japan Promotion to use the telephone and to say goodbye to a few business associates when his eye caught a postcard of a cow – a multicolor cow.

He asked about the artist and was told that he was Danish, and not Dutch, but to Paul Takada the cow was a symbol of the Netherlands because there were so many of them in the country. When he got back to Japan, he sent a fax message to Bo Bendixen. After discussing back and forth, Bo Bendixen agreed to create some designs for Huis Ten Bosch.

Bo Bendixen visited the Netherlands on an all-expenses paid scouting trip, and was asked to develop landscape and animal designs for the park. In particular, he was asked to make a special design for the park entrance cards, which would be in plastic, and he submitted several patterns for this purpose. While the scale for these designs was quite small, one of his most challenging assignments was to create an image for a gigantic hot air balloon.

This was the start of the relationship, and Bo Bendixen found it all very exiting.

Display 3.1 Bo Bendixen's multi-colored cows

The First Trip to Japan – Relationship Building

Bo Bendixen was invited to Japan before the opening of the theme park. As Bo Bendixen recalls, it was a long trip, first by airplane from Jutland to Copenhagen, then to Tokyo and Nagasaki. In Nagasaki, he was met by a Huis Ten Bosch welcome committee with a sign that said 'Bo Bendixen'. They also had a picture of him from his marketing literature in order to confirm his identity. The Huis Ten Bosch people were afraid that Bo Bendixen would get lost in Japan, so two 'bodyguards' kindly followed him around while he was there. They also turned out to be helpful concerning cultural issues. For instance, on several occasions they told him, in a nice way, to take of his shoes before entering traditional restaurants, and they advised him on the dress-code required at formal dinners.

This was in 1991, and the theme park was still just one large construction site with a year of building to be completed before it opened. Since the park hotels were not yet open, Bo Bendixen stayed at a hotel in Sasebo, a nearby city.

Before I left for Japan, I had talked to people who knew about the country in order to get advice on various traditions and how to behave. I was told to dress formally. I was not accustomed to wearing formal business attire, but I bought a suit and tie. I also

*bought chocolates because I was told that I needed to bring gifts.
So I bought four to five packages of the local Elisa chocolates.
One of these was specifically intended for the president.*

Although upon arrival Bo Bendixen was exhausted after twenty-four
hours of traveling, he was invited to a restaurant to eat fish on rice
balls (sushi) and raw fish (sashimi). Once there, he was served a big
plate with fresh fish, and one in particular was cut down the side. It
seemed to be alive and looking directly at Bo Bendixen. Needless to
say, he was quite shocked. His hotel room was just on the other side of
the street so he went to get his camera. Bo Bendixen recalls:

*My host thought I had become sick from looking at the fish, so
they asked 'Mr. Bo are you okay?', and when I said I was fine
they were relieved. But, I must say that it was a shocking first food
experience in Japan. Now, however, going out to eat has become
my greatest pleasure when I am there.*

Bo Bendixen was in Huis Ten Bosch for one week in order to get
acquainted with the employees and the surroundings inside and outside
the park. He was treated well and found it interesting to experience
Japan for the first time, but for him the most important part of the visit
was the formal meeting where he would find out whether or not his
work had been accepted.

The First Meeting
While waiting for the big day to come, Bo Bendixen was invited to go
sightseeing in Nagasaki Holland Village Park. This eight year old park
was going to be replaced by the new one. The initial meeting was also
going to be held there.

At one o'clock, the meeting started with about thirty people
participating and Bo Bendixen the only representative from Denmark.
A welcome speech was made by one of the directors and then the
president entered the room. The president greeted Bo Bendixen and
then quickly started to look at the designs that Bo Bendixen was
proposing for the park. According to Bo Bendixen:

*It all happened in twenty to thirty minutes, in what seemed to be a
very quick meeting. The only one who spoke was the president.
Everyone showed a great deal of respect for the president and the
executives who surrounded him. There was an evident*

hierarchical order, and I could sense this even without knowing the titles of everyone. I had brought my chocolate with me, but I was very nervous and I could not see who was who, so I gave my chocolate to the wrong person. When the president arrived as the last person, I did not have any more presents so he did not get any. The president merely got my briefcase. He did not speak English – there was hardly anyone who did. The president mostly said 'good', and then he said 'I think it is fine with Mr. Bendixen and I can see that he is still a young man so there is still a future in him'. Then everybody sighed with relief because we had been communicating for a number of months and they had asked me to do specific pictures relating to the Netherlands, meaning that they had already invested a lot of money and effort in me. This included getting me to Japan, since they paid everything, so before I even sat down at that table it had been a considerable investment for them.

The director, Paul Takada, and the others involved in promoting Bo Bendixen were equally happy about the positive decision.

But what happened to the chocolate presents? According to the Huis Ten Bosch staff Ai Kawanami and Yuki Araki, Bo Bendixen's presents probably reached their intended destination. Presents in Japan are automatically passed to the president or to the appropriate person in the hierarchy, and the Japanese do not open them in front of others. The most important thing was that Bo Bendixen had made the gesture of offering a gift.

Regarding the park itself, Bo Bendixen was surprised at the scope of the project, as well as at the careful planning and detailed nature of the work. During his subsequent visits to the park he has also been treated with great hospitality. Every time he has visited Japan, he has been invited out for dinner by various department managers, and the last dinner of his stay is always with the president and one of the top directors at a traditional fine Japanese restaurant. In this sense, hospitality is both a Japanese token of goodwill and an invitation for further cooperation. Above all, it is an obligatory activity in any Japanese setting.

Setup in Japan and Market Entry

During the next ten years, Bo Bendixen visited Japan once or twice a year. In particular, once his designs had been accepted, his second visit was for the purpose of negotiating the contract. It took a lot of time to settle on a license agreement and he made a special trip to Japan to sign it when all the details were agreed upon. He also visited the factories that were going to produce the merchandise, and factory representatives came to the park for meetings every time he was in Japan. Huis Ten Bosch produced new products continuously as part of the license agreement. However, Bo Bendixen had to approve the products, as well as a sample, before they started producing. In particular, the choice of colors and their exact reproduction turned out to be a few of the more difficult issues that had to be resolved. For instance, they had many problems in the beginning with t-shirts. Bo Bendixen wanted the Japanese producers to match his colors perfectly, so he went to the factory many times to get the nuances right, and the color combinations were always a problem. Eventually, they stopped producing t-shirts in Japan and bought directly from Bo Bendixen in Denmark.

The first years were extremely exiting, and Bo Bendixen was happy to have had the opportunity to make his business entry into Japan through Huis Ten Bosch. In particular, because he had been contacted directly, he did not have to go through the time-consuming process of finding a partner in Japan on his own. After just a few years, Huis Ten Bosch and Bo Bendixen developed a larger collection, including clothes, bags, porcelain and stationary. With the development of the larger collection, now composed of almost 700 product categories, a special Bo Bendixen shop was opened in the park in order to exclusively promote the full product line.

The License Agreement – Pros and Cons of Exclusivity

The contract Bo Bendixen signed with Huis Ten Bosch included exclusive rights for not only Japan, but also Korea, Taiwan and Hong Kong. Huis Ten Bosch, at first, had big ambitions to sell Bo Bendixen products well beyond the limits of the theme park.

Bo Bendixen, for his part, had signed the contract because it was his only option. Huis Ten Bosch was his only potential connection in Japan. At the same time, he was flattered by their willingness to promote his designs, and he felt that their enthusiasm would create a good basis for future cooperation.

Another important reason for signing the agreement was to protect his designs in Japan. A large organization like Huis Ten Bosch would have the resources to take counterfeiters to court, and he knew that he would not be able to stop infringement in Asia without powerful connections. As he himself said, he would probably not even know if his rights were being infringed, since this had been the case with previous instances of counterfeiting in Europe.[3]

Regarding market expansion, Huis Ten Bosch did manage to sell Bo Bendixen products at the airports in Fukuoka and Nagasaki, as well as in a nearby resort community. However, tourism at the resort was heavily seasonal, with most of its business during the summer, so promotion within the resort was eventually dropped. Representatives from Huis Ten Bosch had been to Denmark to visit his stores, and they tried to make something similar in Japan, but according to Bo Bendixen he did not have a chance to influence either the interior design or the sales promotion. On both of these issues he would have liked to have been actively consulted. In his own six stores and six franchise stores in Denmark, Bo Bendixen has personally designed the interiors, down to the smallest detail.

Eventually, as it turned out, Huis Ten Bosch did not promote Bo Bendixen's products beyond the initial ventures described above because all of their energy went into trying to ensure the future of the park itself. Additionally, Bo Bendixen discovered that the Huis Ten Bosch organization was neither interested in nor capable of distributing his products more widely in Japan, let alone Asia. During the first five years of the licensing agreement, this was not a problem for Bo because business was going so well. However, since the late 1990s, turnover has decreased steadily without the possibility of selling more widely in Asia, due to the exclusivity of the licensing agreement. At the same time, Bo Bendixen has created many new product designs, and the potential for these products, he says, is far from exhausted.

Consequently, Bo Bendixen would like to change the contract – especially the exclusivity agreement. If Huis Ten Bosh were exploiting their rights to the greatest extent possible, that would be one thing. However, since they do not have the capacity to do so, he would like to open the possibility to others to promote his products in other regions. Bo Bendixen is often contacted at trade fairs by Japanese business people who would like to discuss promoting his products, but he is prevented from dealing with them given his contract with Huis Ten Bosch.

Nevertheless, despite his aspirations for the future, Bo Bendixen's present contract with Huis Ten Bosch has provided him with more business advantages than disadvantages. In reality, Bo Bendixen has plenty of work to do, and if he were to make an extra effort in Japan, it would be at the expense of his business activities in Denmark.

A New Business Opportunity – The Asahi Shimbun Contract

In 1994, an opportunity arose for Bo Bendixen to expand his business in Japan. He was asked to create a logo for the Asahi Shimbun, the second largest newspaper in Japan with a daily distribution of approximately nine million newspapers.

The arrangement was initiated by the marketing director of the Asahi Shimbun. The marketing director's hometown is Nagasaki, and every time she was there, she visited Huis Ten Bosch. She was crazy about the park, and when she saw Bo Bendixen's shop she became crazy about it as well. She felt that a design from Bo Bendixen could improve the Asahi Shimbun's image.

Paul Takada, the person responsible for business development on behalf of Huis Ten Bosch, knew that the Asahi Shimbun was a traditional and intellectually-oriented paper, so he was doubtful that management would adopt one of Bo Bendixen's cute designs.

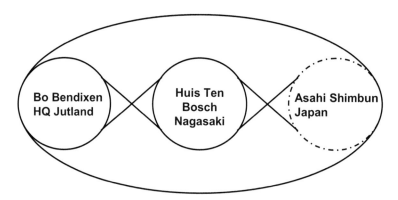

Display 3.2 Bo Bendixen, communication diagram

Display 3.3 The 'Paper Doggie' and the 'Ohayo Dori' at the Sunrise Mountain

The Asahi Shimbun marketing and distribution departments were going to use the logo for posters, commercials, bus and train ads, their distribution trucks and motorbikes, and various giveaways. They wanted a logo and image of something connected to the delivery of the paper and to 'sunrise', which is the literal meaning of 'asahi'. Bo Bendixen delivered two proposals: a dog carrying a newspaper in his mouth, which they called 'paper doggie' and a rooster on top of the morning sun, which they called 'ohayo dori'.

When Paul Takada went to present the proposals at the Asahi Shimbun head office, both designs were immediately accepted. Bo Bendixen remembers the celebration of the agreement:

> *The Asahi Shimbun accepted both proposals and we had to sign contracts again. This time, it was a separate contract between Asahi Shimbun and me. Huis Ten Bosch, who had sole ownership of my designs, agreed to this arrangement. I was at the Asahi headquarters for a big ceremony where three directors signed the contract with pens of gold. Afterwards, we went out to eat on the Tokyo Bay with a boat they had rented for about thirty people. We had to give a toast, and almost everybody had to give a speech. Most of them did not understand English – but the newspaper always provided me with a translator.*

Three years later, the president of the Asahi Shimbun once again invited Bo Bendixen to the Asahi headquarters and asked him to create a number of additional designs for the newspaper. He was to design the animal of the year, based on the twelve animal symbols of Chinese astrology (the Zodiac). He started with the mouse, and each subsequent year he was asked to create the corresponding animal as part of an ongoing contract.

Bo Bendixen was very proud when he saw his 'paper doggie' on subway billboards all over Tokyo as well as on the electronic billboard at the famous Shibuya crossing in Tokyo where millions of Japanese pass by on a daily basis. Thanks to such mass communication and large-scale promotion, Bo Bendixen's animal designs are now well-known throughout Japan.

Superstar Treatment

Bo Bendixen has been treated with great hospitably and as an honored guest in all of his Japanese business dealings, he says. This treatment is in stark contrast to the way he is treated at home, in Denmark:

The first time I visited the Asahi Shimbun in Tokyo they had printed the doggie and the rooster as posters and placed them all around the newspaper building. 'Dear Bo Bendixen, welcome to Asahi Shimbun', it said in my eight colors. They had also carved the dog and the rooster in aluminum and mounted them on the front door of the Asahi headquarters.

When he toured the different departments of the Asahi Shimbun, employees stood up and clapped. He was not at all used to this kind of attention, so as he remembers: "I became pretty red in the face from this sudden superstar treatment". Similarly, when he visits his store in Huis Ten Bosch, he is asked to sign autographs and pose for photos. Bo Bendixen remembers such moments with a great deal of joy. In contrast, when he is in one of his stores in Denmark and customers find out that he is the artist, they may or may not stop to talk, and even then it is only for a second.

Cute – The Key to Success

The word 'cute' was mentioned again and again by all of those interviewed. But what does the word mean, and how does it affect Bo Bendixen's business in Japan?

The Huis Ten Bosch Park is built as a Dutch city and features elements of Dutch lifestyle that make ordinary life in the Netherlands part of the park experience. According to Yuki Araki, assistant sales manager, Bo Bendixen's designs create a positive image which fits well with the overall image of the park. In the same way that Disneyland has Mickey Mouse, Huis Ten Bosch has the Bo Bendixen designs. The happy, positive and cute animals suit the park, she says, and there is no doubt that Bo Bendixen's designs have been well received by park visitors due to the 'cute' factor.

Colorful and Cute – Even Dragons

Everyone at Huis Ten Bosch commented on the colors and strokes used to create the designs and frequently identified these two factors as being responsible for the impact of the images.

Paul Takada found that Bo Bendixen's designs were bright and beautiful because of the colors he uses. Even though the red or yellow or blue are popular everyday colors, they are different from the red, yellow or blue that the Japanese normally encounter. According to Paul Takada, Bo Bendixen's designs are free spirited and created in a way that the Japanese would not be able to create on their own. He explained that Japanese are taught to draw in very straight lines that are properly connected. Bo Bendixen's designs are freedom itself. He creates his characters with a special flair that makes an impact on people.

An example that illustrates Bo Bendixen's use of color is if you have an image of a black and white milk cow. Bo's cow was blue, red and white, and captured in very flowing strokes. This kind of creativity is impossible for the Japanese to conceive of on their own. It moves something inside you if you see such an animal and think of its actual color in reality. Suddenly, although it is familiar and immediately recognizable, it is foreign at the same time.

Paul Takada was impressed and surprised when he first saw Bo Bendixen's work.

It takes talent to design an animal in a way that no one would have thought possible. Bo Bendixen may find Japanese culture very different from his own, and Japan may have a large population with lots of busy people living in cities, but Bo Bendixen, who is not fond of big cities, has found out that people in big cities are fond of animals. And he has kept designing his animals in a particularly cute way. He even makes dragons cute in a way that surprises the Japanese.

The Japanese would never have thought that dragons could be 'cute', he continues, a difference which highlights the importance of cultural perception. For example, the section manager of marketing and retail, Hiroshi Iwashiya, referred to Bo Bendixen's design of a camel:

Compared to our image of the camel in Japan, the combination of shape and color in Bo's camel presents us with something that we Japanese could never come up with. We would never come up with the idea of a 'red' camel, for example! So this kind of difference really catches our attention and creates a strong impact. That is how I feel about it.

Display 3.4 The Dragon

When Hiroshi Iwashiya shows the Bo Bendixen designs to suppliers, their first response is always "that is cute". However, Hiroshi Iwashiya must work hard with the manufacturers to precisely duplicate Bo Bendixen's designs.

I am involved in the design business, and what I like about Bo's products are their colors and simple design. These factors are of particular importance, but also particularly difficult to replicate. The shape and color of Bo's images really catch our attention and create a strong impact. So, even though the design is simple, it is powerful. The Japanese are good at drawing and we are able to imitate – but there is very little originality. In my opinion, the Japanese are good at making 'hard' products and assembling different parts, but not good in the imaginary and creative fields, such as design, which the Europeans are good at.

According to Hiroshi Iwashiya, the park management invested substantial resources in identifying foreign designers to promote it, and despite the decline in park visitors, there are usually many people in the souvenir stores, including Bo Bendixen's.

Although the number of visitors has decreased, the Bo Bendixen store has been remodeled: it is larger, and a Bo Bendixen gallery has been added with information on the artist in order to inform customers about his particular conception of design. Bo Bendixen's products are also displayed in many other shops located throughout the park.

In addition to Bo Bendixen's products, the sales of Dutch cheese, beer and souvenirs have also remained stable, despite fewer visitors. The reason for this, he says, is that Asian people love to bring gifts when they celebrate anniversaries, and other occasions. Most importantly, they always bring back souvenirs when they travel. Besides, he says, customers of the Bo Bendixen store also buy his products for themselves. The most frequent visitors to Huis Ten Bosch are people from the region, and they buy their favorite items every time they visit. Not surprisingly, Bo Bendixen is a favorite of many.

Display 3.5 This design did not work in Japan: a shark eating a 'naughty' girl

Designs That Do Not Work in Japan

However, it would be a mistake to assume that everything is culturally transferable, as several design failures in Japan have demonstrated. In particular, certain designs involving patterns of birds, and starlings specifically have been met with outright revulsion. Bo Bendixen submitted the starling designs for approval hoping that they would be a success. Contrary to his expectations, the Huis Ten Bosch staff did not like them, and wrote back that they found birds in a group to be scary. At the time, Bo Bendixen was producing the birds as patterns for silk scarves, towels and posters, and thought they would be a hit in Japan. However, as much as Bo Bendixen has a clear vision for his own designs, the Huis Ten Bosch staff has an equally clear image of what they think the designs should be like in order to appeal to the Japanese consumer and represent the interests of the park.

A similar story involved what Bo Bendixen considered to be a playful design of a shark. He had designed an image of a shark that was eating a little 'naughty' girl. She was wearing a little pink skirt and red shoes. Every one of his staff at the Danish Design office thought it was very funny – but that certainly did not cross-over in Japan. When Bo Bendixen submitted the design, he immediately received at fax from the Huis Ten Bosch office stating: "We hope that this is not your new style". Bo Bendixen assumes that the design must have been too brutal.

However, it is not always the Japanese who are confronted with cultural differences, as a case involving the Asahi Shimbun illustrates. Bo Bendixen recently received a fax inquiring about the production of doormats with the 'paper doggie' and the 'ohayo dori' designs imprinted on them, and whether or not it was acceptable to him that people wipe their shoes on top of his designs. Bo Bendixen wrote back that he was already selling doormats with animal designs, and since he considered a doormat to be a nice way to welcome visitors to one's home, he did not have any problem with people wiping their feet on top of his designs. As only one of many differences in cultural traditions that Bo Bendixen has encountered while working with the Japanese, this case in particular was motivated, he assumed, by the Japanese tradition of taking off their shoes when they enter a home or traditional restaurant. It might also have been out of respect for Bo Bendixen and his designs in order to determine whether or not this would cause offense.

The above stories highlight some of the differences in taste and culture that have become apparent in fifteen years of collaboration between Bo Bendixen and his Japanese partners. With respect to the influence of Japanese 'cute' culture, Bo Bendixen has been asked to design a variety of ever more 'cute' souvenir items, but there are limits to how 'cute' he is willing to go. While Japanese consumers want small gadgets and cute souvenirs, Bo Bendixen is determined to stay true to his own vision in order to support and develop both his own image and that of his products. While the above concerns product and professional considerations, the following concerns the organization of communication between Denmark and Japan and the cultural issues at stake in the exchange of information.

Organization – Working with Huis Ten Bosch

Only a few people in the theme park administration speak English fluently. According to Bo Bendixen, his Japanese counterparts do not understand his spoken English very well and communicating verbally has been a problem throughout their partnership. For example, when Bo Bendixen is in Japan, he negotiates through an interpreter, which presents its own set of challenges. From Denmark, Bo Bendixen normally faxes or mails the Huis Ten Bosch office two to three times a week, unless he is working on a special project that requires him to be in more frequent contact with the park office.

Three administrators plus a number of people in the warehouse are employed at the Bo Bendixen main office in Jutland. Nevertheless, Bo Bendixen takes care of most of the communication with Japan himself. He writes his messages by hand and faxes them, a system that works well for him. He rarely talks on the phone because it usually leads to misunderstandings. Faxes give the Huis Ten Bosch staff an opportunity to work together on the translation, which he finds generally results in more reliable communication.

The fact that language is problematic affects Bo Bendixen's business in many ways. In particular, sometimes general business information is not conveyed at all. For instance, Bo Bendixen hardly received any information concerning the bankruptcy of Huis Ten Bosch in 2003. He was informed through other Danish channels in Japan, but was never contacted directly by Huis Ten Bosch.

Group Decisions Take Time

Another challenge based on cultural differences, according to Bo Bendixen, is that he is not able to get an 'honest' or direct answer from the Huis Ten Bosch staff. This has improved over the years, but as he points out, he has been working with them for fifteen years now. He has often asked for their frank opinion and for direct feedback on his work. However, it seems to him that individual employees have great difficulty in expressing their personal opinions. They always have to discuss an issue repeatedly with their coworkers before deciding on what the answer should be. They seem to place a great deal of importance on group decision-making that often involves several people in the department, even for issues that Bo Bendixen considers to be mere details. He has also observed this process first hand during his business trips to Japan.

When he has been working on a design, Bo Bendixen wants immediate feedback. However, when he first started working with Huis Ten Bosch several days would pass before he got any response at all. For Bo Bendixen, feedback is part of the process of generating new ideas and insights and improving his designs – a process that, when it functions well, resembles sparing with an equally talented and supportive critic. When he asks the Huis Ten Bosch staff for their feedback, it has nothing to do with their potential purchase of the design – rather he simply wants to know whether or not they like it. Bo Bendixen credits the problem to the fact that the employees at Huis Ten Bosch who communicate with him are assistants rather than managers. This means that they do not have the authority to make decisions on their own. While they are in charge of the correspondence, they have several people above them who have to approve the designs, and altogether this process takes time.

The possibility of using the Internet has made it is easier to send new designs for approval. A digital photo of new products can be sent to Japan immediately. However this advance in technology has not changed the way that Bo Bendixen chooses to communicate with Japan. He still writes by hand and faxes his own messages. Of course physical distance is an issue when dealing with Japan, but according to Bo Bendixen, the cultural distance poses the greater challenge.

Working With a Dane

From the point of view of the Huis Ten Bosch staff, the way they work with Bo Bendixen is an exception. The other artists that Huis Ten Bosch deals with, including the illustrator Dick Bruna, all have their own agencies in Japan who take care of business negotiations. Since Bo Bendixen both creates the artwork and manages the business relationship himself, the opportunity to get to know him personally has been an interesting experience for the Huis Ten Bosch staff.

The first assignment given to Yuki Araki when she joined Huis Ten Bosch fourteen years ago was to contact all the foreigners providing services to the company, one of whom was Bo Bendixen. When Yuki Araki's boss, Paul Takada returned from the Netherlands smitten by Bo Bendixen's work, he asked Yuki Araki to write Bo a letter. Since Bo is considered a girl's name in Japan, they found it quite amusing when they discovered that it belonged to a rather tall and physically imposing Danish man.

Although Yuki Araki had dealt with foreigners in Japan, she felt that establishing a business relationship was a serious matter, and consequently she was quite formal in her correspondence. However, she was nonetheless quite relieved and pleased when Bo Bendixen answered with a handwritten letter, as she found his hand writing to be friendly and the way he wrote the 'characters' of the Roman letters in his faxes was interesting. After three to four months of correspondence, Bo Bendixen finally arranged a visit to Japan. While she was surprised by the sight of this gigantic Dane, she found his personality to be just like his letters – gentle and kind.

After working for a short while with Bo Bendixen, Yuki Araki felt confident that she was able to advise her colleagues on 'how to deal with him'. In this way, communication with him was managed as a group process among colleagues.

Bo Bendixen's contact for the last six years, Ai Kawanami, is a subsection manager in the merchandise sales department head office. She is in charge of merchandise in the Bo Bendixen store. At first it was very hard for Ai Kawanami to read Bo Bendixen's handwriting, but after six years she has become an expert. Her impression of 'Mr. Bo' is:

He is a friendly and funny person to be around, but at the business meetings he is very strict and always focuses on his design. When you see the Bo Bendixen store you can see that his persistence pays off. He is very true to his original style, which is what makes his products unique.

According to Ai Kawanami, Bo Bendixen is a country person at heart, with a gentle personality, but when it comes to his craftsmanship, he is very demanding. He is very conscious about the fluid motions used to create his designs, and he has explained to the Huis Ten Bosch staff and the production factory many times that his lines are *not* straight. The edges of his lines are shaking mildly because he makes them by hand. This shaking is important because it differentiates his lines from computerized straight lines. Bo Bendixen's drawings are defined by the lines, and the lines define his design. She has come to understand the importance of this detail over the years. Fifteen years ago, no one at Huis Ten Bosch either understood or appreciated these nuances.[4] In the beginning, when Bo sent a draft of his designs by fax, the park staff thought that perhaps some of the lines should be modified, or the bright colors changed. Needless to say, Mr. Bo was not interested in modifying his design, and he insisted that they be reproduced just as he had submitted them. Even the size of the design had to match the original size perfectly, she says. When the Japanese manufacturers tried to reproduce his designs with different formats or colors, he asked them to stick to the original.

> *So, we learned through many negotiations that we were not allowed to change Bo Bendixen's designs. Bo Bendixen wanted to be in on every detail. The proportions of his designs in relation to the overall product also had to be just as he had directed.*

Ai Kawanami has worked with several foreigners providing services to the park, but she thinks Bo is unique.

> *Whatever Bo's culture is, he is very easy to communicate with for us Japanese. Japanese people are sometimes shy and afraid of talking to foreigners. When I talk to him, I am relaxed and not worried. Everything about him, from his way of living and his design to his personality is relaxed. He is not formal or official. It seems like we rural people in Japan fit well with Bo Bendixen's atmosphere and his personal character, and that is why we can maintain such a long-term relationship.*

As a bonus, Ai Kawanami says and laughs, Bo Bendixen is good to fight with, even though she always loses.

Manager Hiroshi Iwashiya also says that Bo Bendixen is very persistent in the way he protects his designs, but from Bo Bendixen's point of view, this is just a professional brand strategy. Disney or any other brand conscious company would do the same, he says. If you do not protect what makes you original, then you will only dilute your image.

Formal Meetings

One of the most puzzling issues in doing business with Huis Ten Bosch has been the meetings. Bo Bendixen was surprised to discover the large number of people that are expected to take part. When asked about meetings, and why so many people take part, Yuki Araki explained:

> *There is a whole organization behind the decision-making processes in a Japanese company. For instance, as a secretary I know about the details related to the business, but I do not have a title, so I have to ask my section manager, and the section manager has to ask his department manager, who has to ask his area manager. Sometimes issues go all the way to the director or the president. In the case of Bo Bendixen's introductory meeting, everyone was there.*

In other meetings, the Japanese manufacturers will attend with superiors and senior staff. Sometimes the designer or designers will be present, so five to ten people will be there for meetings.

> *We always have to have a large general strategy meeting first to talk about the direction and strategy of our business relationship. At these strategy meetings two to three people lead the meeting. Then we may split up into smaller groups of three or four people to discuss the details. These meetings may include the section manager, the department manager and the manufacturer.*

In formal meetings, mainly the president and the vice president speak. Paul Takada was there for all the initial meetings. He is fluent in English and was able to interpret for the president. On occasions, when he spoke as the director, someone else would interpret. Interestingly, according to Ai Kawanami, Bo Bendixen just came by himself. He could have brought his staff but he came alone.

In summary, several issues were identified concerning communication and cultural differences. These include language, individual/group responsibility and the purpose of meetings. From all accounts, it appears as though neither side has drastically changed their way of doing business to accommodate the other. Bo Bendixen has not done anything actively to improve his language skills. The Huis Ten Bosch staff still struggle to read his handwritten faxes. The opportunity to use new technology to communicate more effectively has not inspired Bo Bendixen. The Japanese continue to make decisions through lengthy processes, while Bo Bendixen has not relented in the slightest in allowing his designs to be modified. Huis Ten Bosch still gathers many people for meetings, and Bo Bendixen always arrives alone.

However, while traditional cultural values thrive, a mutual understanding of both product and people has emerged over time as shared inspiration has moved business forward.

Inspired by the Japanese Business Model

When asked about lessons learned, Bo Bendixen first claims that he has not been inspired by Japan, at least not with respect to his designs. Although, he admits: "You never know where inspiration comes from!" Rather, he has been inspired by the Japanese way of doing business. He has been motivated to broaden his product line while working with Huis Ten Bosch. When he started in Japan, he only made posters, postcards and a few t-shirts. The Japanese consumer-oriented ways have encouraged him to produce a wider variety of products.

Other parts of the Japanese business model do not make much sense to him. For instance, Huis Ten Bosch usually buys through trading houses and not directly from the production site. This way, they pay an extra intermediary for their products, which mean they can sell it to customers for at most twice the price, and sometimes even this is not possible. In comparison, when stores in Denmark buy something from Bo Bendixen Denmark, they aim at multiplying it by two and a half to three. Bo Bendixen has asked several times why they do not deal directly with the Japanese producers or produce in China, but apparently, for the Japanese, relationships mean more than profit in certain instances.

A Business Question – What Would Be the Ideal Solution?

Bo Bendixen is keen to keep Huis Ten Bosch as a client after almost fifteen years of successful partnership. However if he could find new partners in Japan to share licensing rights with Huis Ten Bosch, it would be ideal.

Meanwhile Bo Bendixen is hoping that the Japanese economy will improve and that stability will return to Japan. He has not seen strong signs of recovery recently, but he is hopeful. It is worth mentioning that the economic crisis in Japan has simply meant a decrease in royalties from Huis Ten Bosch, so in this respect, things could have been worse. On the positive side, the direct orders from Huis Ten Bosch to his head office in Jutland have increased, because it is not cost effective for Huis Ten Bosch to produce in small quantities. The present situation is therefore not a serious financial disadvantage for Bo Bendixen.

Expanding Business

But what happened to the original business idea of expanding the market for Bo Bendixen products through sales in Hong Kong, Singapore, Korea and China? According to Paul Takada, many people would be interested in this enterprise, and there are definitely opportunities in other Asian countries.

In the view of Paul Takada, Bo Bendixen could increase his sales in the future.

Of course he can. It is up to him. But sometimes Bo wants to, and sometimes he does not. He does not want to be busier because then he would have to hire more staff. But it is possible, so why not?

The hurdle for Bo Bendixen in building his business further, says Paul Takada, is that he is 'one dimensional' on several fronts.

First, he wants to do everything by himself. Second, he refuses to venture into 3D graphics which would make his business explode. He could just let us make the 3D graphics and produce the merchandise only if he was satisfied with the product. But he does not want to think about business, so it is difficult for us to make sales arguments. In this case, the ambitions of business and art do not match. The fashion designers at the park want to sell more and become famous, but the graphic designers do not have these same goals, and Bo Bendixen is no exception.

Paul Takada has suggested to Bo Bendixen that he should focus on his design work, and hire a business manager to expand the business internationally. However, Bo Bendixen does not like this idea, as he wants to be involved in *all* the decisions concerning his merchandise.

Paul Takada and the Huis Ten Bosch staff have suggested on numerous occasions that he should make his designs three dimensional for the production of toy animals. But, according to Bo Bendixen, it is impossible to transfer his two dimensional designs into three dimensions because his designs are based on lines. He is not even interested in trying, despite the fact that the market potential for toy animals is enormous, according to Paul Takada.

Concerning the Huis Ten Bosch view of the licensing agreement, Yuki Araki says:

> *We still have the rights to East Asia, but we have not talked about this plan for years. Bo Bendixen has not pushed it either. He likes to develop his designs at a quiet pace and is not keen on development that is too fast or that would radically change his work life. His personal principles, which guide his business, have always been strong in this sense. He does not want his designs to boom and then disappear, so Bo has also been holding back. At the same time, our position in the new millennium is not so strong due to the financial difficulties of the park. Therefore, we have the impression that there is mutual agreement in keeping business at the status quo.*

The future depends on the new management at Huis Ten Bosch, says Yuki Araki, and the new manager of sales and executive director of the head office has yet to publicize his plans. An issue that affects the strategy now, she continues, is the fact that the Bo Bendixen designs have become icons of the park. His t-shirts and postcards can only be purchased at Huis Ten Bosch, so his brand is exclusive in this sense. This promotes sales at the Bo Bendixen store, as the exclusivity increases the value of the products for costumers. In particular, this exclusivity may also be the reason why Bo Bendixen's sales have not been seriously affected by either the economic recession or the financial difficulties of the park.

While a few costumers may ask whether Bo Bendixen is Danish or Dutch, these are few and far between. His store continues to be one of the most popular in the park. The fact is, according to Yuki Araki, that many Japanese customers like his designs, regardless of what his nationality might be.

Conclusion

The chapter has dealt with how Bo Bendixen and the Huis Ten Bosch employees perceive and handle cultural differences both in person and in communication by phone and fax. It is clear that both sides have maintained their national and organizational cultural values during more than fifteen years of cooperation. However, experience over time has created knowledge and understanding of business practices on both sides. The cultural differences have been challenging for both parties, but professional interest has helped the partnership to flourish. In this sense, professional business drive has triumphed over cultural issues.

In conclusion, it is important to emphasize that Bo Bendixen's success in Japan, to a great extent, can be credited to his 'cute' animal designs that now have their own status. There is no question but that his designs have hit a cultural nerve in contemporary Japan. Japanese people like cute things, and Bo Bendixen's simple strokes and happy colors couldn't be a more perfect fit.

Chapter Three: Endnotes

[1] The Dutch theme park Huis Ten Bosch was opened on 25 March 1992. Huis Ten Bosch is Dutch for 'House in the Woods' and it is the name of the Dutch Royal Family's residence, a replica of which has been built in the centre the park. Like forty percent of the Netherlands, the park is built on reclaimed land near the seashore, outside Nagasaki. There are six kilometers of canals, a harbor with impressive Dutch ships, and bicycles are available to tour the park. Everything, including the windmills, is an exact replica of real Dutch buildings and streets. To make the experience complete, 300,000 tulips bloom in the spring.

[2] Paul Takada's ancestors may have suffered for being Christians for the following historical reasons: the first Christian missionary to reach Japan was a Jesuit priest Francis Xavier, who arrived in Kyushu in 1549. Over the next few centuries, Christianity spread rapidly before being banned. During this transition, thousands of Japanese Christians were killed because of their religious beliefs. While Japan was closed to the outside world for more than 250 years, the Dutch alone were allowed to trade. However, they were kept isolated on the small artificial island of Dejima in Nagasaki harbor. In 1873, the ban on Japanese Christianity was repealed and about 20,000 'hidden Christians' were discovered in Nagasaki and the surrounding islands.

[3] In Milan, Italy, Bo Bendixen designs have been found in different books and magazines by business acquaintances of Paul Takada. In Paul Takada's view, the fact that Bo Bendixen's designs have been copied in Italy is an indication of his success.

[4] Over the years Ai Kawanami has developed her own design for the park called 'the traveling man'. The traveling man is made in straight lines on the computer. The figure has been made into a number of souvenir products.

Chapter Four

ROSENDAHL, ROYALTY AND HANS CHRISTIAN ANDERSEN

Year	Event
1984	Rosendahl is established by Erik Rosendahl.
1998	Rosendahl begins exporting to Japan through an importer.
2001	Rosendahl hires Martin Glisby as Asia manager.
2004	Rosendahl launches the official H.C. Andersen bicentennial porcelain series.
2004	First Japanese partner meeting in Denmark.

The Rosendahl Company was founded by Erik Rosendahl in 1984, and it has since become a well-established brand in the Danish market. Rosendahl lifestyle home products, including wine openers, glass vases and numerous kinds of kitchen utensils, are used in more than fifty percent of Danish homes. Erik Rosendahl is in charge of the most important market, the Danish market. His son, Henrik Rosendahl, is now in charge of export markets and was involved in the re-entry of the company into Japan.

The chapter presents the story of how a medium sized Danish company began the millennium with limited exports to Japan, only to build it into their second largest export market in just five years. According to Hans Peter Kay, commercial attaché at the Danish Embassy in Tokyo, the great strategic effort required of any company to compete in the Japanese market makes the Rosendahl re-entry a real success story.

The chapter shows how cultural knowledge, new ways of thinking and not least an H.C. Andersen porcelain series enabled a successful market re-entry. The first part of the chapter concerns considerations about the re-entry mode. Second, the story of the introduction of the H.C. Andersen porcelain idea to partners is presented. Third, cultural issues and the organization of communication are described. The final part of the chapter is an account of the introduction of the dark-blue H.C. Andersen porcelain from a Japanese perspective.

The interviews include headquarter executives, the designer Lin Utzon, a Japanese advisor and five Japanese partners.

Rosendahl Re-Enters Japan

The usual strategy used by Danish small and medium sized companies when they wish to expand business from a saturated home market to other countries around the world is to participate in the European life-style fairs. Exhibitor fees are low and the opportunity to make connections with dealers and buyers is substantial. However, much of the time, this approach results in random connections with many countries and only short-term orders. While this has also been the road to internationalization for Rosendahl which currently sells in fifty-five markets,[1] entry into the Japanese market was handled differently.

Rosendahl's story in Japan started in 1998 when they initially began exports through an importer. For several years Rosendahl sold very little in Japan, and in 2001 they contracted with another importer in the hope of building the brand name in the Japanese market. However, the new arrangement worked even less well than the previous one, and Rosendahl realized that a decision had to be made on how to best approach this complex market.

Rosendahl was looking for new ways to export to Japan when Martin Glisby was hired as Asia manager in 2001. Martin Glisby had just earned a Master's in International Business Administration from the Asian Studies Program at Copenhagen Business School and was fluent in Japanese. He was also familiar with Danish business practices in Japan through an internship at the Royal Danish Embassy in Tokyo.

His first task was to end the collaboration with the Japanese importer, since Rosendahl wanted to create its own business model for Japan centered on direct contact with retailers and department stores. Martin Glisby's next task was to bring on board staff capable of building Rosendahl's share of the Japanese market, and three Japanese nationals were employed and stationed at Rosendahl headquarters,

North of Copenhagen. Together, the team set out to change Rosendahl's approach to the Japanese market.

Making Connections in the Market

The idea at first, in 2001, was merely to follow all interesting leads in Japan to create a network. In retrospect, a lot of time was spent talking to people that did not end up doing business with Rosendahl. Meanwhile, people who seemed to be small-scale players turned out in the end to be some of Rosendahl's biggest business partners in Japan.

Martin Glisby spent a lot of time at Rosendahl headquarters trying to get ideas for a re-entry strategy, but he soon realized that sitting at his desk would not get him very far. He had to go to Japan to meet with people and learn more about the market.

First, he used some of his personal connections. A former professor at Copenhagen Business School, Nigel Holden, had written an article about a famous wine expert in Japan who was the wine advisor to the Emperor. Martin Glisby was introduced to the seventy-five year-old gentleman who subsequently allowed Martin to use his network. This created links in directions that could never have been foreseen. The network encompassed business relations such as retail outlets and smaller design stores, which in turn led to media connections such as design magazines, newspapers, and television.

Rosendahl first started out selling through a number of small design stores. While this did not generate volume sales, the relationships turned out to be useful for building Rosendahl's brand image because the stores often had good connections to the editors of various design magazines. This led initially to full page editorials, and later TV Tokyo visited Denmark with a crew of ten to fifteen camera people and journalists. The result was a twelve-minute special program about Rosendahl that was aired during prime time on a Friday evening. The program was worth a gold mine in advertising money, and was the culmination of Rosendahl's and Martin Glisby's first steps in gaining knowledge about networks and media connections in Japan.

Martin Glisby admits that in retrospect the strategy of building a sales organization was in the beginning 'disturbingly unorganized'. However, in less than three years Japan has become Rosendahl's second biggest export market. Norway is the biggest market followed by Japan, Sweden, Britain, Germany and the United States. Clearly, Japan has become a great opportunity for Rosendahl. In particular, the rapidity with which the market for Rosendahl products grew in Japan far outpaced growth in other markets. While this naturally created support from top management at Rosendahl, the real business results were yet to come.

Exclusive Design Stores and Department Stores

At the outset of 2002, the most important objective for Rosendahl was to create at brand name in Japan. This was much more important than creating high turnover. They had already tried working with an importer who was not actively promoting the brand over the long-term. In particular, Martin Glisby was watching competitors whose market expansion using an agent or wholesaler would come to a halt after the first few years. A distributor or agent in Japan, in Martin Glisby's opinion, would have restricted access to other networks, and he set out to ensure Rosendahl's freedom of action by creating their own network. In this sense, Japan was no different than any other market:

> *If you outsource the sales, marketing and branding to an external partner, you will not control your own network and you will not be able to implement your own ideas. We wanted control of the brand building and needed detailed knowledge about the market in order to do things ourselves,* said Martin Glisby.

In other words, Rosendahl wanted the flexibility and freedom to up- and down-scale the brand through strategic selection of business partners. Further, it is always difficult to estimate the effort that agents put into promoting the brand. You can make agreements about the sales volume, but it is difficult to work together on building a brand with long-term results.

In the pursuit of creating a prestigious brand, Rosendahl approached the top design shops located in up-scale areas of Tokyo. These were small shops and the resulting volume of sales was low. Still, the idea was to start up-scale with renowned design stores in order to encourage the interest of the leading department stores and larger wholesalers at a later stage. The implementation of this strategy was very time consuming and required that Rosendahl was willing to absorb a loss in Japan for several years. According to Martin Glisby:

> *We did business with about sixty different smaller design shops and covered a substantial percentage of the total interior market segment. We were not able grow sales from this market setup, but it has had the effect that we have become quite well known in Japan. We have never done any advertising in Japan. And yet we*

have become among the top ten Danish or Scandinavian brands that the Japanese recognize. This is largely due to our involvement with these prestigious design shops.

Over time, Rosendahl's association with these up-scale boutiques began to result in inquiries from companies at the next level of prestige in the Japanese consumer hierarchy. Within this group, Rosendahl made connections with several department stores and larger chains carrying Scandinavian design. These companies were both prestigious and had the ability to generate a larger sales volume.

These companies would not have wanted to do business with us earlier. We originally tried to contact many of the department stores, but they did not even reply. Now our experience is that they contact us and inquire about the possibility of carrying our products. In this sense, we are where we hoped to be, because there is a limit to how far we can go in our effort to create volume sales. If we deal with mass-merchandisers as sales outlets we will loose our connections at the top, which means that we will loose it all. There is a fine line as to how widely we can spread our business. Aiming for large volumes by selling through mass-merchandisers would be costly for our image.

Working with sixty different small interior design shops that had no experience in doing imports themselves was time consuming. When dealing directly with these smaller retailers, Rosendahl had to handle all the import procedures and payments with all the problems that this entailed. The big professional companies, on the other had, had the resources and expertise to manage the import process themselves. Bottom line, something had to be done to minimize the administrative burden imposed by working with the small design shops.

A Change in Plans

In October 2003, Rosendahl again made an explicit change to their marketing approach in Japan.

The smaller shops that were not strategically important were 'automated'. In other words, design shops were encouraged to order automatically on the Rosendahl homepage, implicitly or explicitly meaning that they would no longer receive the same high level of service and attention. The stores that were a part of larger networks became the primary business partners, and these key account relationships were formally supported.

In retrospect, while Rosendahl could have tried to establish relationships with some of the larger players in the market from the outset, it is unlikely that these large companies would have been interested in carrying a completely unproven and unknown brand. By first building their reputation with the help of the smaller, more exclusive design stores, Rosendahl ultimately succeeded in making the larger players come to them. In addition, the valuable market knowledge that was gained during the initial phase of their market entry strategy allowed them to determine who among the larger department stores and wholesalers would be the right partners to continue to build the Rosendahl brand in Japan.

Making Choices

Rosendahl's cultivation of a business network saved them from getting caught in the complex and bureaucratic Japanese system of intermediaries, and a whole array of middlemen was successfully bypassed.

The choice of business partners was based on subjective criteria. This was possible because potential partners were associated with well-established business groups, and thus the solidity of their reputations preceded them. Some of the questions that guided the choice of partners were, according to Martin Glisby:

> *Do they have the right gleam in their eye when we talk about joint projects? Can we feel their excitement? Are they as engaged as we are? Is it the kind of company that we can offer something to? Is it a company that will work in our interest? And finally, do we have good personal chemistry?*

Another guiding principle was to choose business partners that were experts in their industry. Those chosen for cooperation were specialists in their segments of the market, but not direct competitors with each other. The segments included: department store retail, specialty retail, corporate gifts, bridal gifts, institutional sales, mail order, and e-commerce.

The department store retail segment included interior design department stores that focused on design and furniture, as well as traditional Japanese department stores. Specialty retail was represented by design-intensive exhibition stores. Bridal gifts were managed by a new bridal gift company. Corporate gifts and institutional sales were open to several companies, as was e-commerce, while the mail order business was taken care of by a single firm. Finally, a chain of bakeries included Rosendahl products in their catalogue. When customers purchased bread, they would accumulate points which they could then exchange for Danish design products chosen from the catalogue.

Overall, while the final approach differed greatly from Rosendahl's initial approach in 2001, it had been a natural outcome of the market learning and development processes that had been undertaken.

Gaining Market Knowledge

Although these developments were positive in many respects, one fundamental question remained: how was Rosendahl to sustain their competitive advantage within this cooperative network? This fundamental business question required an answer.

Most companies, according to Martin Glisby, focus on 'functional' expertise. They work within core areas of a market such as corporate gifts, or mail order. In Rosendahl's case, each business partner represented a different segment of the market. For instance, one had exclusive rights to department store retail, another to direct retail, another to hotel and restaurant business, and so on. Of course there were grey zones in between, and segments would overlap to some extent, but basically each one covered well segmented areas of the market. Besides, in Martin Glisby's view, any overlap would simply serve to keep the partners on their toes and force them to pay attention to what others were doing to promote and sell the brand. The advantage of this segmented arrangement was that each company had significant functional expertise and knowledge about their share of the market. The bridal company, for instance, knew everything about the bridal market and wedding gifts.

Overall, the knowledge gained through these network partnerships was invaluable to Rosendahl. As newcomers to the market, they would never have been able to obtain the same kind of sector specific knowledge that local companies could provide. Thus, Rosendahl's competitive advantage was ultimately due to their ability to link together and to extract knowledge from a diverse network of business partners whose interests they had aligned with their own. Rosendahl had also managed to avoid potential conflict or competition within the network.

In fact, when the partners were invited to Rosendahl headquarters in 2004, unexpected synergies between them materialized. Each partner had been specially invited to discuss becoming a sales representative for the official H.C. Andersen bicentennial porcelain.

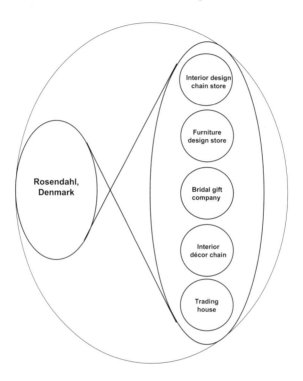

Display 4.1 Rosendahl, communication diagram

Challenging Cultural Stereotypes

The idea of the meeting was to launch the H.C. Andersen porcelain as the official dinnerware of the bicentennial celebration in 2005 of H.C. Andersen's birthday. Dinner plates, coffee cups and plates had been designed by Lin Utzon in dark blue with abstract artwork depicting six Andersen fairy tales: The Little Mermaid, the Nightingale, the Ugly Duckling, Thumbelina (Little Tiny), the Snow Queen and the Butterfly.

Preparing for the meeting was a nerve wrecking experience because Rosendahl had no prior experience with bringing together diverse Japanese retailers and wholesalers. In particular, they were greatly concerned about potential cultural issues. Would the partners be interested in working together? Would they speak honestly and contribute in the meetings or would they hold back? Would they be interested in finalizing business commitments? And on top of it all, would they even be interested in carrying the H.C. Andersen porcelain series?

On 13 March 2004, the presidents and CEOs of the partner companies arrived in Denmark. They spent a week at Rosendahl's headquarters participating in seminars and meetings. They met the Rosendahl management team, as well as the designer Lin Utzon, who had also agreed to do sales promotion locally in the stores in Japan.

This was Rosendahl's first attempt at hosting a sales meeting for all of their Japanese partners, and it turned out to be advantageous that they were conducting it far from the structured formality of the Japanese business environment. During the meetings in Denmark, the Japanese companies contributed actively, sharing their professional experience drawn from each company's market focus. Based on preconceptions about Japanese business and social behavior, Martin Glisby had expected less dialogue during these meetings between senior executives. However, to his surprise, CEOs, presidents and sales managers contributed actively with questions, advice and good ideas. No one seemed reluctant to share their experiences, and they talked directly with one another.

The H.C. Andersen porcelain and the promotional events which were to accompany the launch turned out to be of great interest to each of the potential business partners and soon became a common frame of interest and reference. The H.C. Andersen bicentennial project[2] was to include several Royal events in Japan: first, the visit of Queen Margrethe II and Prince Henrik on 17 November 2004 in Tokyo, to be followed by the visit of Princess Mary and Crown Prince Frederik on 18 April 2005 at the World Exposition in Aichi Prefecture in Japan. With the combination of Royal visits to Japan and the opportunity for commercial events, the chance to present the H.C. Andersen porcelain series created a great deal of excitement among the selected group of Rosendahl partners. Of course 'selected', according to Martin Glisby, is not the correct way of describing Rosendahl's connection with these companies, as they are not usually 'selectable'. Rather, they do the selecting themselves. However, in the case of the H.C. Andersen project, these business giants were the only ones offered exclusive rights in their market segments to sell the blue print porcelain with the six Andersen fairy tales. Potentially because of this status and exclusivity, the group worked well together and was both more outspoken and accepting of ideas than the Rosendahl staff had even hoped they would be.

Another fortuitous opportunity arose during the visit, one which promised to further enhance the H.C. Andersen collaboration, namely the appointment of the Danish Queen Margrethe II as the protector of the H.C. Andersen bicentennial. The appointment ceremony, which overlapped with the visit of Rosendahl's Japanese partners, was to be held in Odense, the birth place of H.C. Andersen. The business partners were invited to join the event, during which they had a once in a lifetime opportunity of having their pictures taken with the Danish Queen. The experience of meeting the Danish Royal Family in person was considered an exceptionally special event by the Japanese, even more so because the Japanese Imperial Family is much less approachable on the rare occasions when they perform public appearances. The Japanese partners also had the opportunity to see the H.C. Andersen museum in Odense, which combined with the meeting of the Danish Royalty led to such a feeling of collective optimism that most of the partners committed to the project on the spot. It is worth highlighting that in Japan none of this would likely have been possible.

Most of the Japanese had never been to Denmark before and some did not even speak English. Rosendahl's Japanese speaking staff guided them throughout their visit, and all meetings were conducted in Japanese. Among all of the factors already mentioned, this may have been one of the most important in contributing to the success of this first encounter. Speaking Japanese may have provided a sense of familiarity in a foreign business environment.

The Andersen Porcelain – Upgrading Rosendahl's Image

Rosendahl's idea behind the production of the H.C. Andersen porcelain was to create images and associations with something perceived to have greater value than the porcelain itself, according to the president, Henrik Rosendahl. In other words, the idea was to take advantage of the opportunity to create a higher perceived value for the Rosendahl brand in Japan. Over the course of the promotion activities to come, the Rosendahl fairy tale porcelain would be associated with celebrities ranging from its designer Lin Utzon to the Andersen Ambassadors and the Danish Queen.

The H.C. Andersen project was handled as a completely separate project from Rosendahl's other retail activities in Japan, and the rest of the network consisting of approximately a hundred smaller shops continued to carry just the traditional Rosendahl product line. In fact, the whole organization of sales in Japan *was very much about choosing what not to do*. According to Martin Glisby, it was very important not to be all things to all people. Rosendahl had already declined proposals from a number of potential retailers because the look and the image of their stores did not reflect the image that Rosendahl wanted to create and be associated with in Japan.

Although it was tempting to choose the easy solution and sell to fifty mass-merchandisers all over Japan to generate large volume sales, Martin Glisby's ambition was somewhat different, namely to create a stronger brand name and image. In this setting, the H.C. Andersen event came as a timely and significant opportunity. However, that is taking the historical perspective – during the planning of the launch itself, nothing could be taken for granted.

Support from Headquarters – A President's Perspective

The business approach taken by Rosendahl in circumventing the multiplicity of intermediaries, as Martin Glisby saw it, was new in Japan. However, the strategy was not only new to the Japanese – it also entailed certain requirements for Rosendahl's operations. Martin Glisby had to stress repeatedly at Rosendahl a number of critical issues related to meeting Japanese expectations, including the production of large quantities which could be used to manage supply and ensure on-time delivery, and the provision of first-class quality products. On time delivery and first-class quality were simply expected in Japan and seen as basic requirements for doing business.

With relatively few resources, Rosendahl had managed to reach customers in a large percentage of the Japanese market. However, this was only possible because they had acted through a network of relationships. Alternatively, if Rosendahl had attempted to use its own sales force, they would have only reached a small portion of the market, or they would have had to use a lot of resources that were not available to the family run business at the time. For example, Martin Glisby did not have the budget to open a flagship store in Japan similar to the Rosendahl store on the walking street 'Strøget' in Copenhagen. Alternative approaches, such as franchising, were not even considered. Direct control was too important, and although a chain of company owned stores would have been ideal for building the brand, success would have been far from guaranteed and the financial risk would have been enormous.

Needless to say, for the success of the chosen approach, it was important to have the full support of Rosendahl management. The idea for Japan was to set it up as a home-market and operate it as such. This included sourcing production and carrying inventory in Japan, which provided an opportunity for the company president, Henrik Rosendahl, to get involved directly. As orders were outstripping current capacity, Henrik Rosendahl went to Japan to set up production.

In the view of Henrik Rosendahl, substantial financial resources were invested in building the Japanese market. In fact, much more was invested than the market share justified at the time. While Henrik Rosendahl was convinced that the H.C. Andersen event would play an important role in building the brand in Japan, as well as lead to future opportunities, he also had to set limits to the scope of involvement.

Naturally, the H.C. Andersen project is upgrading the brand, and the business network is interesting. However, Japan is not an easy country to access. It is an interesting market in many ways, but a difficult one to open up.

Concerning the development of the H.C. Andersen porcelain, Henrik Rosendahl wanted the product line to be of high quality, without catering exclusively to the elite segment of the market. In other countries, Rosendahl targets a fairly broad range of consumers, but in Japan it was important to establish a brand name synonymous with refined quality. Overall, he was convinced that the flexibility of his company would enable Rosendahl to establish itself in the Japanese market:

We work with different retailers and wholesalers in Japan, which means that things change continuously and opportunities arise. We are flexible and work to differentiate our product in cooperation with our customers.

Like his father, Henrik Rosendahl is a venture capitalist. He supports business ideas that he believes in by allocating capital and resources. He gives his managers a lot of autonomy, and he trusts them, but he also expects them to reflect on their work in order to become better at it. There is room for making mistakes – as long as they do not make the same mistake twice, he says and laughs. As a sort of 'business angel', Henrik Rosendahl tries to mediate between the different units inside his company in order to ensure a level of cooperation that furthers the interests of the company as a whole. Henrik's father, Erik

Rosendahl, has always worked to initiate new business opportunities, and his ways guide the spirit and setup of the company.

The IT system is set up so Rosendahl staff can check the sales of any product around the world. The total company turnover day by day can be followed closely. Activities from initial brainstorming and strategy formation through sales and marketing are run independently by regional managers and key account managers, with Henrik Rosendahl motivating and directing his staff through the allocation of financial resources. While Japan is the current area of investment, China is up and coming.

A future aim is to work more on conceptualization and image creation in the marketing of products. In the future, Rosendahl does not wish to merely sell Danish Design – they want to tell stories. The H.C. Andersen porcelain was a big first step in this direction.

Designer Lin Utzon as the Storyteller

The H.C. Andersen fairy tales are well known in Japan, to the extent that Rosendahl's association with the fairy tale writer through the porcelain series was a major coup for the company. The involvement of the world renowned artist Lin Utzon was another. In connection with the Danish business delegation's visit to Japan, Lin Utzon told her stories to customers in Japanese department stores, and she later had the opportunity to be in company of the Danish Queen and the Japanese Emperor to talk about the creation of her art and her personal vision for the H.C. Andersen porcelain. Equally importantly, Lin Utzon's involvement also made a great impression on the Rosendahl business network.

The creation of the porcelain took Lin Utzon three years. In her own words, she found it to be a "very challenging and difficult assignment". The three years included many long periods of reflection and discussion relating to design, color and conception.

Lin Utzon has previously worked with different kinds of design and textiles, including the creation of a very popular series of vases for Rosendahl. When she is working on a new product line, she is completely focused and absorbed, she said when I interviewed her in Japan. However, with respect to the H.C. Andersen porcelain, she was not accustomed to working with figurative design, namely the depiction of human or animal characters. Making the fairy tale designs for the Andersen plates was difficult in many respects. First, Lin Utzon had to be careful not to make her designs so abstract that people would be unable to recognize them as representing H.C. Andersen fairy tales.

Consequently, she created a number of mermaids and butterflies and tried to fit each one into a single pattern. Second, it was difficult to find factories that could reproduce the dark blue color that she found so attractive and exclusive. Finally, Rosendahl wanted a product that was affordable. Eventually, all three demands were reconciled and she was able to successfully complete what had been one of her most difficult and challenging assignments.

Lin Utzon took part in the Danish Business Delegation and Royal visit to Japan in November 2004. On this occasion, she had the opportunity to talk about her work with Queen Margrethe II and the Japanese Imperial Family at a reception at the Imperial Palace in Tokyo.

It was an outstanding experience to meet the Imperial Family. They were so mild that I had a sense that they were divine. I was very pleased to meet them. It was something that I had not dreamed of experiencing. I was very moved and just wanted to stay in my own little bubble after having met them. It was a fantastic experience and I left with a very happy feeling. The fact that I could talk to Queen Margrethe about my work was a great pleasure. To share my thoughts with the Imperial Couple who were so gentle, left me with a very happy feeling. It made me want to be even better at my work.

While in Japan, Lin Utzon participated in a promotion tour for Rosendahl. Her personal stories about design, Danish customs and table-setting traditions were followed by her signature in a H.C. Andersen fairy tale book (Rosendahl had printed ten thousand copies of the book in Japanese for customers purchasing the porcelain). Rosendahl also arranged for her to be interviewed by a number of design magazines. Overall, the combination of Rosendahl's network and Lin Utzon's talent and reputation proved to be a winning one.

Display 4.2 Lin Utzon at a prestigious department store in Tokyo

A Japan Unit within Danish Headquarters

With respect to Rosendahl's operations in Japan, the company made the decision to concentrate their market and cultural expertise at Rosendahl headquarters north of Copenhagen. In other words, cultural translation between what is Danish and what is Japanese is managed in Denmark rather than in Japan. In particular, Rosendahl has become culturally enabled by focusing on the language and cultural competencies of prospective employees during the hiring process. Everyone involved with Japan at Rosendahl is, at a minimum, bi-cultural and bi-lingual.

Specifically, of the Rosendahl employees focused on the Japanese market, several are Japanese nationals, most of whom have been working and living in Denmark for some time. Consequently, they are to varying degrees also fluent in Danish and knowledgeable about Danish culture. The process of crossing cultural boundaries, which challenges most companies, is managed internally at Rosendahl and dealt with on a daily basis.

Internally at Rosendahl, the Japan unit is almost a company within the company, as it largely works independently of other units and autonomously pursues its own strategies. The Danish and the European Export units, for instance, are built around agents and importers and focus on selling in large volumes. For Japan, the current focus is the building of the brand name.

Organizationally, the Japan sales unit within Rosendahl is driven by key account managers, each of whom is responsible for a number of close business relationships. These clients get first priority and they are attended to immediately – in Japanese. One of the key components to Rosendahl's success is that culture and language are dealt with almost seamlessly. Appreciation for this approach to business is clearly reflected in the statements made by various members of Rosendahl's business network in Japan (highlighted at the end of the chapter). If someone in Japan has a problem, they know who to contact and they get service immediately. This way the Japanese staff take care of order processing and business development at the same time. One of the advantages of knowing the language and the culture according to the account manager, Hiroki Saito, is that sometimes his costumers do not state explicitly what they think. In such cases, he has to 'see' what they think instead of just asking them. This ability to step back, watch and wait to see what they come up with is important, he says. He has to know when to stop pushing his argument. This comes with practice, but also with cultural sensitivity.

The Real Business Coup – A Japanese Advisor
It is well known that the number one criterion for success in Japan is local connections and networks. It may take two to three years of continuous effort to even get an introduction to department stores in Japan, and the traditional distribution system obliges you to go through two to four intermediaries before you reach the consumer.

The opportunity for Rosendahl to work directly with prestigious department stores was arranged through an introduction by Rosendahl's advisor in Japan.[3] Through him the Rosendahl management was able to meet with the top executive of the Department store group. The advisor has been *the* promoter of Danish design in Japan for decades, and he was recently contracted by Rosendahl. He is also a senior advisor to giant Japanese trading houses *(sogoshosha)*.

Needless to say, the advisor is well connected – many of Japan's business elite can be found in his rolodex – and his endorsement has instantly secured business opportunities for the companies he advises. Rosendahl's biggest coup in Japan, according to Martin Glisby, was to hire him. He made important introductions to two department store chains, as well as other partners that Rosendahl identified as 'high flyers' with great potential:

> *It is usually problematic to even find out which intermediaries to contact. We tried previously to ask some department stores directly about which intermediaries to contact to do business with them. They did not volunteer the information. Now with the endorsement of our advisor, we were able to arrange a meeting. We deliberately invited them to the big conference room at the Royal Danish Embassy in Tokyo[4] where we were formally introduced. The sales manager seemed genuinely interested in the Andersen project. It is difficult to say whether or not this interest was generated because of the presence of our advisor, because of the formality of the meeting at the Embassy or whether it was because of the H.C. Andersen name. But he instantly accepted the package of ideas that I presented. One meeting was basically all that was needed*, according to Martin Glisby.

After the introductory meeting, the department store representatives were ready to work with Rosendahl and they provided the contact information for employees within the stores responsible for import administration and transactions. They also immediately arranged for exhibitions to take place at different department stores.

The Rosendahl setup, according to the advisor, is different than that for other Scandinavian companies. While it is very common for foreign companies to hire agents who will get their products to retailers and finally reach the customers through several intermediaries, Rosendahl deals directly with retailers and saves intermediary interference. However, concerning the time required for a brand to blossom, he is conservative. From his experience with other clients, he knows that building a brand in Japan takes time, and he would like to see Rosendahl push for another five years in order to gain real brand recognition.

A Japanese Perspective

The production of the H.C. Andersen porcelain was already in the pipeline at Rosendahl when they decided to use the events surrounding the H.C. Andersen bicentennial as a special opportunity to cooperate with their business network.

Type of company	Importance of H.C. Andersen, Royal visit and Lin Utzon	Impressions connected to Danes/Denmark	Impression of Rosendahl's communication and culture
Interior design chain store	H.C. Andersen products interesting Queen's visit important Utzon's products are already popular	Positive, easy going people Earnest and sincere compared to other foreigners	Orders are flawless and on time Positive about frequent contact in Japanese
Furniture design store	H.C. Andersen important – in newspaper articles Utzon designs match Japanese traditional, simple style	'Slow life' Danish and Japanese simplicity are complementary	Easy access to decision makers Japanese is appreciated
Bridal gift company	H.C. Andersen stories good for wedding gifts Lin Utzon also interesting for other business	Fairy tale country Romantic	Similar business minds
Interior décor chain	H.C. Andersen upgrades other Rosendahl products Lin Utzon important for special promotion	Design a natural part of Danish life Fond of classic Danish designers	Frequent contact in Japanese
Trading house	H.C. Andersen porcelain a hit with top management Lin Utzon promotion important	Previous business with Erik Rosendahl builds trust, even if long ago	Trust and easy communication Knowledge about Japanese culture is appreciated Good quality

Display 4.3 Working with Rosendahl and the H.C. Andersen project – A Japanese View

The following is a Japanese view of events. Just the day before the Royal Family and the Danish Business Delegation held their main event at the Grand Hyatt Hotel in Roppongi Tokyo, on 17 November, I went to the display rooms and main offices of Rosendahl's business partners in Tokyo to interview them. Here are their experiences of the H.C. Andersen project.

The Interior Design Chain Stores

The interior design chain store was one of the first Japanese companies to carry Rosendahl products, beginning in 2000. They were contacted in Japan and immediately agreed to market the product line. They already knew about Rosendahl from a trade fair in Germany which they attended during the 1990s and where they bought ten of the classic Kay Bojesen monkeys sold by Rosendahl.

They have stores in Tokyo, Nagoya and Osaka. When you step into the reception office, six bright-blue Fritz Hansen Danish design chairs greet you in a room that is otherwise white in the simplest of Scandinavian style. The chairs draw the attention in the room, despite the fact that one wall frames a view of Tokyo. The interior design chain store is a very successful up-scale furniture chain that in addition to carrying Danish design furniture also carries Bang & Olufsen audiovisual equipment and Louis Poulsen lighting products, all of which are fashionably displayed along with other top-rated European brands. The H.C. Andersen porcelain is positioned in the most important spot on the ground floor and Rosendahl products are granted a considerable corner display where many of their products, from bottle openers to vases, are featured prominently. Over the years, the classic Kay Bojesen Monkey and Elephant have been faithfully on display, and while not sold in great quantity, they are nonetheless popular. According to the merchandise manager, the Japanese are familiar with H.C. Andersen's fairy tales, but they do not connect the stories with Denmark, although the publicity surrounding the choice of the Andersen Ambassadors may make this connection more apparent.

Regarding the partnership, the merchandise manager, who is female, comments:

We were invited by the Danish Royal Embassy last year to meet with Rosendahl at the Embassy because they wanted to choose us as partners for the H.C. Andersen promotion. We were seven partners. We have displayed all the products in our store and also on our homepage. The background of the porcelain is explained on the homepage. It turns out that the people who are interested in this background information also tend to buy.

The most popular, naturally, is the Little Mermaid, while the second most popular is the Ugly Duckling. Two stories unfamiliar to the Japanese are the Butterfly and the Snow Queen. Sales of products started in June and were good at first. The merchandise manager is expecting sales to pick up again at Christmas. Some people buy on the homepage, while others have read about the porcelain in magazines or visited the stores. The fact that the Danish Queen is going to visit Japan is important. However, Rosendahl has discouraged promotion of the Queen's visit due to security reasons. After the Royal visit, the merchandise manager expects the mass communication activities to once again boost sales. Optimistically, she estimates that the appointment of the H.C. Andersen Ambassadors will mean a thirty percent rise in sales. The promotion of Hans Christian Andersen will affect sales over time, although the peak is naturally expected to be the Andersen bicentennial in 2005.

The merchandise manager studies reports on consumer trends regularly. Today, Japanese consumers are interested in intriguing design, interesting facts and gimmicks. Most Japanese want to buy things that they will keep for a while, but they do not generally value older items with history the way Europeans do. They have traditionally liked to buy and throw away. However, mass media discussions of environmental issues have had an impact. 'Less is more' is a trend in Japan that is connected to being concerned about the environment, and today more Japanese think about preserving and protecting the natural environment. For example, they now buy higher-quality design products and do not just 'buy and throw away' as was the trend during the 1980s and 1990s.

Concerning the use and purchase of the Andersen porcelain, the merchandise manager says that it is very rare for the Japanese to have table settings of six to twelve pieces as may be common in the West. The Japanese like to mix a range of colors, sizes and patterns for their meals, and this has an influence on their buying behavior. They select and combine their porcelain depending on the eating habits of the family. Families who like to eat a lot of different foods such as Italian, Chinese and Japanese also like to have different plates. These plates have to match the colors and styles they already have. In particular, blue colors are easily matched in Japan because they are similar in color to the traditional Japanese Arima pottery. It is also common to own one piece from several manufacturers as collector's items. A couple of glasses or a cup and saucer are often bought both for collections and for daily use.

The business arrangement with Rosendahl works well for the interior design chain store. They are used to ordering from abroad and, compared to other European partners the Rosendahl staff has an earnest and sincere attitude towards conducting business. In certain respects, the merchandise manager feels that the Danish staff is almost Japanese in their thinking, and she finds it very easy building a personal connection across the physical distance that separates them. In addition, the Rosendahl sense of quality is of great importance. "There are hardly ever any problems with our orders", says the merchandise manager. The cultural aspects of their communication are positive and communication with Rosendahl is frequent. There are many phone calls from Rosendahl, and the interior design chain store receives a visit every other month. As the relationship was developing, Rosendahl was in contact every week. When asked about the partnership idea and the potential competition between partners, the merchandise manager said that it is an advantage for the interior design chain store that Rosendahl is sold through different channels. This creates brand awareness and product knowledge among consumers. Furthermore, when the interior design chain store has an exclusive contract, it requires a lot of work to sell the minimum amount agreed upon. With the Rosendahl partnership, the responsibility for marketing is divided between participants, and this is a great advantage, she says.

A Furniture Design Store – Simplicity

The second partner I went to see in Tokyo was a furniture design store. It is one of a chain of six furniture retail stores. Two of the stores are directly connected to the main company, which produces traditional Japanese furniture. Four of the stores are interior design stores with lifestyle concepts. The cooperation between the furniture design store and Rosendahl began at the Tokyo exhibition Interior Lifestyle in June 2004.

The furniture design store carries most of Rosendahl's products, and the Rosendahl plates and cups and vases are nicely displayed at the front of the store. According to the director, they had found the Rosendahl products to be stylish, and they therefore immediately agreed to cooperate when they were contacted and asked to be a partner in the sale of the H.C. Andersen porcelain. The blue color of the Andersen series fit well with both traditional and modern Japanese interior styles.

A big article about H.C. Andersen had been printed in the Asahi newspaper. The director said that according to the article, the Japanese know of H.C. Andersen but they do not know that he was Danish. The director believed that the sales of the H.C. Andersen series would boom for two to three months, and then the Japanese would forget about it. Of course, if his sales people kept working with H.C. Andersen theme, then the boom might last longer. It was important, he said, that the staff make a special effort to talk about the Andersen stories. Leaflets with the Andersen stories in Japanese are placed by the porcelain, and many had already been taken home by customers. The effect of the PR surrounding the Queen's visit and the Andersen Ambassadors would make the Japanese more aware of Copenhagen and Denmark. However, whether or not this would have an effect on sales was another question, he said.

According to the director of the furniture design store, Danish design products are easy to mix with Japanese furniture and lifestyles. To prove his point, he pointed to a traditional Japanese lacquer piece and a transparent vase with white patterns by Lin Utzon. They complimented each other nicely.

> *European design, in contrast to American design, is easy to match. When you look at the Japanese lifestyle in general, there are only a very few Japanese who have their own design style. Our interior design store caters to a small niche of Japanese customers who like individual taste. Not even five percent are in this group.*

The Japanese are brand adoring people; for instance, they love Louis Vuitton bags. However, according to the director, the Japanese do not know the culture or the story behind the brand – they buy it because it is popular. His store caters to a different audience. They manufacture very traditional Japanese style furniture and they want to include some European items that match this Japanese style in order to add color and atmosphere. The Japanese traditional furniture he was referring to was predominately sofas and tables in natural colors that match *tatami* floor mats. Japanese living quarters in general, compared to those in European countries, he said, are different in size and setup. Japanese houses and apartments are simple and functional. Simple, '*kanzo*', also means stylish and elegant. The Japanese who travel and stay at the top European hotels and have this sense of simple elegance are his preferred costumers. The notion of comfort and cozy atmosphere *(kokochii)* are the core values of his store concept, and he was convinced that the Japanese in this category of lifestyle consumers would like the simplicity of Danish design. He associated the image of the 'slow life' with Denmark. "Time flows slowly and the pace of life is relaxed in Denmark. But is that really true?," he asked with a laugh.

Wedding 'Return' Gifts and Storytelling

The Kay Bojesen Monkey was greeting customers at the bridal gift company situated a few hundred meters from the Royal Danish Embassy in Tokyo, but the classic monkey served more as decoration that as a gift item.

The bridal gift company was organized as a 'select shop' in the bridal gift market. In Japan, it is customary that guests bring a gift for the newlyweds and take home at *return gift* when they leave a wedding party. The 'select shop' offered suggestions for these return gifts in many variations.

The bridal gift company started in 2003 when a young man, only thirty years old at the time and now president, developed a new concept for gift giving at Japanese weddings. He branched out from his father's trading company and works with his younger brother on his new ideas.

The gift market is growing in Japan. According to the president of the bridal gift store, about one million couples get married every year. Divorce is also becoming more common with a divorce rate of thirty-three percent in 2003 (twenty-nine percent in the rural areas). Consequently, the wedding gift industry is booming. The president of the bridal gift company and his brother were trying to break away from offering the traditional five pieces of porcelain, among other traditional items, that are usually given as return gifts.

Storytelling was the main tool in their new concept. The brothers build stories with heart around their presents. The idea was to go beyond the traditional gift ideas to include stories and create added romantic value. The H.C. Andersen porcelain provided a great opportunity for doing this, although the creative writers at the bridal gift company had to rewrite the ending of some of the fairy tales, since happy endings were not always what the pedagogic H.C. Andersen was aiming for. One of the stories, namely the Nightingale was not represented in the bridal gift catalogue. The Little Mermaid and the Snow Queen were carried, but their stories had been given a slight twist to ensure a happy ending.

The cooperation with Rosendahl soon included ideas of working with the designer Lin Utzon to make special products in Japanese black and brown lacquer ware. According to the president, frequent meetings, easy access to Rosendahl decision makers in Copenhagen and Tokyo, and an initial invitation to visit Copenhagen had all contributed to creating a business relationship which now ran very smoothly.

An Interior Décor Chain – Natural and Simple

The interior décor chain, in addition to producing their own brand, imports Scandinavian design, including tableware, kitchen utensils, furniture and gifts. In 2000, when the interior décor chain opened their first stores, they began to carry a few Rosendahl products, including the wooden monkey and the Global knife line designed by the well-known Japanese artist Komin Yamada. The H.C. Andersen tableware became the next Rosendahl breakthrough with the chain and it was displayed in the storefront in five stores. The interior décor chain deals with Scandinavian interior design and their products include many well-known Danish brands. According to the general manager of merchandise and sales, the H.C. Andersen porcelain was a welcome idea and they immediately committed to the project:

As our business is to sell and promote Scandinavian products and lifestyle this was an outstanding opportunity. The promotion of H.C. Andersen was a good idea that we wanted to share with our customers and we found that the promotion was good for our image and products in general. We want to carry Scandinavian products that have motivation.

'Motivation' was used by other interviewees in reference to good sales. The general manager had great expectations for the store's sales because of the Queen's visit to Japan. The nomination of the H.C. Andersen Ambassadors in November 2004 also added to his excitement.

Naturally, the trend for sales depends on how successfully stories are carried by the media and how well this penetrates to consumers.

The general manager is personally a great fan of Danish design and he was fascinated by the experience of its practical use in Denmark. In his mind, there was an indication of design everywhere in Copenhagen. Products designed by Arne Jacobsen, for instance, were used in many of the institutions he had visited. The life of people in Denmark seemed to revolve around design, and every product had a unique character. One of the ideas of the interior décor chain, he said, was to join with Scandinavian designers in the future to co-design products for the Japanese market. The interior décor chain also planned to carry Rosendahl's products in the future – in fact, the general manager had wanted to deal with Rosendahl for a long time. The Andersen products fit the image of the interior décor chain particularly well. The value of a brand like Rosendahl would rise, he said, because of the H.C. Andersen events. Rosendahl, according to him, was unknown in Japan, but the H.C. Andersen porcelain series would build the brand name as well as consumer awareness. The events connected to the porcelain were the biggest promotion idea that Rosendahl had presented since his interior décor chain started doing business with Rosendahl, and he thought it was a great opportunity 'to stretch the business' for everyone involved.

The interior décor chain stores had engaged the Japanese trading house, described below, as their agent because they had successfully worked together in the past. Although it was cheaper (and often quicker) to import directly from Rosendahl, the interior décor chain wanted a stock-function and an importer to take care of logistics and import operations. This distribution arrangement enabled them to order large quantities and to service customers immediately. The interior décor chain's marketing and sales people were regularly in touch with Rosendahl by mail or phone, and they got a great deal of information directly from the Rosendahl staff Hiroki Saito and Kuniko Matsushima Rasmussen. Martin Glisby also visited frequently, which meant that the interior décor chain management and sales people were continuously updated about new products and promotion activities, the general manager said.

According to the general manager, Scandinavian design is popular in Japan. The simplicity of Scandinavian design strikes a natural chord of affinity with the Japanese and should be a success for a long time to come.

A Traditional Trading Company – Building Trust
The fifth partner, a traditional Japanese trading company, was originally in the steel business, and the conglomerate had a very strong network with the prestigious department stores and chains in Japan.

The trading company was very supportive of the H.C. Andersen project and the general manager was very involved with the promotion of the H.C. Andersen porcelain. The president was invited by

Rosendahl to the reception dinner held at the Imperial Palace by the Japanese Emperor and Empress, and he participated personally in sales promotion activities. He had read the H.C. Andersen fairy tales when he was a school boy, and he still remembered sitting at the library until it closed in order to finish the fairy tales full of the Danish author's wisdom. Naturally, he was quick to give his support to the H.C. Andersen porcelain promotion.

One of the appealing aspects of working with Rosendahl, according to the general manager, was the opportunity to work with the world famous designer Lin Utzon. However, quality was also of paramount importance. The trading company had developed an in-house brand in conjunction with a Japanese designer and the relationship had lasted thirty years. According to the general manager, the quality of the two product lines was very similar, and while Rosendahl had not been in Japan for thirty years, it was well-established and reputable internationally.

We have now included Rosendahl in our wholesale business. We did not choose Rosendahl due to the name or due to the amount of business that we can do. Rosendahl produces fantastic products, but this it not why it will sell. There are many other firms and brands and it is impossible to choose them all. It is essential, in my opinion, to disseminate good design. Rosendahl is not a new firm and it makes quality products. We will be working hard to sell H.C. Andersen porcelain in Japan.

The general manager stressed the fact that it took thirty years for their designer products to be ubiquitously appreciated by the Japanese consumer, and emphasized that companies, such as Rosendahl who are new in Japan and must start from scratch, should not assume that their products will sell just because they are being displayed in prestigious places.

It is true that by placing your product in a department store it will be accepted as a high-quality, fashionable product, but it will not automatically sell.

Display 4.4 Promoting the H.C. Andersen porcelain at a department store

Rosendahl's design draws people's attention, he said, but the question is whether or not their products make the desired impression. Do people need them – and do they purchase them? The general manager's vision was to build the brand to the point that "people feel satisfied to own a Rosendahl". In particular, he stressed the fact that the Japanese brand mentality is different from that of other countries:

> *A product does not have value if you are the only one that knows about the brand.*

The question of whether or not to market and sell the H.C. Andersen porcelain was decided by the executive management at the trading house. The idea was discussed back and forth in-depth before the decision to join the launch was made. An important reason for the immediate trust in Rosendahl was the fact that the trading company had done business twenty years earlier with the company's founder, Erik Rosendahl.

The trading company had been doing business with companies from a number of countries, including France, Britain, Germany, Italy,

China and Korea. One of their largest partners is the American company Dansk.

Incidentally, Erik Rosendahl was the marketing manager of Dansk in the United States. This was before he founded Rosendahl in Denmark in 1984. We have been the sole agency for Dansk for ten years, so I feel it is a turn of fate. The name Dansk comes from Danish design, as the design is mainly Scandinavian or Danish. I hope to do business in the future where I can carry these and other similar brands. It is one of the core concepts that I have in mind, and a brand like Rosendahl will fit in to this circle naturally. That is what I think.

It is the first time that the trading company has worked directly with a Danish company. According to the general manager, Rosendahl was very accommodating and easy to do business with, not at least because of the Japanese speaking staff.

I think Rosendahl felt attracted to the Japanese market and therefore they emphasized it in their work, for instance by employing Japanese staff. Compared to other firms that we deal with I feel more sympathy for Japan from Rosendahl.

According to the general manager, Americans were sometimes late with their deliveries and they did not understand the Japanese requirements for product quality. He also felt that it was problematic to explain to Americans that their quality was not considered good enough in Japan. Another advantage of working with Rosendahl was the quick response to correspondence. Rosendahl's sales and marketing department exchanged e-mails with the trading company staff every day *in Japanese.* The general manager felt, he said, that Rosendahl was a serious business partner, and the use of Japanese was important in this respect. Everyone from Rosendahl who dealt with Japan could speak Japanese, and as he emphasized, they were also able to take part comfortably in the informal social activities.

My English is not too great, so when I get an e-mail in English, I do not perfectly understand everything that is being conveyed. For this reason, I hope that our relationship with Rosendahl will succeed not just for business reasons, but because of good personal relations as well. For instance, when we went to our distribution centre together, we could have stayed in an ordinary hotel, but we checked in to a Japanese style hotel with hot spring baths. The rooms were furnished with tatami and they had a large public bathroom. I was wondering how Martin Glisby would manage, but he enjoyed the hot springs and acted completely naturally, which is to say Japanese. I thought he was a great person. I am sure he felt some hesitation, but he managed to adapt.

Clearly, the language and cultural adaptation were appreciated and contributed to the creation of the business relationship.

In summary, the views within the trading company regarding the partnership with Rosendahl surrounding the H.C. Andersen project reflected mutual commitment and efficient professional communication. It was emphasized by all that the H.C. Andersen name and the Royal visits had an impact on their quick decision-making and strong engagement in brand building events. Although the large-scale promotion surrounding the events may have been short-lived, according to most it was a great opportunity to introduce the Rosendahl name. The Rosendahl staff described similar observations regarding accessibility and smooth communication. Overall, the shared viewpoint was that the partnership's success rested to a great extent on the cultural and communicative capabilities of the Rosendahl staff.

Lessons Learned

The H.C. Andersen porcelain launch became a fantastic opportunity for Rosendahl's re-entry to Japan.

Japan is a country infatuated with brands, but competition is fierce. Rosendahl's association with H.C. Andersen through the porcelain designed by Lin Utzon gave the brand an edge in upgrading its image while at the same time building brand awareness.

The events surrounding the Hans Christian Andersen bicentennial enabled Rosendahl to treat their business partners to something special. The fact that Rosendahl was focusing exclusively on a single product series facilitated the clear communication of ideas and the ease with which decisions could be implemented. The connection with the H.C. Andersen events also provided the launch of the porcelain series with a set time schedule that had to be met. This accelerated commitments that under ordinary Japanese business conditions might have taken considerably longer.

From their experience, Rosendahl acknowledges that creating a new organization in Japan posed a lot of new questions that in the beginning had no clear answers. At the point of departure in 2002, the concept was undefined, none of the partners were definite, and the advisor who would play such a key role was not even their advisor yet. On top of this, the plan of activities was closely related to the Royal visit, which had not yet even been confirmed. Lin Utzon was designing the porcelain, and that was the only thing that Rosendahl knew for sure.

However, Rosendahl took the risk, and as we have seen they are well on their way to success in the Japanese market. It is even possible that their current success has exceeded their own expectations, as in the beginning they had nothing but some new ideas and generally good intentions. As it turned out, fairy tales, Royalty, a world renowned designer and solid knowledge of Japanese business practices became a platform for a very successful re-entry.

Bibliography

Børsen (2004) "Vejen til success i Japan går via netværk", 5 November [The Road to Success in Japan Goes through Networks]

Børsen (2005) "Danske designere har flere muligheder i Japan", March [Danish Designers Have More Possibilities in Japan]

Glisby, M. (2004) "Interplay: From Market Penetration to Co-Creation of the Market", in Dansk Industri Rapport om Japan, Confederation of Danish Industries, October, pp. 41-49

Glisby, M. & Holden, N. (2005) "Applying Knowledge Management Concepts to the Supply Chain: How a Danish Firm Achieved a Remarkable Breakthrough in Japan", *Academy of Management Executive*, Special Issue May, The Global Transfer of Management Knowledge

Chapter Four: Endnotes

[1] Rosendahl works with agents in eighty to ninety percent of their markets. The exceptions are Japan, China and other Asian markets. Agents, of course, carry many other brands apart from Rosendahl, and may promote other competing product lines, including Menu, Stelton, and Eva Trio, among others.

[2] The H.C. Andersen Foundation rented a conference room at the Grand Hyatt in Tokyo, and on 17 November the Queen participated for thirty minutes during the nomination of the eight Japanese H.C. Andersen Ambassadors by the Danish minister. A Japanese theatre group then did a Japanese interpretation of selected Andersen fairy tales, after which Lin Utzon presented the porcelain series to each of the Ambassadors. The Ambassadors were Japanese celebrities famous not only in Japan, but also internationally, and approximately 160 media related people attended to cover the event.

[3] As requested by Rosendahl the advisor and business partners are referred to by title rather than by name.

[4] The Royal Danish Embassy in Tokyo makes a room available furnished with Danish design for business and diplomatic encounters. The opportunity to use these facilities is valuable to the Danish business community as corporate Japan has great respect for diplomacy and embassy authorities.

Chapter Five

SCANDINAVIAN TOURIST BOARD: CREATING A VIKING MASCOT

Year	Event
1970	Danish Tourist Board (now VisitDenmark) starts promotion in Japan.
1986	The office is called Scandinavian Tourist Board but is still owned by the Danish Tourist Board.
1995	Søren Leerskov becomes the regional director of Scandinavian Tourist Board, Asia.
1999	Scandinavian Tourist Board becomes an established company owned by the national tourist boards of Denmark, Norway and Sweden.
2002	Scandinavian Tourist Board starts development of the branding process.
2004	Takk-kun, the Scandinavian Mascot, is approved by Scandinavian Tourist Board's board of directors.

The study of intercultural communication within a tourism organization is both interesting and challenging because the product is intangible. The promotion of tourism is a process of image creation and storytelling about countries, cultures and people involving authentic and exotic claims designed to attract as many visitors as possible to cities, seasides, and other tourist destinations. It requires both a great deal of knowledge about, as well as intercultural negotiation between, several cultures in order to best position the destination, as well as package and sell the associated experiences. Furthermore, the business of tourism and its related promotion and communication involve a number of stakeholders, in this particular case both in Denmark and Japan.

The working relationship between VisitDenmark in Copenhagen and Scandinavian Tourist Board in Tokyo is complex, and a substantial effort is being made in the internal organization to deal with cultural encounters between the two countries. In addition, as this chapter will demonstrate, those strategies local to the Japanese market differ in several instances from the tourism strategies of VisitDenmark in the rest of the world.

In summary, this chapter deals with issues of global strategy and local adaptation, as well as communication between the headquarters in Denmark and the regional office in Japan. It also deals with internal communication within the Japanese office itself. These perspectives are then used to investigate how Danish and Japanese culture, as well as intercultural knowledge and understanding, influence decision-making processes. The interviews were conducted with everyone at the Danish headquarters that works closely with Japan. At the Tokyo office, almost everyone participated in the interviews.

Scandinavian Tourist Board Asia – Background

Scandinavian Tourist Board in Asia (hereafter STB Asia) is situated in Tokyo and provides several Danish, Swedish and Norwegian tourism organizations with services in Japan through its extensive network within the travel trade, media, government and non-profit organizations.

STB Asia is a regional office that provides services in all of Asia and has offices in Korea, the Philippines and China. According to the director of STB Asia Søren Leerskov, the future aspirations and mission statement of STB Asia are twofold:

- To ensure STB Asia as the main promotion coordinator, main hub for product and market development and main tourism know-how center in Asia for partners;
- To be the organization responsible for branding Scandinavia in Asia with the objective of turning Scandinavia into a household name.

The office in Japan is operated in collaboration with the other Scandinavian national tourist offices of Norway and Sweden. The Scandinavian joint venture in Japan started in 1986. According to

Flemming Bruhn, the chief financial officer at VisitDenmark and person responsible for the overall operation in Japan, the Japanese operation was and is still very dependent on the business knowledge and cultural expertise of its director. The previous director, Lars Sandahl, and the present director, Søren Leerskov, are both very knowledgeable Japan experts. The latter has been in charge of the Tokyo office for the last ten years. This tenure and experience as well as his language competence, have earned him the respect of his colleagues. His knowledge regarding Japan has become a strategic advantage when negotiating with the tourism partners in Japan, with his team at the Tokyo office and not least with headquarters, says Flemming Bruhn.

Promoting Scandinavia – A Headquarter Perspective
The Danish Tourist Board is situated on the waterfront of Islands Brygge. It overlooks Copenhagen's canals and bridges, the spires of old buildings and the glass fronts of new landmark architecture. The Danish Tourist Board recently changed its name to VisitDenmark thereby emphasizing its core business focus, namely encouraging tourists to visit Denmark. Flemming Bruhn explains the strategy of promotion in Japan:

> *The office in Japan is promoting all of Scandinavia for three reasons. First, market research shows that the Japanese perceive Scandinavia as a single entity rather than three independent countries. The countries are perceived as being situated far up in the North of Europe. They are cold, expensive and far away. Second, Scandinavia also stimulates positive associations, namely that the Scandinavian way of living is safe. This is of great importance to the Japanese who have a record of high safety and low crime. Third, the Scandinavian countries work well together and it makes sense financially to have one setup instead of three.*

STB Asia thus administers a joint venture of activities in Japan. A board of directors guides these activities, and consists of a representative from each national tourist office, namely VisitDenmark, Innovation Norway and Swedish Tourism and Travel Council, as well as the director of the office in Tokyo. These directors meet two to three times a year to discuss business plans and the economic situation of the Tokyo office. One of these meetings takes place in Japan or Asia.

Business Model and Strategy for Japan

The business model in Japan differs in many respects from the setups in the rest of the world. Every Scandinavian national tourist office invests DKK 2.2 million in direct subsidy to the Asian setup. As a public tourism organization STB Asia does not have a financial bottom line that has to be maximized. Instead they have to maximize the number and quality of activities they offer. According to Flemming Bruhn:

> *It is the task of the regional director of Asia, Søren Leerskov, to implement as many activities as possible with the end goal of generating as much tourism to Denmark from the Asian market as possible. The target group is composed of high-end Asian tourists, the so-called profitable tourists who spend money on hotels, sights and shopping.*

High-end tourists have been chosen as the target market, as opposed to focusing on backpackers or other travelers, to gain a higher return on investment. The activities supported by the government funding include: 1) research in Asian on tourism trends, 2) a basic marketing platform, 3) technical visits, 4) finance and administration, and 5) general project development. Besides government funding, the Scandinavian tourism industry also supports the Tokyo office financially. This government-industry business model works well in Japan, according to Flemming Bruhn:

> *The director Søren Leerskov has been able to involve the tourism industry and business in Denmark in order to cover additional expenses. Japan boasts an investment in activities from the industry of more than 130 percent. In other words, on top of the activities the tourism partners buy, they also cover more than thirty percent of the basic organizational setup. That is an exceptionally good arrangement, and a good way of getting financial support on top of government funding.*

The emphasis of the Tokyo office strategy, according to the director Søren Leerskov, is to qualify its decision-making based on research facts rather than mere intuition about trends in the market. Danish tourism partners get insight into this pool of knowledge about the market when they participate in the various programs. Partners are also able to participate in activities called Spearhead Projects in Japan.

Special projects include H.C. Andersen 2005 and special visits by government officials. However, as already mentioned, the focus of project development is not limited to Denmark. For example, Wonderful Copenhagen is one of several important STB Asia tourism business partners that have also cooperated with Stockholm on projects, while Norway has invested heavily in promotion projects focused on the fjords and northern light. These Norwegian destinations in particular have already captured a great deal of interest among the Japanese.

High Return on Investment

With respect to the Danish tourism industry, Japanese tourists represent only a marginal share of all tourists, with Japanese bed nights totaling 100,000 a year. However, the Japanese are some of the biggest spenders. They spend roughly DKK 2000 – 2500 per person per day versus an average of DKK 400, and they contribute a considerable sum of money to Copenhagen and its vicinity.

The Japanese also spend only a few nights relative to other tourists visiting Denmark.[1] In particular, Scandinavians and Germans often book extended stays in summer homes along the coast of Jutland. Even though Copenhagen mostly hosts tourists from far away markets, including Japan, Japanese tourists still make up only a very small percentage of the total.

Nevertheless, promoting Denmark as a tourist destination for the Japanese is considered a good investment. According to Flemming Bruhn's calculations, the DKK 2.5 - 3 million invested in the Japanese market generate DKK 250 million back in turnover for Denmark. This provides approximately DKK 80 million in taxes to the Danish state. Shopping brings in another DKK 60 million in sales, which in turn means another DKK 20 million in taxes. Therefore he feels the return on investment to be high, even though he admits that it is impossible to know exactly how much STB Asia is able to influence the market, or where exactly the investments have the most impact.

We do not have any precise measurements for tourism results, and do not know how many would visit us if we did not carry out marketing activities in Japan – or the United States for that matter, says Flemming Bruhn.

Although Japanese tourists are attractive clients because they spend a lot of money, the number of Japanese travelers decreased for several years beginning in 2000 - 2001. The decline was due to terrorism and SARS. Since 2004, the number of Japanese tourists has been increasing once again.

Long-Term Investment

The best argument for investment is usually a growing market. However, this is not the case for Japan, according to Karim Grau Nielsen, marketing director of VisitDenmark:

> *Even in times of decline, it is important for us to be consistent in the Japanese market. When the Japanese travel, they build up a relationship with their tour operator. That is a very important part of the experience. The Germans for instance do not care about relationships. They care about prices. The cheaper the better. A Japanese tourist builds up a relationship that he will never break, unless you do not keep your end of the agreement. To work with Japanese tour groups is a long-term process. First, you do not just enter the market for one or three years. You have to enter with a commitment of ten years, no matter if it goes up or down. Second, it is a slow process to build up a network of clients and to close deals because business is based on trust. That is the most important sales argument we can make to the tourism partners in Denmark, but it is also the most difficult, because their interest is primarily short-term gain.*

According to Karim Grau Nielsen, STB Asia's promotion package for Japan is significantly different from other packages because tourism partners in Scandinavia have to sign up for three years. For example, VisitDenmark also works with tour operators and hotel groups in promoting their products in other parts of the world, but the promotion contracts are much shorter-term.

Communication from Headquarters

At headquarters, all interviewees agreed that tourism promotion in Japan was different in many respects due to Japanese culture. Also, the corporate values and decision-making processes differed in Japan. Several people from the VisitDenmark headquarters are in regular contact with Japan. These include the chief financial officer, who has the overall responsibility, the marketing manager, the press manager, the Japan-coordinator and the Wonderful Copenhagen key account manager. Besides daily communication, VisitDenmark holds three to four market directors' meetings a year to gather all country directors. Søren Leerskov, the director of STB Asia in Tokyo, does not have the time to join all the meetings because he also has a similar number of meetings every year with each of his Norwegian and Swedish colleagues. Consequently, Flemming Bruhn is not expecting Søren Leerskov to implement ideas and strategies as strictly as he expects them to be implemented in other markets.

It is a general problem to communicate with market offices in order to get the synergies we want and to get them to implement the strategies we have agreed on. We are continuously contemplating whether we are sending too much or too little information. We sometimes forget to inform each other on both sides. This is a general problem, but the problem is bigger concerning Japan, because they have agreements with three countries, so their information flow is three times as big.

VisitDenmark continually works to communicate more effectively with its markets. They distribute meeting summaries from the market directors' meetings, and include an in-depth summary to all market offices. They also have a market director's communication group on the Intranet. This means that every time they email market directors around the world, Søren Leerskov in Japan is included.

While information is beneficial, digesting it is also time-consuming. It is understood at headquarters that it is a major task for Søren Leerskov to filter all of the information that he receives. Although there may be no correlation between workload and e-mail etiquette, he often does not answer when he is traveling to China or Korea or when he receives VIPs from Norway, Denmark or Sweden. Flemming Bruhn concludes:

One of the challenges we have to work with continuously is communicating. Communication is simply a difficult thing.

Danish as the Corporate Language

Language is another communication challenge, according to Flemming Bruhn. The corporate language of VisitDenmark is Danish, yet only two of the permanent employees in Japan speak Danish.

In the other markets, the directors can distribute information without modification; in the Tokyo office, Søren Leerskov is faced with a substantial translation problem. Every day he has to skim messages and documents from the incoming information flow, and he has the choice of answering himself or translating messages and documents for his staff.

That is where things go wrong. We have discussed the language dilemma at VisitDenmark, but Japan is the only place where this is a problem. There are a few non-Danish speaking employees at other destinations: one in London, two in Italy and one in the United States. Besides these, everyone else understands and writes Danish in all our market offices. That is the reason why we do not intend to change our corporate language to English.

At any rate, direct communication is considered particularly important with Japan because it seems like it is far away. The decisions made at headquarters meetings, according to Flemming Bruhn, should be explained better and in more detail to make sense in a Japanese environment. Dealing with the press and the politics of tourism are complex matters. Often he feels that it is important to get on the phone to straighten out issues. Direct contact and keeping in touch are even more important with far away offices, according to Flemming Bruhn.

In Japan, the Scandinavian employees do not feel the distance, while the Japanese staff does. The feeling of distance, in other words, may have more to do with feelings of closeness to people and practices than physical proximity.

Panic Solutions Are Not Suitable for the Japanese Market

Several conceptions of Japan and the Japanese market are commonly shared among the people at headquarters who deal with Japan on a regular basis. One of them is the requirement of planning and investing for the long-term. According to Marketing Director Karim Grau Nielsen, panic solutions do not work in the Japanese market.

As a rule of thumb, the tourism business is often driven by short-term thinking: if there is no return on investment within three months, you have to come up with something else. For example, hotel rooms have to be filled for the season. In Japan, the strategy is to look at efforts as a long-term investment of resources. While the way VisitDenmark works in Japan is not that different from the way they work with other markets, what makes a difference, according to Karim Grau Nielsen, is whether or not you know the culture.

It is of course very beneficial for the Danish tourism industry that we have Søren Leerskov, who knows the language and the culture. If you were to send me, who does not know either, it would be at the risk of making mistakes. We have learned this as a basic rule about Japan. In that type of complex market, it is important to have a person who knows the language and the culture. There is a big difference between operating in Europe or Asia or the US, but what is interesting is that all the basic activities, the way we work with the markets, is basically the same no matter where we are. So there is no difference in this respect.

SARS, terror and the Japanese financial depression have each had their effect on tourism, but throughout it all VisitDenmark has maintained the level of their effort in Japan. Karim Nielsen credits Søren Leerskov for pursing this long-term vision, and he both trusts Søren Leerskov's judgment and believes in the way he negotiates and promotes the tourist packages within the Japanese business culture.

One never knows if a sales pitch has been accepted, but Søren Leerskov has been dealing with the Japanese for a decade and is good at reading the responses from his clients.

Flemming Bruhn's comment on the business situation is that the head office is cut off from knowing what is really going on, and consequently there is over reliance on Søren Leerskov in Japan. Flemming Bruhn has to rely on Søren Leerskov for decision-making concerning Japan. On top of this, the Scandinavian countries make different demands of STB Asia, which means Søren Leerskov often has to make compromises. Flemming Bruhn, who is also a member of the board of directors, says:

Of course the culture is very different, but we are also three different tourist organizations with different demands. Therefore, I cannot decide unilaterally regarding a market, which means I have to compromise on solutions.

This is the dilemma faced by the board of directors, because Sweden wants to go this way, Norway would like to go in that direction, and Denmark wants to go in a third direction. They usually meet somewhere in the middle.

Building Relationships and Trust

During one of his visits to Japan, Karim Nielsen had the opportunity to witness the relationship that has developed between the Tokyo office staff and the Japanese travel trade industry representatives. This reaffirmed his respect for the professionalism of the office and pointed to a difference between building business relationships in Japan and other countries:

> *When I visited Japan last time, I was very impressed with the trust and commitment that existed between our office staff and the industry people. Søren Leerskov has built up these relationships over the last ten years. When we were invited for a travel workshop, all the top directors in the Japanese travel industry were there. That would never happen in our other markets. You would not be able to gather VIPs to this extent. The fact that they show up is based on a strong relationship of trust. The Japanese clients are committed to making Scandinavia a part of their program – and even a large part of their program. This means that before you even begin to focus on business in Japan, this loyalty and trust has to be gained – which is what it is all about.*

On his business visit to Japan, Karim Grau Nielsen also participated in a formal evening reception complete with speeches.

> *It was an amazing experience to see how the Tokyo office was in contact with the top people in the Japanese tourism industry. About 150 people participated. That is something you only dream about in Denmark. The fact that a CEO takes his time to appear at a reception is something you would not experience even in Germany, our largest supplier of tourists. The top executives there would not make the time, even though we accommodate sixteen million Germans in bed nights annually. This is compared to 100,000 Japanese bed nights.*

Karim Grau Nielsen found the experience interesting and unique. The reception went well and Søren Leerskov formally presented all the guests in fluent Japanese. In the view of Karim Grau Nielsen, it must have made a positive impression on the Japanese that a "Dane speaks their language".

A Japanese Hand at Headquarters

VisitDenmark and STB Asia work with activities in Japan, as well as many other Asian markets. Tanja Ibsen Nørskov is VisitDenmark's marketing manager for Leisure & Asia. She has been the coordinator for several years and talks about the importance of having a person at headquarters who can speak in the interest of Asian activities.

Only Asia has a coordinator at headquarters. The only other market where a coordinator may be relevant is on behalf of the United States. The other markets, with Italy the furthest away, seem closer and easier to coordinate from VisitDenmark.

> *My task is to make sure that there is a focus on the Japanese market in our organization and to remember Japan and China when we develop business plans, decide on activities and plan to do workshops. It is important to integrate our Asian offices into our daily work so they do not disappear into the background compared to our neighboring markets. There is a clear focus on the markets that generate the most income, but it is also important that we do not forget the Asian market. It is also my task to contact our press officer and our editor to provide them with news on the Japanese and Chinese markets. When we wish to step up our activities in Asia, we need to signal this through information provided to the tourism industry, to government offices, and to different stakeholders in our environment. That is something you can do from Tokyo, but it is much easier to do from here where you are informed about all the activities. Therefore, I am the person who is responsible for integrating our Asian activities into our daily work,* says Tanja Ibsen Nørskov.

It is an established part of VisitDenmark's strategy to work in Japan and Asian, and there is no question about the importance of developing activities in Asia. Rather, it is a question of how to handle information about Asia in the best way.

Working with Partners

Partners may include Radisson SAS hotels, Wonderful Copenhagen, incoming operators such as Tumlare, the Tivoli garden, the tax free company Global Refund, different local tourist boards and SAS. These companies are often STB's partners for activities in the Japanese market.

The display below shows the communication flow between VisitDenmark and the Tokyo office. To the left, the Scandinavian countries are displayed. VisitDenmark represents smaller Danish partners, whereas STB Asia in Tokyo communicates directly with Wonderful Copenhagen and Hotel Imperial in Denmark. Scandinavian partners with offices in Japan communicate directly with STB Asia in Tokyo, bypassing VisitDenmark.

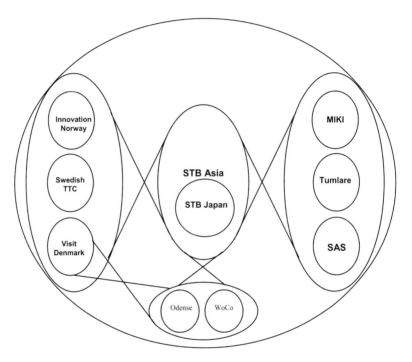

Display 5.1 Scandinavian Tourist Board, communication diagram: national tourist offices, Scandinavian Tourist Board, partners (e.g. incoming agents: MIKI, Tumlare; Airline: SAS; destinations: Odense, Wonderful Copenhagen)

Every year a substantial effort is made to secure backing from Danish partners for activities in the Japanese market. If there is no support from the tourism industry, activities will not be carried out. This provides two imperatives for VisitDenmark and STB Asia: 1) Secure continuous backing from commercial businesses, which requires that marketing activities be sold to the tourism industry; 2) Create new partners.

VisitDenmark and STB Asia need to maintain their relationships with existing partners in Scandinavia, as well as create new ones. This follows a cycle similar to all other markets: a strategy for the marketing activities is developed, and then the programs are sold by bringing the partners onboard and securing their financial commitment.

The Tokyo office develops the framework for the kind of activities that will be for sale. In cooperation with the marketing department, Tanja Ibsen Nørskov then identifies potential partners in Denmark. The Tokyo office is in charge of administration and they communicate directly with the partners. Tanja Ibsen Nørskov invites partners to Tokyo when a workshop is being held. She also contacts Danish partners and updates them during the year to help foster a sense of security and stability.

We have to keep telling the good stories. We have a lot of good ones from Japan. Among others stories, we have the Green Santa Claus and the technical visits. We have to keep a positive spiral of information going. If only one more hotel joins and has a successful experience, then it is worth it. These are the conditions for communication in an organization with experience as the product.

The Green Santa story is described in the introductory chapter. It was mentioned as a success story by everyone at VisitDenmark headquarters.

Cultural Differences
From the Japanese perspective a cultural difference that is difficult to understand is the fact that no one works in Denmark after five o'clock p.m. or on weekends.

Scandinavian people prioritize their private time more. Sometimes it is a bit frustrating when we come with a big group of Japanese and they say, 'well we are on vacation so we cannot meet with you', said Kjell Ellefsen, Senior Executive at STB Asia.

Danes see it as their human right to spend their free time as they please. Most Japanese people are more willing to sacrifice their free time for work.

Training in Tokyo – Cultural Insights

According to Tanja Ibsen Nørskov, knowledge about Japanese culture and personal introductions to her colleagues in the Tokyo office have been paramount in facilitating her daily communication with them. It has minimized not only the physical distance, but also the mental distance.

When she started in her position as the coordinator for Japan, she was sent to the Tokyo office to learn how the business and the company were structured, as well as how the daily work was performed. The stay at the Tokyo office enabled her to establish personal relationships with the office staff. During the day, she would sit with one of her colleagues to learn about their specific projects and areas of responsibility. She spent nearly a day within each department and gained substantial insight into each individual's work responsibilities. There were also opportunities in the evening to be more social with colleagues after work. Overall, she found the experience to be very helpful, and there was a lot to learn. She recalled:

> *I was treated, and also felt, like a new employee who had to start with a two-week orientation program. It was interesting to witness the work routines carried out from a Japanese perspective in a company which I have worked in for many years. It was a great eye-opener. Japan is not around the corner. There is a great distance between us, and it was a treat to spend time there. It was good to get an understanding about the practical work, but it was also interesting to find out who my colleagues were. It was good to see how people worked and what their day looked like, as well as get to know their views on various issues. When I am at VisitDenmark, 10,000 kilometers away from Japan, and talk on the phone, I can imagine people at their desks. I know if their desk is messy or tidy [she laughs] and how they spend their day. I know if they are part of the group that stays after hours to chat and brainstorm. It is nice to be able to picture the faces of the people whom I am talking to. It is also important for the cooperation we have now developed.*

The training period was valuable, and Tanja Ibsen Nørskov spent a total of ten days in the office. Additionally, she spent a couple of days seeing clients together with some of the visiting Danish partners.

Scandinavian Management Philosophy – A Danish View

When asked to talk about specific Scandinavian management characteristics in light of her stay in Tokyo, Tanja Ibsen Nørskov said:

> *Scandinavian culture is a part of the Scandinavian management style, which is characterized by flexibility, the way you expect employees to work independently, and also the way you reward them with freedom, responsibility and decision making. The Japanese employees are dedicated and hard working. They focus and seem more disciplined in their physical posture, for instance the way they sit up straight at their desks. There is a form of authority which is simply a part of the ambiance among the Japanese. They laugh and joke once in a while, but they seem to have another level of respect for those who are their leaders or top managers, something you would not find in Danish companies. They seem to be respectful, obedient and wishing to be of service. It is almost beautiful – very different from the way people act at the VisitDenmark office where employees sometimes slouch over their desks, put their feet up and talk out loud or yell to their colleagues when they feel like it.*

The Europeans and the Japanese at the Tokyo office seem to have different relationships with the director, Søren Leerskov, and their actions towards him as a superior also differ. They each have their own ways of approaching him with equally good results, but each group does it in their own way.

> *I sense,* Tanja Ibsen Nørskov continued, *that the management style I experience in the Scandinavian part of the world places a larger responsibility on the individual. We have a great deal of independence. In return, there is a great expectation that you will solve the tasks you are assigned. Scandinavians do not need to get permission and no one looks over your shoulder. You may check back with your superiors or co-workers once in a while when you are in the process of solving the problem, but they trust you and expect you to get things done. Communication styles are very democratic actually, while the Japanese employees expect an authoritarian leader. The Scandinavian style is to focus on individual competencies through project work and project organizational styles. There is a general acceptance of an individual need to both be different and to be a part of a group.*

Both strategies focus on the individual. If an employee expresses an interest in developing in a new direction, the organization tries to accommodate this wish. On the other hand, if the lack of respect for authority turns into an undisciplined and uncontrollable attitude among the employees, this can become a problem for managers and for the company. But if managers are able to deal with conflicting views and differing opinions, it is an enormous strength because it enables the company to draw on the resources of independent co-workers who can think for themselves, take initiative, and also to stop something when they do not want to participate any longer.

According to Tanja Ibsen Nørskov, the Scandinavian communication style enables employees to take initiative, to ask questions about what others are doing, and even more importantly to question their leaders. In a Danish company, you can say "I do not agree with what you are saying. Can you please explain it to me one more time, or push your arguments further if you want to convince me to work in this direction".

Even though it can be annoying at times that people always have an opinion, she finds that it is important to challenge ideas from management. In Scandinavian companies you work with other employees more as consulting partners and as a source of inspiration in order to enhance your own work.

Employees in Scandinavian companies, in Tanja Ibsen Nørskov's opinion, are to a large extent able to influence the direction of the company, and a high level of personal participation characterizes Scandinavian management style. While the director in the Tokyo office automatically has authority over his Japanese employees, he has to earn it from the Scandinavians.

On the other hand, jealousy among colleagues and the Law of Jante do not exist among the Japanese according to Harro Christensen, director of economy and administration at VisitDenmark. Although he admits that emotions may be difficult to assess during his relatively short annual visits to the Tokyo office in connection with year-end closing of accounts.

Technological Communication Bottlenecks
In Asia, there are mobile phone networks which use different standards than those in Europe, and this significantly complicates communication, particularly with the director who travels a lot. When

Søren Leerskov travels to Europe, he has to have a telephone for the European network; when he is in Japan he has to have a telephone for the Japanese network; and when he is in Korea, he has to have one for the Korean network. In other words, it is not easy to know where and how you can get a hold of him, because he has three different telephone numbers. He is often traveling so where does one call? The same problem occurs with e-mail, since depending on where he is he may not have network access.

This means that we have a bottleneck, which we now try to solve by developing closer cooperation between the market office and headquarters. Earlier, we tried to decentralize more because it had certain advantages, but in the new millennium we would like to handle some issues centrally to ensure that our Danish partners experience quality service, said Karim Grau Nielsen.

Providing quality service according to Karim means that partners should always be able to get in contact with Japan. While advanced technology may enhance global communication access, it still depends on technical availability and personal efforts to communicate.

Overall, enhanced cultural perceptions and knowledge about Japanese business practices facilitate communication between the Danish headquarters and the subsidiary in Japan. Visits to Japan have provided several employees with knowledge about professional practices and, even more importantly, they have become acquainted with people at the Tokyo office. Information and stories are continuously circulated back and forth to keep Japan fresh in the minds of stakeholders in Denmark. Meanwhile, a coordinator at headquarters ensures that the Asian perspective is well represented.

Creating a Mascot – In Tokyo

Two processes of image and value creation were ongoing when I visited the Scandinavian Tourist Board office in Tokyo. These were the image branding process, based on external images of Scandinavia and its individual countries, and a product marketing process, based on the creation of a mascot. These are described in turn, with greater emphasis placed on the process of creating a mascot.

The Scandinavian Tourist Board office in Tokyo consists of twelve employees. They naturally have professional contacts at the Danish headquarters connected to their area of responsibility. Most have been to Denmark several times either for business or on holiday. However, their perceptions of Scandinavia and Scandinavian management are based to a great degree on their relationships with Scandinavian co-workers at the Tokyo office.

The remainder of this section will present how various individuals became involved in the internal processes of branding Scandinavia and creating a Scandinavian mascot. It describes various cultural encounters as they were experienced in the Tokyo office by both Japanese and Scandinavians alike.

Branding Scandinavia

In 2003, STB Asia decided to launch an effort to brand Scandinavia. The director of STB, Søren Leerskov, tells the story of the branding project:

> *In 1999, STB conducted an analysis in cooperation with SAS to estimate the level of recognition connected to Scandinavia as a name – not as a destination. At that time, merely two percent of those surveyed could recognize the name Scandinavia; however, this number increased drastically in 2002 to twenty-three percent.*

Based on the findings of the 2002 survey, STB developed a branding strategy which was accepted by the board of directors. A three year plan and a budget of DKK 2.5 million were approved with the overarching goal of branding Scandinavia as a region. In cooperation with Dentsu, the largest advertising agency in Japan, STB started preparations.

Early in the process STB Asia found that it was too expensive and too difficult to create a brand with substance for all of Scandinavia. Dentsu suggested that STB Asia should create a single brand for all the countries. However, based on findings from the previous survey that each country individually had greater recognition than Scandinavia as a whole among the Japanese, STB Asia decided to brand each country – Denmark, Norway and Sweden – separately. Sweden in particular was already well known to the Japanese. Twice as big as each of the two other countries, Sweden also had by far the largest number of companies placed in Asia. In addition, according to Søren Leerskov, the Swedish companies promote themselves as being Swedish, while Danish companies do not. Since large Danish companies such as Lego, Maersk and Novo do not promote their Danish nationality, Denmark and Danish companies secures less of a place in the minds of the

Japanese than their Swedish counterparts. The Swedish company Volvo, for instance, is promoting its new cars in connection with the wide-open and beautiful Swedish countryside. Norwegian companies also do not promote their nationality, with the exception of products such as salmon and other specialty fish. However, as names, Sweden, Denmark and Norway were known by the Japanese more than the name Scandinavia. Thus, it made more sense to brand nationally than regionally.

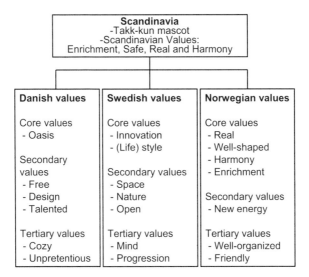

Display 5.2 Scandinavian values

Consequently, STB Asia decided to change their focus from a regional brand to one that would also include national branding. The national values displayed in display 5.2 serve to illustrate the national tourism promotion values that were identified for each country as a preliminary exercise to create an umbrella brand for Scandinavia.

According to Søren Leerskov, STB Asia still uses Scandinavia as a brand of origin, in the same way that SAS uses Scandinavia. However, on a strategic level, STB Asia decided that the *product marketing should be on the regional level, whereas the image marketing should be on the national level,* enabling a greater degree of synergy. The common denominator which underlies all these is thus the brand of origin, which is called *Scandinavia.*

Image Creation – The Internal Process

STB started a branding identification process by setting up certain branding guides based on the tourism promotion branding values from the three Scandinavian headquarters (see display 5.2). Both qualitative and quantitative interviews followed this. The ultimate conclusion that the working group came up with, according to Kjell Ellefsen, senior executive at STB Asia, was that the branding values were rather high-browed in a way that they did not make sense to most of the Japanese focus groups. After an hour of explanation, some focus group participants would say "That is very interesting!", but their reactions to and understanding of the concepts were not immediate. *Nature* stood out as something they identified with Scandinavia, but again, nature is a very ambiguous concept. What could STB Asia do to pursue *Nature* as its image? STB Asia went through an internal process of brainstorming and most people thought that these values actually had a lot of depth and therefore had to be elaborated. When the Japanese, for instance, hear about Scandinavians being very in tune with ecology, they find this very interesting. And, of course, Scandinavia does have abundant and well-protected natural capital, so there was a sound foundation for this affinity. The Danish *Hygge*, 'cozy', also stood out as a new but interesting concept.

> *'Hygge' is a very typical Scandinavian cultural component. The Japanese have never heard of it, and it has to be explained. But once they hear about it, they find it interesting. It is a new experience. We came up with a lot of fundamental concepts, but we did not agree on any concepts that immediately worked for a lot of Japanese people,* says Kjell Ellefsen.

Japanese Images of Scandinavia

It was difficult to define brand values that were wide enough to cover all three Scandinavian countries, and at the same time representative of each country's identity and idiosyncrasies. According to Tue Paarup, manager of research and communication, it put pressure on STB Asia to code the promotional message in such a way that it would be decoded 'correctly' by the Japanese traveler.

STB Asia ended up terminating the collaboration with Dentsu and working instead with the promotion agency Vector until 2005. Dentsu's results were filtered by Vector and some of the material was used. Vector's suggestions for values were delivered in the form of mind maps illustrating what the Scandinavian images meant in Japan.

Four sets of values were then put together: the unique Danish image, the unique Norwegian image, and the unique Swedish image, together with the Japanese perception of all three countries. The combination of these four pieces and the previously defined branding values of Denmark, Norway and Sweden made up one picture which became the Scandinavian brand in Japan. In other words, the core values formed the foundation for this exercise, and the brand was built on top of this foundation.

Display 5.3 Mascot prototypes from the Asahi newspaper competition

The Scandinavian brand values ended up being *enrichment*, *safe*, *real* and *harmony* (see the final national and Scandinavian brand values above in display 5.2).

The Mascot

Developing a mascot suddenly became a natural continuation of the branding exercise, and this is where the staff really got involved. People remember mascots much better than slogans, and unless you have the slogan in continuous advertising rotation, people tend to forget it. This was the reasoning behind STB Asia's decision to develop a mascot who could be a storyteller for all three national brands. The idea was to try different icons to see what would communicate most effectively. It had to be a cartoon character of some kind, and it had to be something people would identify as being uniquely Scandinavian, not something which might be, for instance, perceived as German or Polish. A number of activities were undertaken, and in particular STB Asia sponsored a competition in one of the larger Japanese newspapers, Asahi Shimbun, from which it received hundreds of suggestions for mascots (see display 5.3). Based on these, STB Asia conducted several staff meetings to evaluate the suggestions, well knowing that the staff was biased both in its professional outlook and in its knowledge of Scandinavia. However, this was an occasion where everyone had the opportunity to engage in a discussion about what was uniquely Scandinavian.

Two icons were typical of the submitted ideas for a mascot – a Viking and an Elk. However, it was known in advance that the Elk would not be approved by Denmark as being sufficiently representative. Therefore, the Viking was chosen as an icon that was immediately and uniquely identifiable with Scandinavia. However:

> *The mascot was not approved by the board of directors when it was first presented, because the Viking concept is recognized by us, and by the politicians in particular, as something we want to distance ourselves from, and we are an organization which is controlled by political money,* says Søren Leerskov.

It deserves mentioning that the mascot was to be connected to the promotion of tourism products and not to the STB Asia corporate image.

The Viking Image – Excellent in Japan

The Japanese like cute things, according to Kjell Ellefsen. Therefore, if STB Asia were to come up with a cute mascot, there would be a natural affinity with the Japanese consumer. They could easily connect the main Scandinavian values to the cute character. But the reaction to the Viking from the Scandinavian point of view was naturally, he says: "Come on this was a thousand years ago let us move on". Nevertheless, Kjell Ellefsen still liked the Viking idea:

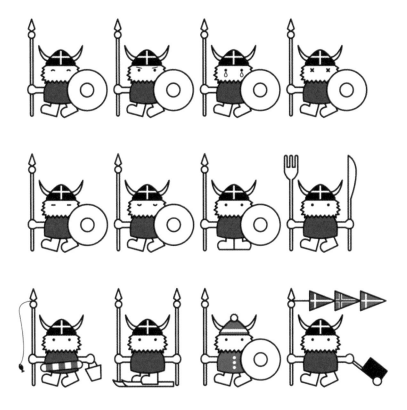

Display 5.4 Takk-kun the Scandinavian mascot

The Japanese still see the Viking as the one icon of Scandinavia, and we know for a fact, for instance, that Vikings were rather progressive in their thinking about women. Women had a lot of rights in Viking times compared with other societies, and this could be an interesting story that this particular character could talk about! The mascot could present this story in a fun way, although the issue at hand it is actually quite serious. We could talk about Viking technology and the way they built their ships. The character could explain Scandinavian ideals and brands, down to a very gut level that the Japanese could immediately identify with. We need to reach outside the centre of a costumer focus to regular people. If we want more Japanese people to come to Scandinavia, and not just deal with the Japanese who are already fans of Scandinavia because we have already captured them, then we need to reach further. While we have not previously embarked on this new type of mascot-promotion, it might be the way to accomplish this. That is how I and the staff feel.

However, headquarters just did not like the idea of the Viking. An extremely strong icon would be the Little Mermaid because she is well known in Japan. However, something so intimately linked to Denmark would obviously not satisfy the 'Elk countries' – Norway and Sweden.

This is where we found that all three countries could pride themselves on being Vikings. We thought this was the least controversial mascot that all three countries could identify with, said Kjell Ellefsen.

The director Søren Leerskov was content with the process of creating and choosing the mascot, but the Viking image continued to cause problems. The common denominator that could unite the Scandinavian countries and immediately trigger Scandinavian associations among the Japanese was the little Viking, and that was both good and bad.

Søren Leerskov thought it was ugly and almost perverted to use a person from the middle ages, where ninety percent of the population was peasants and the rest were robbers. However, that part of Scandinavian history is not known in Japan. What the Japanese know is that Vikings are exotic, like their own *samurai*. They know the word Viking from buffets – which are called 'Viking style' in Japan. Thus, the concept had all the right connotations in the Japanese market, and that is why the mascot was both a solid fit and the best character to tell stories. The Viking was also tested on a significant part of the population – 1200 people chosen independently of STB by an advertising agency.

Takk-kun is Cute

There is no doubt about it – the Viking is loved by the Japanese. This has now been confirmed through tests in connection with the different STB Asia events and gatherings. Clients have clapped their hands and said: 'Oh, so kawaii (cute)'. The Viking character has also been found to be cute in larger surveys conducted by Vector.

The designer who won the competition was quite imaginative and thorough in his development of the Viking concept. He has presented Takk-kun, the mascot, in action in different contexts such as fishing, eating out and skiing (see display 5.4). The designer also made a Takk-kun in clay as a sculpture. All this was thoughtfully conceived in the view of Tue Paarup, manager of research and communication, but he is still skeptical:

You have to ask why we keep using the Viking as the ambassador. It is clear that we overuse the Viking, not so much in Sweden, but certainly in Denmark and Norway. Go to a Danish tourist shop and there are tons of small statues of Vikings.

But Tue Paarup respects the fact that the Japanese like the mascot, and because they do, it is the right choice. As he says: "We do not have to sell Scandinavia to me – we have to sell it to the Japanese market". A downside of using the Viking, he says, is that STB Asia keeps referring to something that happened in the past, instead of something that is going to happen in the future. In retrospect, Tue Paarup would like something visionary, something that looks into the future; however, he does not know what it should be, and this is his only regret. As far as he is concerned, Takk-kun looks very nice and cute – and he grows on you.

An advantage to using the Viking is that STB Asia draws on knowledge that the Japanese already have about Scandinavia. With a little creative retelling, the history of what happened a thousand years ago can be rewritten into new stories about Vikings who lead exiting lives.

Regarding the Viking concept, the comments from partners such as VisitDenmark and Wonderful Copenhagen were positive. Their observations were simply that if this will work in the Japanese market, the mascot should go ahead and sell stories. Of course some people had concerns about the image that STB Asia would project by using a Viking, even if only a distant relative to the bloodthirsty barbarians who went to Britain to kill, rape and plunder. However, if the Japanese see it as a cute and enchanting character then it was okay.

As mentioned previously the board of directors at first did not like the idea of the Viking. However, it has now been approved since Japanese consumers perceive it to be so incredibly cute, and it is currently being used in the new promotion material.

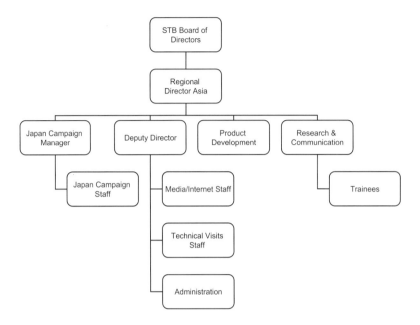

Display 5.5 STB Asia, Tokyo office organizational chart (own development based on hierarchy)

The Organizational Process

The process of choosing a mascot involved everyone. Søren Leerskov, the director, had sessions with the Scandinavian staff, and Shoko Itoh, the deputy director, had sessions with the Japanese staff. In particular, she met with the young female staff and with the managers. The meetings were divided into these two groups because the staff has different ways of behaving in front of the director, Søren Leerskov. It is, for example, difficult for younger Japanese women to express their opinion in a general meeting. If they do, their co-workers think that they talk a lot. In addition, in any group setting, including staff meetings, it is difficult for the Japanese in general to say that they disagree or do not like an idea.

All in all, there were five group meetings, after which they finally decided on the mascot in a shared session. While Shoko Itoh was in all the meetings, Søren Leerskov only participated in those meetings involving the managers or the office as a whole.

At the managers' meetings they talked about strategy, budgeting, and financial issues. In the staff meeting for the female Japanese employees, the issue was the emotional appeal of the mascot, and in particular, how cute he was. The opinions and impressions of the young females were seen as important, as this age and gender group represented a new target market for STB.

Other Staff Opinions about the Mascot

Some Japanese staff liked Takk-kun, the mascot, while others disliked him but were willing to accept the majority opinion. Nagisa Imamura in information management commented:

I like the Viking. It is a really good idea because it is the image of Scandinavia.

Yuko Sato, in travel trade promotion also liked Takk-kun, as well as the process of choosing him:

The Japanese know about the Vikings, so it is a good choice. Also the process of choosing a mascot was great fun.

Yoshiko Asakawa in media promotion did not personally like the choice of Takk-kun, but she was already thinking about ideas of how to further incorporate him into project development:

I am working with media people as well as some Scandinavian related companies in Japan, such as Illums, Carl Hansen, Lego, and Royal Copenhagen I have had very positive feedback using this character, and it is very useful in this sense. Some female editors of travel magazines also like him and think he is very cute. Takk-kun is perfect for Japanese women. While some Japanese people have an image of Scandinavia as a country famous for its design, most Japanese do not know what Scandinavia is like. Most link the traditional image of the Viking to Scandinavia. Personally, I would like to promote a more modern image, but we have ended up with a very cute and familiar character. When we support press trips or media coverage we sometimes get free space for stories. It will be nice to develop the mascot in these channels so that the Japanese recognize Scandinavia through our mascot. We are now developing a strategy to take full advantage of him.

163

Finally, Shoko Itoh, the deputy director was not fond of the idea of a Viking Mascot, but she gave in to the opinions of the younger generation:

> *Actually he is not my favorite, but I accept the choice. I am forty-three years old. Until I was thirty-five I believed that I knew everything and that I could make decisions by myself. But now there is a generation gap, so I listen to the twenty or twenty-five year-olds and I accept their opinions even if I do not understand them. They may have spotted a trend. My function is better as a mediator, so this is the role that I am taking. I listen, and even if I do not agree or like it, it is okay.*

According to Shoko Itoh, although the people in decision making positions in Japanese companies are usually men between forty and fifty years old, they are under increasing influence by their younger staff. Following the Japanese tradition, the older managers often go out to drink after work, and this is when they listen to workplace opinion, as well as learn about new trends from their younger female employees. Clearly, Japan is no longer an old man's world. The younger generation has the buying power, and even the older segment of the population knows that the younger generations are both the trend setters and the target market for most consumer goods. This means that even fifty or sixty year old men have to listen. Otherwise, they cannot be successful in their business activities – and they know that, says Shoko Itoh. Since even older executives must listen to the younger generations, a cute mascot may work and eventually have an effect on the Japanese consumer in a way that transcends the various generation gaps.

Decision-Making Processes – Lessons Learned

Søren Leerskov emphasizes the fact that the process of choosing a mascot was perceived as less abstract than the earlier process of defining corporate values in connection with the creation of a new STB Asia logo.[2] This may have been due to the bottom-up decision making that was utilized, and there is no doubt that the response from the office staff demonstrated that everyone was both engaged in the process and supportive of the result. Therefore, in his opinion, there is a much stronger chance that the Takk-kun program will be implemented successfully than if it had been a top-down decision.

The way decisions are made has a great impact on the implementation and motivation of employees. Undoubtedly, processes are important. The idea that I make the decisions without listening to everybody is accepted by the Japanese, but not always by the Scandinavians, Søren Leerskov says.

This goes back to Tanja Ibsen Nørskov's comment that Danish people are brought up to express their opinions. In return, they also want to be part of decision-making processes.

However, Søren Leerskov is against making committee work for every issue STB Asia has to deal with. In principle, he works with three types of decisions: the ones he makes on his own, the ones he makes after consulting with his staff, and the ones the office staff decides together. As he has the responsibility for all decisions, one of the most important criteria is that processes are right. It would be cruel, for instance, to ask the employees to re-arrange the office setup and decide who sits where. This would create a lot of conflicts, and some people might end up hating each other. The same is true for bonus allowances. He confers with his managers, but makes the decisions himself in order to save the managers from problems with their subordinates.

In conclusion, soft matters such as the creation of the mascot turned out to work well at the STB Asia office when carried out as bottom-up processes.

From Local to Global – A Final Note

The Viking mascot, Takk-kun, has finally been officially approved by the Scandinavian board of directors and a recent survey in Japan has shown that potential Japanese tourists both love the Viking and find him absolutely 'cute'. Takk-kun may in time become a best practices example of the co-creation, or re-creation, of an image for Scandinavia – just like the Green Santa Claus.

Bibliography

Lyck, Lise (2003) *"Turismeudvikling og attraktioner i et strategisk perspektiv"*, Nyt fra Samfundsvidenskaberne [Tourism Development and Attractions From a Strategic Perspective]

Lyck, Lise (2003) *"Turistattraktionsstudier i et økonomisk perspektiv"*, Nyt fra Samfundsvidenskaberne [Tourism Attraction Studies From an Economic Perspective]

Ooi, Can-Seng (2004) "The Poetics and Politics of Destination Branding: Denmark", *Scandinavian Journal of Hospitality and Tourism*, volume 4, no. 2, pp. 107-128

Ooi, Can-Seng (2005) "A Theory of Tourism Experiences", in O'Dell, T. and Billing, P. (eds.), *"Experiencescapes: Culture, Tourism and Economy"*, Copenhagen, Copenhagen Business School Press, pp. 51-68

Chapter Five: Endnotes

[1] Dividing Danish tourism by nationality, ninety percent of the bed nights per person are tourists from Denmark, Germany, Norway or Sweden, and ten percent are Americans, Dutch, Italians, British, Japanese, Chinese, or Koreans.

[2] The corporate STB Asia logo creation process was also in progress but it is not described here.

Chapter Six

BANG & OLUFSEN: QUESTIONING THE ORDINARY

Year	Event
1960s	Bang & Olufsen employs Danish and Japanese trading partners.
1970	Bang & Olufsen uses a Japanese importer.
1983	Bang & Olufsen starts a subsidiary in Tokyo.
1993	Bang & Olufsen closes the subsidiary and switches to a Japanese agent.
1997	Marantz represents Bang & Olufsen. Lars Myrup joins Marantz as a consultant.
2000	Re-establishing a Bang & Olufsen subsidiary in Japan.
2002	Chiyuki Komuro is made responsible for retail and marketing activities in Japan.
2003	Lars Myrup creates a new regional office for Asia in Singapore. Japan is part of the Asian region.
2005	Global celebration of 80-year anniversary of Bang & Olufsen.

Bang & Olufsen's vision statement is expressed as: "Courage to constantly question the ordinary in search of surprising long lasting experiences".

About Bang & Olufsen

Bang & Olufsen[1] audio visual products have been sold in Japan for more than forty years. The initial business was the export, through

Danish and Japanese trading partners, of pick ups for gramophones. During the 1970s, Bang & Olufsen established a larger presence in Japan through the use of importers, and in 1983 the subsidiary Bang & Olufsen Japan K.K. was established. However, ten years later in 1993, Bang & Olufsen closed the subsidiary and left their business in the hands of a Japanese agent. Subsequently as business improved, Anders Knutsen, the CEO of Bang & Olufsen from 1992 - 2002, felt that representation through an agent was a suboptimal approach for developing the Japanese market, and a subsidiary was reestablished in 2000. This chapter presents the story of how Bang & Olufsen went from being present in Japan only through a local partner to establishing a fully owned subsidiary on two separate occasions.

This chapter presents a cultural studies approach in analyzing Bang & Olufsen's presence in the Japanese market by providing answers to the following questions. What were Bang & Olufsen's considerations in organizing a subsidiary in Japan? What were the lessons learned? Did national and organizational culture matter? How did they deal with national and organizational cultural issues? Did Bang & Olufsen try to implement their corporate organizational culture in the Japanese subsidiaries, and if so, what were the outcomes? How are global strategies communicated and adapted locally? What is the status of the regional office for Asia in Singapore in relation to Japan? And last, but not least, how do employees deal with cultural specificities?

The material presented in this chapter is based on in-depth interviews with the Danish president of Bang & Olufsen Japan, Lars Myrup, who is now stationed in Singapore, as well as interviews with the retail and marketing manager, Chiyuki Komuro, and three of her colleagues in the Tokyo office.

1983-93: A Decade of No Profit

During the decade from 1983 to 1993, Bang & Olufsen operated a Japanese subsidiary that did not register a single year of profit. Needless to say, this was a difficult period from both a local and corporate perspective. Later, there was ongoing conflict of interest between Bang & Olufsen and their Japanese partner and agent and cooperation between the two parties was severely impaired.

Lars Myrup, the current president of Bang & Olufsen Japan, started with Bang & Olufsen in 1984 and has since worked for them in Denmark, Germany, Belgium, Saudi Arabia, Japan and now Singapore. From 1995 to 1997, Lars Myrup left the company to work in Japan for the Danish company Coloplast. However, he was rehired by Bang & Olufsen in 1997 in order to develop the strong potential of the Japanese market. Lars Myrup recalls:

> *In 1983, we started our subsidiary based on the conviction that if you want to be recognized within the industry you need to have a one hundred percent owned subsidiary in Japan. That was resolved by the previous management, and Bang & Olufsen operated the subsidiary for ten years from 1983 to 1993 with Japanese management and Japanese staff.*

The failure to turn a profit, according to Lars Myrup, was due to both communication problems and a general lack of market understanding. In his view, Bang & Olufsen headquarters was unaware of both Japanese business practices and the challenges specific to the Japanese market. The result was a lack of cooperation from headquarters that translated into a lack of leadership from within Bang & Olufsen with respect to operations in Japan. In hindsight, according to Lars Myrup, it was an unnecessarily costly lesson. Since the first subsidiary was established before the economic downturn in Japan, the subsequent failure cannot be blamed on outside factors. Rather, it was purely a lack of management and leadership. Despite this lesson, there remained a number of others related to the impact of culture that Bang & Olufsen would also have to learn the hard way.

1993: Break Point[2] – Restructuring Business

By 1993, it was time to make a decision concerning Bang & Olufsen's strategy in Japan. The very same year, Bang & Olufsen as a whole was undergoing a very difficult reorganization as part of a management turnaround headed by Anders Knutsen and described in the book 'Break Point: Anders Knutsen and Bang & Olufsen' (Poulsen, 1998). Anders Knutsen was with Bang & Olufsen for twenty-five years. He was the CEO from 1991 to 2002 and in accepting the position it fell to him to get Bang & Olufsen back on its feet. At the time, one of his greatest challenges was to introduce precaution into the company mindset: Bang & Olufsen could not take success for granted. In emphasizing attention to detail together with cost consciousness, Anders Knutsen added to the company soul in a way that continues to influence operations worldwide today. In 1993, Bang & Olufsen had been operating in Japan for ten years without a profit and, according to Lars Myrup, something had to be done:

> *It was not a matter of adjusting the organization. It was a matter of stopping the bleeding or dying. Everything that was not profitable here and now or that would not become profitable within a half to one year had to be shut down.*

It was a difficult process, but there was no other choice. The strategy was still to be represented in Japan, since starting from scratch would be too costly if Bang & Olufsen wanted to re-enter the market at some point in the future. Therefore Bang & Olufsen found an industry partner to be their agent. They closed the subsidiary, incurring substantial costs in the process. Unfortunately, the new partner's way of doing business, with all due respect says Lars Myrup, was very different from the Bang & Olufsen business model. In particular, Bang & Olufsen wanted a more exclusive retail environment as part of their global retail strategy.

1997: Breaking Partnership

In 1997, Anders Knutsen asked Lars Myrup to break up the unhappy marriage with the industry partner Marantz. For more than three years business had not improved, and although Bang & Olufsen had been the one to propose the partnership, they now wanted to end it as it was not working on several fronts.

Marantz had not grown the business and did not understand Bang & Olufsen's long-term brand-enhancing strategy, choosing instead to concentrate on short-term profits. Marantz intended to expand the number of sales outlets from one hundred to four hundred, distributing the products through low-quality, high-volume retailers using a wholesale philosophy which was adverse to Bang & Olufsen's branded-retail philosophy. In fact, Marantz was using Bang & Olufsen as a 'door opener' for getting its own products into new retail outlets. As an added complication, Marantz's management structure was complex and missing certain key competencies within branding and retail marketing. The bottom line, however, was simply the fact that their promotion of the Bang & Olufsen brand was not consistent with Bang & Olufsen's corporate strategy.

Knowing that he was to end the partnership with Marantz, Lars Myrup evaluated a number of options for alternative representation in Japan. One possibility was to continue to work with a Japanese partner, but this time require them to establish a dedicated sales division to promote the Bang & Olufsen brand and products. Another option was to form a joint venture with either an industry partner, one of the big retailers or one of the traditional trading houses. However, all ideas basically pointed in the same direction: Bang & Olufsen wanted management control, and consequently Lars Myrup ended up choosing the solution of a wholly owned subsidiary.

2000: Restarting a Subsidiary

As was demonstrated in the previous chapters, as a manager working with Japan you not only have to see opportunities in the market, you also have to present convincing arguments to sell your ideas to headquarters.

Lars Myrup soon learned that knowledge about the market did not mean immediate support from home. After having initially screened the different options for Bang & Olufsen in Japan, Lars Myrup and his superior at the time, a Spanish gentleman named Manel Adell, presented their case to the board of managers at the head office in Jutland. The key person to convince was the corporate CEO, Anders Knutsen. The investigation of opportunities tapped a vast number of connections from Danish and foreign companies and showed that if Bang & Olufsen had the resources a wholly owned subsidiary was the best option. However, the more presentations Lars Myrup made for his board of managers in Denmark, the more he realized that this would be an uphill battle. Anders Knutsen had already closed one subsidiary in Japan and he had paid a lot of money to do so. It took two years of PowerPoint presentations to convince Anders Knutsen that the chosen business model was solid. Ultimately, the most convincing part of the proposal may have been the capabilities and backgrounds of the people involved, says Lars Myrup. The combination of a company person like himself, who was born and raised within Bang & Olufsen culture in Struer, and a similarly growth-oriented, aggressive and commercially minded gentleman with strong industry experience was a good combination. The facts presented by Lars Myrup, who had strong credibility within the organization, and Manel Adell, who had experience from one of the big corporations in Europe, convinced Anders Knutsen.

In fact, Anders Knutsen was knowledgeable about Japan himself and had been conducting business there for more than twenty years with a total of more than fifty visits. Although his particular line of expertise was purchasing rather than the retail side of the business, he had a very good understanding of Japan. When Lars Myrup and Manel Adell presented the final proposal, it had become crystal clear: it was based on Bang & Olufsen's position in Japan, future strategy and cost conscious outlook. Equally important, the plan was presented without painting too rosy a picture, emphasizing instead a balanced projection of obstacles and opportunities. Anders Knutsen signed the check and Bang & Olufsen Japan K.K. started operations in 2000. According to Lars Myrup, this was the best decision that Bang & Olufsen could have made, and the numbers prove it. The second time around, Bang & Olufsen Japan was profitable the very first year of business.

Within just a few years, Bang & Olufsen managed to reduce the number of existing dealers from 130 to twenty, while at the same time adding twenty new ones. Although this represented a drastic reduction in the number of retail outlets, profitability increased and Japan became an extremely profitable market, says Lars Myrup. Today, Bang & Olufsen deal with thirty-five percent of their audio visual product portfolio in Japan; they sell 2500 music systems a year and have accumulated approximately 20,000 customers over the last decade.

Re-Establishing a Subsidiary – Cultural Issues

Despite all the hard work that Lars Myrup and Manel Adell had put into just getting Anders Knutsen's approval for their proposal, in reality the hard work was just beginning. The next major hurdle was to establish a good sales and marketing team for the office in Tokyo. However, the lack of flexibility of the Japanese workforce was a major obstacle and this turned out to be one of the main problems facing Bang & Olufsen Japan. Lars Myrup explains:

> *Once you hire people, you need fingerprints and recorded misbehavior on video before you can let them go. It is very difficult to say goodbye to unwanted staff. This condition makes it difficult to fine-tune and build the team you need for new tasks.*

On top of it all, Bang & Olufsen had made a deal with the Japanese partner, Marantz, to hire their entire staff. In other countries where Bang & Olufsen have taken over distributors or agents within the last ten years, such as Germany, Spain or Italy, Bang & Olufsen was able to cherry-pick one or two key people from the team and let the rest go. But in Japan, Bang & Olufsen was asked to hire the entire team. Setting up a new team by educating the old one while simultaneously integrating new competencies was a real challenge. It took Lars Myrup three years to rearrange and put together the team that he needed. As if this was not enough, according to Lars Myrup, all the 'classic conflicts' between Japanese and Western national and organizational culture were encountered during the transition.

The Human Resource Challenge

From 1997, Lars Myrup had been part of the Bang & Olufsen team situated inside the Marantz organization. He was working as an onsite consultant from Bang & Olufsen and was there to provide support, as well as monitor operations. Starting in 2000 with the wholly owned subsidiary, Bang & Olufsen took over seven employees from Marantz. Out of the seven, five left within four years. A long process was required to establish a capable team and the period was filled with many positive and, without a doubt, negative aspects of human resource management.

In other countries, as described above, Bang & Olufsen would have discontinued employment for the vast majority if not all of the employees, and hired new staff to assist in the transition. If Lars Myrup had had to startup operations in Germany or in the UK, where he personally had a better understanding of the local culture and spoke the language, he would have been able to monitor the process in much more detail. In Japan, the case was different and Lars Myrup had to convince CEO Anders Knutsen of the impact of local culture with respect to the transition, and in particular the necessity of retaining the Marantz employees.

First and foremost, according to Lars Myrup, it was important to keep the Marantz employees during the transition phase because of the close relationship between Bang & Olufsen and the Japanese retailers. Lars Myrup, as a blond *gaijin* and non-native speaker, found that he was not able to simply take over in order to maintain and strengthen existing relationships. It was important that Marantz representatives continue the operation to make sure that the retailers were comfortable with the transition process. Lars Myrup sensed that Bang & Olufsen's distribution partners would not be comfortable suddenly dealing with a foreigner, especially in the early days and months after the transition.

Japanese Group Responsibility and Hierarchy

The Bang & Olufsen management style provides its employees with independence and a high degree of responsibility. With this responsibility, according to Lars Myrup, employees are expected to take initiative, push their performance and deliver. In Japan, he saw two possible scenarios with the new team:

A) The Marantz employees would blossom when hired by a Danish company. Freedom and responsibility would turn them into dedicated and outstanding employees, or
B) The team would assume that this new freedom meant that Japanese rules no longer applied, and with the more relaxed Danish management style they would lean back and fail to perform.

Two of the employees loved the new responsibility and challenge – and they blossomed. The remaining four fell into the second category. They were very unproductive and simply did not fit in. One of the employees who had trouble adjusting to the Danish management style said openly to Lars Myrup that he felt it was not fair that he should be responsible for his own budget. He was expecting more support from his boss and felt that Lars Myrup was not backing him up. Lars Myrup wanted him to create an action plan based on Bang & Olufsen corporate strategy, but the employee felt that he was better at executing plans and budgets than creating them. Lars Myrup found that the Japanese employees in general were afraid to assume individual responsibility. They seemed more comfortable the greater the number of people that shared any given responsibility. However, in Lars Myrup's mind, the logic was that *if more people have responsibility then no one has responsibility*, a perspective grounded in his Scandinavian management values.

Despite the adjustment difficulties, the choice of bringing the Marantz team onboard was the right one. In particular, it was successful in maintaining good relationships with the retail channels throughout the transition. Most employees did their best, but some eventually realized that they did not fit into the new strategy as it started to accelerate. Thus, Lars Myrup started to bring onboard new profiles to complement the organization. In particular, he hired young Japanese, 28-32 years old, who had been abroad and were fluent in English. Some of them were even bi-cultural and tri-lingual. Not surprisingly, their profiles were the diametric opposite of the profiles of the team members that Lars Myrup had taken over from Marantz, a conservative Japanese company. Marantz's business culture was very traditional and had been built on the cultural heritage of the Japanese company from the post-World War II era, incorporating classical structures of hierarchy and formal business conduct. Lars Myrup hired young Japanese that had not been with the company for more than one day before they were suddenly promoted to management positions in charge of the employees in their department. This was like throwing a grenade into an organization that had run according to well-established, traditional Japanese culture. But Lars kindly provoked them on purpose, and threw the grenade in anyway, because he felt it was needed in order to make the next leap forward. It was a very stressful and unpleasant experience for the traditional Japanese staff – but according to Lars Myrup it had to be done.

The Advantage of First Working for a Japanese Company

When I conducted interviews at the Tokyo office, the last manager had only just left his position. One of the original Marantz employees that stayed, Miyoko Okuno, is now the marketing manager at Bang & Olufsen. She has been with Bang & Olufsen for twenty-two years, and her historical knowledge of Bang & Olufsen's operations in Japan are an important asset. Given her experience, she is well placed to highlight some of the cultural differences between the two companies:

> *When I started to work for Bang & Olufsen, it was very small. Then we moved to Marantz. When I worked with Marantz Japan my job was basically the same, but the relationships in the company were completely different. The last year with Marantz Japan we had fifteen staff members. We were basically sitting in one room so it was easy to communicate with each other. It was easy to communicate with general management and people responsible for different areas. But with Marantz we also had many departments, and the organization was very hierarchical, so it was difficult to get consensus even on small matters. It was a unique and interesting experience, but I did not like it. With Bang & Olufsen, the community of people and the setup is simple. We are able to communicate directly to the person in Denmark who is in charge of our area.*

Miyoko Okuno reports to Chiyuki Komuro, the retail and marketing manager, but she is often in direct contact with colleagues in Denmark, for instance regarding marketing material or logistics when PR people visit Denmark. When she worked with Marantz, she had to get a seal from each manager to approve even small decisions. Communication in this respect is more effective at the Bang & Olufsen subsidiary. The development and use of IT has also created a change. Instead of shuffling papers and getting a seal from each manager, she is now able to send e-mails to get comments directly from the people involved.

The advantage of having worked for both companies, she says, is her knowledge of both company cultures. Also, she understands the history of the brand strategy and is able to tell the brand story in her promotion activities. She understands less about the technical aspects of the products, but it is enough to get by, and more importantly she understands the mind of Japanese consumers. As she modestly admits in classic Japanese style: "I am not a specialist in any one field, but I have been taking care of PR, customer relationships and sales support for more than a decade". Needless to say, her network and her knowledge of consumer behavior, press relations and retail mechanisms are a goldmine for a foreign company.

Before I introduce the organization of communication at the Tokyo office, I will look at the Bang & Olufsen brand image in Japan.

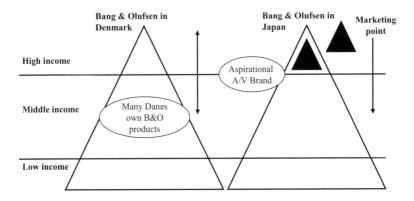

Display 6.1 Bang & Olufsen, an aspirational brand in Japan

Aspirational Brand Image in Japan

Bang & Olufsen uses global branding strategies and standardized tools for image creation in their markets. Bang & Olufsen cater to consumers who appreciate high quality audio visual products and exclusive sound, according to Lars Myrup. The global marketing platform is situated in London and from here activities are coordinated worldwide. However, while Bang & Olufsen is promoted as an upscale brand in Denmark, for instance, promotion is targeting an even more exclusive image in Japan. Specifically, Bang & Olufsen is being promoted as an aspirational brand in an effort to reach the Japanese elite (see display 6.1).

In addition to a number of activities each year, Bang & Olufsen contributes to the creation of an exclusive, glamorous book which they then mail to 2000 of their top clients. The *White Book*, exemplifies the local branding effort particular to Japan. Bang & Olufsen cooperates with eight other companies to build both closer relationships with each other and to build a brand community with costumers. The other participants include Porsche, Giorgio Armani, Harry Winston Jewelry, Citibank, Don Perignon Champagne, Cassina Italian Furniture, and Peninsula Hotels. Recently, JAL has joined as the first Japanese member, and their *White Book* members fly first class – not only on business, but also privately. The companies have one point of common interest – shared costumer profiles (they do not share client information, as this is illegal due to privacy laws). According to Lars Myrup, the other companies each cater to customers who appreciate good things in life. Sub-textually, this translates to consumers who have high disposable incomes, a Western-oriented life style, and are open to non-Japanese products and technology.

The *White Book* provides an advanced form of direct marketing via an eighty-page, art-quality book. Each book has a theme. The first issue was dedicated to 'origins' (2003) and dealt with the history of the companies and the in-depth stories behind the brands. According to Lars Myrup:

> *The Japanese are extremely interested in what is behind the product. They want to know about the core values of the companies, the corporate history, and the origin of key ideas. They want the story of the efforts we put into creating unique product concepts.*

Clearly, if this sort of promotion is able to create a personal connection between the brand and the consumer based on lifestyle, then the investment will have been well worth it. Other themes have been 'passion' (summer 2004) and 'reflection' (winter 2004). There is always an 'educational story' in each of the *White Book*s, and there are always testimonials from elite representatives of Japanese society who enjoy the products 'advertised'. Ultimately, the *White Book* is a visual symbol and a vehicle for building a brand relationship with customers.

With respect to specific joint promotional events associated with the *White Book* and the companies' elite clientele, there is a lavish Christmas dinner every year with entertainment and ball room dancing. Customers are also invited to the various headquarters and factories of the participating companies to experience the brands and brand stories first hand. Finally, the various companies support each other with joint branding events in a way that the *White Book* becomes a very exclusive club to which only these top-flight companies and their top-shelf clients belong.

The Tokyo Office Today

What is the status of the Tokyo office today? The office in Tokyo is not just considered a remote sales office, says Lars Myrup. It is part of Bang & Olufsen's global strategy, and as such it is critical that the staff feel connected to the people at headquarters.

The office is situated with a nice view of the Tokyo Tower on the seventh floor of an office building. The office furniture and design is modern. The walls are glass and everything is transparent. A soundproof show room displays recently developed audio visual equipment including flat screens. The Tokyo office is a sales and marketing office. There are twelve employees in the Tokyo office – all Japanese. Some regional stores in Japan are also operated from the Tokyo office with about nineteen employees in total. From time to time, Bang & Olufsen assumes control of retail stores if they are mismanaged by their partners. In such cases the partners are dismissed and the Tokyo office staff manages the store until it gets back on track. At such times there is more staff in the office. However, direct retail operations are only temporary. In general, the Tokyo office has a staff of twelve across four functions: retail, marketing, product service and administration.

Out of three managers two are female, which is not unusual in Japan within foreign owned companies. A fourth manager was part of the Marantz team, but never fit into the new organization, in large part because his superior was female. This was a deliberate strategy, according to Lars Myrup, because Japanese females are generally "more efficient, culturally intelligent and higher performing than the men". Due to their traditional Japanese mindset, some Japanese men are not able to perform with a female manager. The male manager left shortly after Chiyuki Komuro was hired in 2002 to be in charge of the retail and marketing activities. According to Lars Myrup, it is common knowledge among expatriates in Japan that you give yourself every advantage possible if you recruit Japanese women.

With respect to being a female manager, Chiyuki Komuro says that of course it has been an issue. At first, she had to deal with resistance from some of the Japanese dealers. She has overcome this by being 'professional'. In her words, she has concentrated on delivering a clear message and being consistent in her business communication. Through this approach she has managed to overcome apprehension on the part of the dealers and to get on good business terms with them.

Display 6.2 The Bang & Olufsen office in Tokyo

Cultural Issues in Organizational Charts

Two organizational charts are in use for the division of tasks and responsibilities in the Tokyo office. One chart shows the formal hierarchy of the organization and the other show a matrix of responsibilities. The first indicates titles and the reporting structure of the organization. This is important to the Japanese staff because status and place in hierarchy have a great deal of influence on their sense of commitment and organizational behavior. However, the traditional organizational chart (display 6.3), according to Lars Myrup, does not say much about how the organization actually works and what the daily tasks are. That is why he prefers the matrix configuration (display 6.4).

The nature of the matrix chart is more interesting. It tells you what your responsibilities are and who you are to support. It places you in brand marketing, retail marketing, finance or sales and service. It shows how everyone has special areas of responsibility with B-1 stores, shop-in-shops or key accounts. The subsidiary's function is mainly to support the people who bring in the sales and who present the solutions to the customers, whether it is with financial support or marketing support or service and training support. These people bring in the money for our salaries and we are here to ensure that we sell more by making our customers happy. We are not here to please the next layer of management.

According to Lars Myrup, it was quite a radical move to present this matrix in Japan. It does not show who reports to whom, nor does it pay attention to organizational hierarchy. According to traditional Japanese business culture, hierarchy and the number of years that someone has been with the company are of great importance. The matrix does not show who the managers are, and this is very confusing for the Japanese staff. Therefore both charts are displayed on the whiteboard in the office so that everyone knows who manages whom.

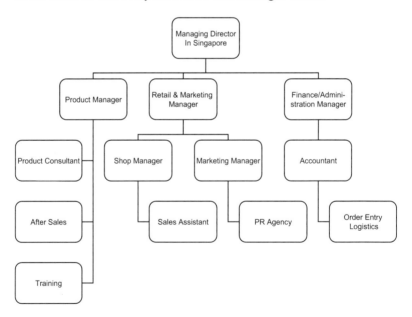

Display 6.3 Traditional organizational chart – hierarchical

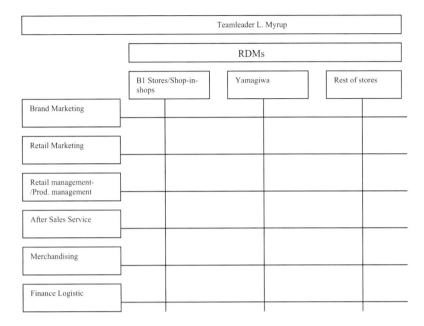

Display 6.4 Organizational matrix – operations and core business activities

The matrix is closely related to operations and the core business activities of the organization. It shows how the support functions are connected to the three legs in the organization: the shopping malls, the shop-in-shops and others key accounts such as department stores. The employees that have daily contact with retail partners are called retail development managers (RDMs), and they are in important communication positions for sales and market sensing.

In the matrix chart all functions have a supporting and educational role to make sure the brand is developed according to global standards. The employees that are responsible for brand marketing, for instance, take care of the window displays and campaigns in accordance with global Bang & Olufsen activities. Marketing employees are responsible for direct mail and in-store events. Product training employees ensure that the frontline staff is fully up to date on product features as well as general sales skills. It is, however, the RDMs that have overall responsibility for the performance of their individual accounts.

The matrix "highlights the core business functions, as well as where the money is". For Lars Myrup, it makes much more sense to organize the staff in relation to operations rather than in a static, hierarchical organizational chart. However, the chart has divided the office in two. While Lars Myrup has his 'dynamic', matrix organizational chart, the twelve office members prefer the line organizational chart because it describes hierarchies and decision-making processes in more traditional ways.

Thus, Danish egalitarian and straight-forward business culture is not always naturally adopted by Japanese staff that has a tradition of male dominated, hierarchical ways of thinking. The Marantz managers who were able to adapt were few, but they have become outstanding resources for Bang & Olufsen with their knowledge of the two business cultures and their local networks.

A change in hierarchies and information flow is also taking place through the use of e-mail. The change is subtle, but nonetheless is having an influence on traditional hierarchical structures and lines of communication. Thus, technological advance is making communication both across borders and within organizations more efficient, but with potentially unforeseen side effects which may be viewed as both positive and negative. These pro and cons of internet communication are discussed in the following section.

Organization of Global Communication

Implementation of new technology has changed communication across borders at Bang & Olufsen dramatically within recent decades. This section will highlight the effects that advances in technology have had on communication, and how Bang & Olufsen is using this technology to spread a global message and strategy, as well as to discuss the management implications at both a global level and in the Japanese subsidiary.

From 1983 to 1993, the first Bang & Olufsen subsidiary in Japan was operated solely by Japanese staff. Communication would typically go through the proper hierarchical routes from the sales and marketing assistants to the marketing manager. If anyone had a question or a problem to solve that required input from headquarters, they would go through the sales manager. The sales manager would talk to someone of the same position in Denmark, in other words either the sales manager or the CEO. The sales manager and the CEO were the only people who traveled to Japan at the time, and a great deal of courage would have been needed to bypass this line of communication. For the Japanese sales manager, contacting someone else was simply out of the question. The result was that issues that should have been dealt with by line managers were often communicated to top executives in Denmark that were busy dealing with global operations or issues from more important markets (Japan is the thirteenth most important market in sales). There was also a problem of language and interpretation. Finally, since several Japanese managers typically had to be involved as a message bubbled up through the hierarchy of Bang & Olufsen Japan (a system still found in many Japanese companies today), it was very inefficient and time consuming. According to Lars Myrup, it simply did not work.

In 2000, when Lars Myrup took over the subsidiary in Tokyo, one of his key goals was to hire people who were able to pick up the phone and call Denmark or write an e-mail in English. He also sent new employees to Struer for training in corporate values and marketing strategies and, perhaps even more importantly, to meet their counterparts. Today, communication goes directly to anyone concerned at headquarters, with a copy to Lars Myrup to keep him informed. The e-mail structure facilitates mutual information sharing, which has made communication between the subsidiary and headquarters more efficient.

If communication does not run smoothly the company will not grow. There is still a great deal of reluctance to contact headquarters in Denmark directly if you hire people from other Japanese companies who are accustomed to the Japanese hierarchical system. If you hire young graduates out of university and train them for a year or two and then send them to Struer, it helps tremendously, says Lars Myrup.

Lars Myrup found that it was important to hire people that were able to interact directly with their counterpart at their organizational level in Denmark – people with international mindsets. This international mindset is further encouraged through training in Demark, as described in the next section.

One Global Message
At Bang & Olufsen, technological advance is accelerating. The current CEO, Torben Ballegaard Sørensen, communicates directly not only with managers but also with employees connected to retail outlets and end customers. Utilizing these new lines of communication, the CEO can both address the appropriate information to, and gather it from,

employees throughout the organization, and this virtual yet direct contact has had a substantial impact on the organization as a whole. Lars Myrup observes:

> *In the old days we would have to call everyone in and the CEO would make a speech. Now with one click, he can address three thousand employees directly in one second. Of course there is the language issue in some cases, but basically he can address employees directly, and this is healthy for the organization. He is a very hands-on person. He likes technology and he understands how to use it in the right way. So in order not to dilute any key messages in the company through the next layer of managers – including me and yet another layer, namely the local management in Japan – he can talk directly to the retail development managers – who are the employees closest to our retailers.*

As a new communication initiative, the CEO has a yearly meeting where he briefs the retail development managers directly with the global strategy and message that they are all expected to communicate to the retailers. This means that in many instances there are only two people between the CEO at headquarters and the end customer in Japan: the retail development managers and the sales people in the store. In the old days, particularly in Japan, a greater number of intermediaries were involved in the retail channel and there were more layers of communication within each company. According to Lars Myrup, the communication value chain has dissolved. In this new scenario, the Bang & Olufsen CEO could be included in the matrix in the organizational chart above. He can deliver the corporate message company wide and, with equal facility, choose to send a brand message directly to the three people in Tokyo who are in charge of the retail stores.

Technology enables communication methods that make information available to all and ensures message consistency across borders and across markets. The CEO, Torben Ballegaard Sørensen, is skillful at taking advantage of these lines of communication but, according Lars Myrup, this process can also undermine the traditional role of middle managers who typically coordinated information flows between headquarters and the subsidiaries for which they were responsible. Given that the same information is often available to everyone, it may be a challenge for the middle managers to stay on top of the communication which now flows around them.

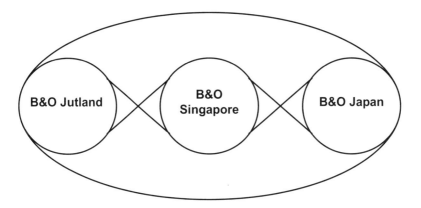

Display 6.5 Bang & Olufsen, communication diagram

Global Information Flow

There are several challenges for international managers presented by this new flow of corporate information. It puts substantial pressure on middle managers to a) know even more to maintain some kind of control and to b) be able to choose the right information to conduct properly informed local leadership. Ultimately, when everyone has access to the same level of information, it can raise questions about the chain of command as well as how to use the information, according to Lars Myrup.

> *You do need local management to coach and lead the process of enforcing messages from headquarters. I think it will be very interesting to see how it will work in the future. I am still flying to Japan to ensure that we implement the global strategy as the CEO has dictated. It demands a new way of thinking for our Japanese employees to be addressed directly by the CEO and my task is to make sure that they understand one hundred percent what the consequences are, and what they have to do now in the local market.*

It is a corporate objective at Bang & Olufsen to convey messages that are uniform throughout the global organization. Executive management believes that this global, uniform communication of information and strategy is the key to the future destiny of the company, and the CEO personally spearheads this activity.

It is important to avoid complicated filters and bottlenecks as well as misunderstanding in this new form of communication, says Lars Myrup. Hence, as part of this new communication network, middle managers become important mediators between the global message and the local interpretation(s) and execution of the indicated strategy.

The use of direct and broadcast communication channels can lead to a streamlining of the flow of information. At the same time, it is acknowledged by headquarters that there is still a need for regional offices to interpret, lead, and monitor global strategy at a local or regional level. For Bang & Olufsen in Asia, this has now been implemented through a regional office in Singapore.

Asia Pacific Regional Office – Singapore 2003

While Bang & Olufsen intends to create regional offices for the United States and Europe, this strategy has already materialized in Asia. After the establishment of the Tokyo office, Lars Myrup was given the task of managing all the markets in Asia from a new regional office opened in Singapore in 2003.[3] Virtual management will become even more important when Bang & Olufsen completes a new intranet system that will enable employees to communicate directly with one another visually and verbally from their PCs. For instance, from Japan employees will be able to see Lars Myrup in his office in Singapore, or any other manager sitting in their office in any other location. Physical office structure, according to Lars Myrup, is becoming obsolete:

> *If I stretch my neck, anybody in the Japan office will be able to see it. My financial controller is in Tokyo at the moment, but I just have to click and ask if she is there to get a visual connection. The Internet helps me merge the two offices. My assignment is basically getting the most out of the two teams in Asia located in Singapore and Tokyo. Of course, there is a seven hour flight between the two physical locations, but I see them as one.*

Several functional areas are managed from Singapore. Product and training related areas are managed from Singapore. In addition, the Japanese controller has recently been moved from Tokyo to Singapore. Via Bang & Olufsen's SAP system the financial controller can operate from anywhere in the world. From Singapore, she controls financial transactions and the accounting in Japan, including the monthly closing of accounts. In fact, as part of this new setup, only one out of the four managers at the top level will physically be in Japan.

However, just as the face to face interaction is an important basis for effective virtual communication internally, time, effort and physical presence are important for building company culture, and this will ultimately form the basis for organizational communication and coordination.

National and Corporate Values

Bang & Olufsen culture is grounded in the countryside of Denmark, and more specifically in the small village of Struer, situated in the Northern part of Jutland. Outside the modern glass factory, Jutland's natural abundance hosts a large dairy industry, plenty of wheat fields, and the beaches of the nearby North Sea. England is just across the Channel, and Germany borders the Jutland peninsula to the south. Inside the high-tech glass buildings, a substantial portion of the administrative staff come from the surrounding area, while engineers are recruited nationwide. The pace and atmosphere at Bang & Olufsen headquarters are influenced by the quiet countryside mentality of the Struer villagers, although the present CEO, Torben Ballegaard Sørensen, was educated in the United States and is a fast-paced, energetic leader.

While it is difficult to measure just how much the Bang & Olufsen culture is influenced by the surrounding Struer mentality, according Lars Myrup, Bang & Olufsen culture is unique – in fact, it is almost a religion:

> *The best that we can do is to educate and train our staff so that they be become dedicated evangelists. If you want to be a Muslim you go to Mecca. If you want to be a Catholic you go to Rome. And if you want to be a true Bang & Olufsen employee, you go to Struer. Here you become transfused with the right blood as if by osmosis. You meet all the company heroes that are part of our corporate culture, from the creative designers to the people on the factory floor who produce the products for you to sell.*

According to Lars Myrup, Bang & Olufsen management cherishes the feeling of being 'one big family', and it feels good to be where it all started and where it is still going on. He finds the experience of a visit to be an important source of knowledge for people who work outside Denmark, and a critical part of their becoming an ambassador for the brand. The more of a transfusion you have had from Struer, the more convincing and credible you will sound, he says. The whole experience leads to a professionalism and dedication that are essential when talking about the brand to both retail partners and customers. When the retail staff from Japan is sent to Struer for a week of training, their sales go up when they return because they have stories to tell, according to Lars Myrup.

It is therefore important to train employees with the objective of creating a shared organizational history and background. All of these objectives are enhanced by the regular visits, as well as the daily phone and internet communication that takes place across the distance separating the two organizations.

Questioning the Ordinary – Vision
The vision statement of Bang & Olufsen is: "Courage to constantly question the ordinary in search of surprising long lasting experiences". It is a very powerful statement, according to Lars Myrup:

> *You can read it in again and again, and it is actually embodied in everything that we do. We want to challenge the ordinary. We want to be different, and we want to create these magical experiences and surprises. But at the same time, we do not just want to surprise with a transitory gimmick, but rather want to make an impression that creates a long lasting experience. And this long lasting experience is often based on the seriousness with which we select the highest quality technology. Another value is excellence; excellence is in everything we do. And passion.*

The mission statement, the brand identity value[4] and the core competence areas basically form a 'three layer rocket' that encompasses the soul of Bang & Olufsen (the brand identity values are performance, design, humanization, craftsmanship; the core competence areas are quality, picture, sound, user interaction, design, integration, mechanical movements, materials and finish, as cited on the homepage).

While the products themselves are in some sense the end result of what Bang & Olufsen employees do, the characteristics of these products both influence and are influenced by the employee behavior and creative mentality that lie behind their creation. In this sense, the concept value chain goes all the way from the employees, through the products, to the end customer. This is the primary reason why knowledge of the core values is critical, and why they are stressed in employee training aimed at spreading and strengthening the Bang & Olufsen corporate culture, says Lars Myrup.

Nevertheless, it is reasonable to ask whether or not the Japanese office staff know the corporate values? According to Lars Myrup they may not know them by heart but they know what Bang & Olufsen stands for:

> *They might not be able to remember the values by heart but they are continuously reminded of them through meetings and everyday work. The longer they have stayed with the company, the more they know about the Bang & Olufsen way of doing things. It is not so much the ability to remember the values by heart and to be able to list them with your eyes closed in the middle of the night. Rather, they are an integrated part of employees' daily work and an inner guide to how they should behave and operate.*

This assumption was confirmed in the interviews at the Tokyo office. In particular, the mission statement, 'questioning the ordinary', was mentioned by most of the managers. However, according to Chiyuki Komuro, questioning the ordinary is not a part of Japanese culture. On the contrary, being similar (ordinary) and not sticking out are virtues for most Japanese. So, although the concept is ingrained as a form of knowledge in the employees' heads, it does not have the same connotations or influence in Japan as it may have in Denmark.

Other values were mainly mentioned in relation to branding, retail promotion and costumer relations. For instance, the value statement that "technology is made for the benefit of man – and not the reverse" was mentioned several times as a core value related to the products. However, as we have seen, meaning is often culturally bound and influenced, and the ultimate interpretation of many of the values may change, even significantly, in the Japanese context.

Shared Values

The most important way to get people to share company values is to hire people who are willing and able to adapt. When Lars Myrup hires new employees, he evaluates them according to the following criteria:

> *I was born, spoiled and raised in the system so I feel that I have the values in my blood* [the parents of all of his best friends worked for Bang & Olufsen]. *When I interview people for a job, I immediately have a feeling of whether they will fit into our culture*

191

or not. You can compare a cultural system to a living organism. If you inject a new cell or medicine into it the organism, it may be accepted and become a part of the organism. However, if it is not healthy for the system, it will be rejected after a while. If you station staff in Struer or in any other organization, you soon find out whether they have been accepted or rejected by the system. They may be the nicest people at the interview, but if they behave in a un-Bang & Olufsen way, they will not be able to work in the culture or be a part of it. They might think they are, but eventually they will find out that they are not, and will thus not be able to survive.

According to Lars Myrup, employees from both cultures have their rituals in the way they work and behave that are corporate as well as national.

I am sure that you can find many tribes around the world but the Struer headquarters and the office in Japan both represent a very unique company culture and a unique country culture. In both cases you really need to go there first and take the temperature. You have to test the waters on your own and observe people's behavior. Before you start behaving and acting on your own, you need to see what surrounds you and what the rules are. You may like the rules; you may dislike them. Maybe your job is actually to change the rules, but before you start changing the rules you need to understand what they are there for. Whether you go from Tokyo to Struer or you are sent from Struer to Japan, if you want to change the game and the rules, then you have to figure out what is going on first and be sensitive to it.

Sensitivity, according to Lars Myrup, is a key component of intercultural competence. He also believes that his strongest tool in maintaining the culture is to hire people who can internalize company beliefs.

You cannot control culture and you should not try to, but if you hire people who are fundamentally in agreement with you and the company values, you are on the right track. If they share the values, it is okay that they have ideas of their own that are not immediately part of the dynamics of the organization. This will add value. It might create conflicts at first, but these conflicts are healthy for the system. However, if you hire people that you do not feel share the company values a hundred percent, then you have to be there more as a police man to control things, and this takes time away from the forward looking vision and the search for growth. So, you have to make sure that the people you work with are natural evangelists. If they are, it is okay that they run wild as long as it is broadly in the desired direction we want the company to take.

The only introductory material to the company for new employees is the book *Break Point*. After that, visiting Struer and meeting the family suffices. Normally the introduction lasts two to three days, but every visit to Struer is part of a process. Walking in the corridors at headquarters, going though a factory, having breakfast Friday morning with colleagues, saying "Hi" to the CEO and chatting with him and other colleagues over coffee – all these things are part of the training to be an 'evangelist'.

The Danish Way – A Japanese Perspective

The present manager for marketing and retail of Bang & Olufsen Japan, Chiyuki Komuro, was hired in 2002 to take over the next phase of expanding the retail network and securing the quality of the brand and retail marketing. Her core competency is product branding, a competency which has been her specialty with several international brands, including the French brand Cartier Jewelry and the American apparel brands Calvin Klein and the Gap. Although the company had already made significant strides by 2002, she joined Bang & Olufsen with the charter of taking the brand 'to the next level.' She was not part of the 'cultural revolution' at the Tokyo office because the last two male employees who had problems adjusting left just as she was starting with the company.

Chiyuki Komuro sets out to 'question the ordinary', she says, and to make the Bang & Olufsen brand even more attractive among Japan's elite consumers. In reading *Break Point*, she understood that even a well-established brand is vulnerable, but she knows how to capitalize on the fact that Bang & Olufsen is a foreign brand and plans to utilize this to the utmost. In particular, she promotes Bang & Olufsen as a high-profile design audio visual product, and this promotion is done in the most attractive way possible in order to showcase the connection between exclusive design and an exclusive lifestyle. As part of this effort, she has already used a variety of events to associate the Bang & Olufsen brand with highly esteemed Japanese artists, including the Japanese designer Tadao Ando, among others. Chiyuki Komuro has also been able to cooperate with other prestigious companies, such as Louis Vuitton, to promote Bang & Olufsen in joint branding activities in Tokyo.

However, Chiyuki Komuro also sees challenges, as she is now for the first time working with a Scandinavian brand and with Scandinavian management. Bang & Olufsen costumers (approximately 20,000) have a difficult time even pronouncing the brand name, and few people in the population at large even know where Denmark is. However, she finds that the professional similarities to her previous positions are greater than the differences. Further, the simplicity that characterizes the lifestyles and design of the Danes and the Japanese is a common cultural trait – and a likeable and sellable one:

> *Although the company Bang & Olufsen is far away from us physically, their mentality is familiar and close. Danish cultural traditions include simplicity, which allows us as Japanese to feel close to Danish culture and the Danish people. Simplicity is a common denominator. People who discover Bang & Olufsen's character feel comfortable with the products and the aesthetics of the design.*

Not surprisingly, however, some business practices are new to her. The Danish way of life both at work and at home seems quite relaxed compared to that of the busy Japanese. It is her impression that Danes are also more casual and open than the Japanese. They may not be open underneath it all, she says, but on the surface the Danes she has meet are relaxed and casual. Bang & Olufsen top executives are open to new ideas and they leave space for their international managers to voice their opinions. American companies by contrast are very straight forward: "You have to do this and do that. If you don't do it, you may not have a job tomorrow". If Chiyuki Komuro wants to take a new approach to implementing an idea for the Japanese market – and if she delivers the right arguments – she gets to try:

> *Danes can also be direct in some ways. It seems to also be part of their mentality. But when it comes to business, they will try to make you understand their point of view in your own way. They do not just force you by power to accept the importance of the*

corporate strategy or business direction. They let you feel that your work is being appreciated and they delegate responsibility to you. I have learned that, and I am doing the same with my people at the office. That way, they feel positive about getting direction. The American way is to say 'you have to do it', but the Danish style is to sort of develop consensus around business ideas. My superiors will say 'Yes I know, it is different, but this is really important to Bang & Olufsen, because of this and that'. This is the Scandinavian way of being forceful.

Display 6.6 Tadao Ando designed the exhibition 'Styling Danish Life' in the Mori Hall of the Grand Hyatt Hotel in connection with the business delegation and Royal visit to Japan in November 2004. From left are the exhibiting partners Lars Myrup, Bang & Olufsen; Flemming Lindeløv, Royal Copenhagen; Henrik Holm, Fritz Hansen; and Erik Holm, Louis Poulsen Lighting

Negotiation with Danes in this manner takes more time, and eventually she is often forced to implement the corporate strategy anyway. But her motivation is higher, and that is the difference in styles. Chiyuki Komuro also emphasized that Danes are consensus-minded and that this is a commonality between Danes and Japanese that makes cooperation easy.

When asked about the Struer culture, she laughs and says that she could live there for a limited period of time – if she had to. The countryside, the many cows and the quiet do not attract her nearly as much as the busy metropolitan sprawl of Tokyo. However, for her the key differences between Struer and Tokyo are not so much the surroundings as the mentalities of the people. Specifically, she feels that she needs to make an extra effort to find a common platform for the exchange of business ideas. For instance, at the global marketing meetings she encounters a lot of Danes who have never been to her part of the world and who do not understand the situation in Japan:

> *It is a challenge because they say 'Okay but', and I do not know what comes after the 'but', because I do not see the other half of the sentence. So the situation needs work. When I am with people at headquarters, I single them out and talk about the situation in Japan. I keep talking and making friends with them. And show them how our sales figures are growing to help them understand how they can help us. I always do this, but it takes time to pursue ideas and convince them because they have not been out here. They do not know my staff. I wish I could show them the differences because we are reading things in a different way. Our readings depend on our way of living and our mentality. At least I try to let them understand the difference, but going far beyond that is difficult. They say 'Yes, I understand but . . .'*

According to Chiyuki Komuro, this is not at all due to a Danish or Scandinavian lack of cultural knowledge. People anywhere in the world who stay in their own little corner their whole lives have this same gap, although they may have the best intentions of working together. Basically, it is difficult for her to really share the Japanese culture and way of thinking with people who have no prior knowledge or background with which to relate to what she is telling them. One of her examples from Japan is that, when required, the Japanese will sacrifice their holidays or weekends to meet a deadline. If Chiyuki Komuro receives a complaint from a customer, she may have to apologize personally and she will 'sacrifice her free time' – in Danish terms – to make sure that the customer is satisfied. In Japan, this is a responsibility that is simply considered to be a natural part of any job. In Denmark, however, free time appears to be a sacred human right.

Another example is the importance of timely product delivery. In Japan, being on time is of the utmost importance and is an important part of the national identity (just look at the punctuality of the trains and media attention surrounding a single late arrival).

However, these are examples that are easy to explain and are just as easy to forget. In particular, the nuances of the cultural differences which they underscore are significant, but not necessarily easy to remember or understand unless experienced.

The Role of the Local Manager

As part of the management group, Chiyuki Komuro sees her most important responsibility as a mediator between Bang & Olufsen Denmark and Bang & Olufsen Japan. Hierarchically, her role and responsibilities comprise four levels of management that she must attend to: headquarters and global management are the first level; the middle managers whom she represents form the second level; the commercial, retail and retail development managers at the Tokyo office are the third level; and finally the retail-customers are the fourth level of management. Communication at each of these levels varies from being very international, European or Danish to being very conservatively Japanese.

> *One way to think about my role is that of an interpreter. I have to know about the European* and *the Japanese way of doing things. If I only knew one culture, it would not really work. Japan differs in a lot of respects. The Japanese language for one is very ambiguous for foreigners. For instance when the Japanese say 'Yes', it means: 'Yes I understand what you are saying'. It means that they understand the statement. It does not mean 'Yes I agree'. Our words are vague, which is difficult to understand for someone who does not know about Japanese culture. When the Japanese say 'Yes' (I understand) foreigners think that means 'Okay, they agree', but they do not necessarily agree – not at all.*

Similarly, the Japanese 'No' is expressed in roundabout terms such as 'We will think about it' or 'we will consider it'. It is very important that mediators and translators explain the implications of these nuances and complexities to mediate not only language but also the cultural implications of what is communicated. In this sense, there is a substantial distance between the language spoken by headquarters executives and that spoken by the Japanese dealers.

Language, says Chiyuki Komuro, does not only mean English or Japanese, which of course are the common means of communication. It also means professional or personal language. Although she speaks English fluently, and has many years of experience abroad as well as in European companies, she encounters problems of understanding between people who are from different professional backgrounds. For instance, financial managers oriented towards numerical bottom lines and people like herself who are creative people working with emotional bottom lines in their branding efforts often experience a communication gap.

She encourages her office staff to learn English, but says that international understanding only comes after many years of experience in an international and professional environment.

From Danish to Japanese Subsidiary Management

The move of the Danish managerial staff to the Singapore office has influenced the mindset of the Tokyo office employees. When asked how it has influenced the work culture, Emiko Fukuda, the financial controller says:

> *To be honest, I really enjoyed having somebody from Denmark in the office. It was a good mixture of the best of the two cultures. Of course, our most important asset in the Tokyo office is that we are Japanese and we work with the Japanese dealers. But having the immediate input from Denmark directly from a Dane was motivating. When Lars was here it was a completely different environment. The everyday international link and influence is missing.*

One of the biggest differences according to Emiko Fukuda is the fact that English is not used at the office anymore. This means that "the office mentality and way of thinking can get very local". Most people in the office have connections with staff in Denmark, but these often remain virtual. Before, when Lars Myrup was in Tokyo he would tell a lot of stories from Struer or other Bang & Olufsen locations in the world, and Danes from headquarters would visit the Japanese office more often. Now, Singapore is the Asian headquarters and it has become the important stop-over, and the Tokyo office has the status of a satellite operation, she says. At first, the restructuring also resulted in behavioral changes from some staff members, says Emiko Fukuda:

Lars always wanted to know everything that was going on. He did not close his door, which meant that he could hear what was going on. He was always watching or at least this is what we thought. We were used to it and everybody worked so hard. Since he is no longer here, you need a different kind of discipline. It is so much a part of Japanese mentality to work harder when someone watches you. That is why most Japanese offices are arranged so the superior can watch over their employees and vice versa. Your boss can continuously follow you. If the manager is away, we regress to student behavior – just like when the teacher is away and the playing starts.

When asked about the change from Danish to Japanese management in the Tokyo office, the product manager Taketoshi Hashimoto says:

But Lars Myrup is Japanese!! Well in principle, anyway. Lars was working as president here in this room for three years and I never found a gap in our viewpoints. Lars himself worked for Marantz for three years building the basis for the subsidiary before we opened Bang & Olufsen Japan. He has been living in Japan for many years, so he shows a good understanding of our way of thinking. His approach as a president has been to lower the gaps in the hierarchy in our office. He also has good communication not only with managers but with every employee.

Despite his claim about Lars Myrup's ethnicity, Taketoshi Hashimoto considers his boss' style of communication to be much friendlier than the traditionally formal communication that takes place between managers and staff in most Japanese corporations. In his view, Lars Myrup's approach and frequent communication with his staff at all levels have helped to fill possible cultural and linguistic gaps and avoid misunderstandings. Although restarting the subsidiary was difficult and followed by a period of substantial conflict, Lars Myrup's style helped to smooth communication in the office, he says. He takes the restructuring as a sign that the Tokyo office is doing well.

The marketing and retail manager, Chiyuki Komuro, deals with motivation in the same way that Lars Myrup did. She offers her staff substantial freedom in carrying out their duties, in return for which they must accept responsibility for their performance. In this way, she is working to help them realize some of the benefits of working for a Danish company.

Cultural Change Does Not Happen Overnight

In retrospect, Lars Myrup views the overall decision to reestablish a subsidiary to be a success story. In reasserting their control of the operation in Japan, Bang & Olufsen started from a period of seven years without growth during which the brand had been diluted by their former agent's short-term strategy. However, he does not blame the agent, as it was Bang & Olufsen that chose and approached them, rather than the other way around. While it was not a good match, it was a necessary stepping stone on the way to implementing the company's chosen strategy in Japan. The fact that results improved drastically during the first year of the new subsidiary was an exception for the Japanese market, where it typically takes much longer to engineer a turnaround.

The shift in organizational culture, however, was a long and uphill battle. It is not possible to set an exact date for the transformation, but it took about three years starting from the day when Lars Myrup brought in new team members. After three years, it was clear that the more entrepreneurial Bang & Olufsen spirit had prevailed, although to this day in Japan it must be tempered with a respect for the relationship building that is a part of traditional Japanese business practices. Ultimately, a culture which is seventy to eighty percent new has emerged, and Lars Myrup considers this progress a success. In his opinion, it is one thing to get the finances turned around, as this simply requires market knowledge, capable execution and hard work. Cultural transformation, however, is another matter altogether, as it requires a deep understanding of both cultures: the culture you operate in and the culture you wish to infuse. "It was a long walk", according to Lars Myrup. It was not a question of just hiring new people, but also of hiring new people that would function well within the new setting. The main lesson learned was:

You cannot just eliminate culture. You cannot make jumps and leaps to make a new culture because then you risk loosing it all. You need to take it from where you are, making sure you know where you want to go, and bridge that gap, concludes Lars Myrup.

Bibliography

Jensen, J., Olesen, C. H., Harder, K., Pedersen, B.M., & Skifter, P.U. (2003) *"Bang & Olufsen 1960-1990. Fra dansk kvalitetsmærke til international ikon"*, [From Danish Quality Brand to International Icon], Viborg Denmark, Forlaget Hovedland

Poulsen, P. T. (1998) *"Break Point. Anders Knutsen and Bang & Olufsen"*, Haslev, Denmark, Nordisk Bog Center A/S

Chapter Six: Endnotes

[1] In 1925, Bang & Olufsen was founded by Peter Bang and Svend Olufsen. Today Bang & Olufsen has 2500 employees and annual turnover is USD 600 million. Bang & Olufsen is listed on the Copenhagen Stock Exchange and all production – except for one factory in the Czech Republic – still takes place in Denmark. Bang & Olufsen sells high-end home entertainment solutions. They are present in seventy countries with 1400 stores around the world, of which approximately 700 are exclusively selling Bang & Olufsen products.

[2] 'Break Point' was the name of the corporate turnaround strategy begun in 1993 by CEO Anders Knutsen. The corporate turnaround of global operations became an important part of Bang & Olufsen business culture. The experience was an important lesson highlighting the fact that even the best companies can go down if corporate management gets out of control. By straightening out management and refocusing strategy and operations, Bang & Olufsen came out of the crisis a stronger company (Poulsen, 1998).

[3] Bang & Olufsen does not have its own subsidiary in Hong Kong, Korea, Taiwan, or Australia, where a single representative office in each country distributes to and manages local retailers. The biggest markets in Asia are Japan, Hong Kong, Australia and China. The next group to be focused on for development includes Taiwan and Korea, as well as the smaller markets of Singapore, Thailand, and Malaysia.

[4] The corporate values today are based on the internationalization policy and value discussions of the 1970s. The corporate identity components, CIC, then were authenticity, audio-visuality, credibility, domesticity, essentiality, individuality, inventiveness. At the time, the fact that Sony and six other Japanese companies were the main competitors made Bang & Olufsen decide to craft a clear distinction that would make their identity and market position clear both internally and externally (Jensen *et al.*, 2003).

Chapter Seven

ECCOES OF THE WORLD

Year	Event
1982	ECCO (Eccolet) sign the first license agreement with Achilles.
2002	A new subsidiary established in Hong Kong to oversee ECCO activities in the Asia Pacific region, including Japan.
2003	A new license contract between ECCO and Achilles to provide for expansion through 2013, as in 2013 Japan is still projected to be the no. 3 market in sales worldwide.

From Small Shoemaker to International Brand

In April 1963, ECCO was founded by Karl-Heinz Toosbuy in the town of Bredebro in Southern Jutland, Denmark. Karl-Heinz Toosbuy[1] passed away in May 2004 just as this research project was taking form. However Toosbuy's vision and ground breaking ideas continue to drive today, as they always have, ECCO's explosive growth.[2] In 2003, Toosbuy decided to double global production within ten years, and every manager was required to make a business plan to reach this goal by 2013. Needless to say, operations at ECCO are still carried out in the spirit established and nurtured by Toosbuy, a spirit which extends to ECCO's business in Japan, which Toosbuy personally initiated and directed.

Nonetheless, ECCO is currently facing several challenges to the continued success of Toosbuy's ideas. Turning the tide and building upon these ideas to realize even greater success will depend on management control of the company and the communication of ideas worldwide, issues which have direct implications for operations in Japan.

Over the last decade, Toosbuy made several hundred trips to visit ECCO subsidiaries and partners all over the world at a time when ECCO was undergoing rapid development. Toosbuy, as the owner of the company, was able to establish the right contracts with the right people in order to sell millions of shoes. Today, ECCO produces twelve million pairs of shoes a year and 1.2 million pairs are sold in Japan.

This chapter describes the history and background of cooperation between ECCO headquarters and the Achilles Corporation in Japan. First, there is an account of ECCO's entry to Japan. Next, the main cultural and organizational challenges facing the partnership are discussed, followed by an overview of the challenges related to import quotas and the distribution system. Subsequently, the importance of the Hong Kong office to global communication flow is highlighted, and the chapter concludes with a discussion of the Japanese implementation of 'global strategy' as well as lessons learned.

The chapter is based on interviews with executive managers, operational staff and trainees in Denmark, Hong Kong and Japan. The interviews present individual perceptions of the national and organizational cultural issues facing the partnership between ECCO and Achilles. Employees also offer suggestions on how to best communicate to reach future organizational goals.

ECCO in Japan – Background

In 1982, ECCO entered Japan with production and marketing through a license agreement with the Achilles Corporation. Today, Japan is ECCO's third most important market in terms of sales. The communication and cooperation over the last two decades between ECCO and their license partner, Achilles, is explored in this chapter.

ECCO is a company characterized by an entrepreneurial spirit, open communication, and a relatively flat organizational structure. Achilles, on the other hand, is a traditional Japanese company with several organizational layers and complex decision-making processes.

The two companies have different ways of thinking and doing business that are deeply rooted in the Danish and Japanese cultures respectively. Language is a clear barrier to communication. However, ECCO headquarters and the Achilles Corporation have one important thing in common – they both want to do business. Hence, collaborative efforts include human resource development initiatives to enhance cultural competencies in order to improve communication. Junior employees from both organizations have been exchanged as trainees whose mission is to learn the business practices of the 'other' in order to bridge the gap between different national and organizational cultures.

EXPANSION

The human brain is man's best and most important raw material.
The effort to exploit the optimum potential of the brain's resources is tomorrow's great challenge – and a source of new creativity, strength and epoch–making results.
ECCO sees it as its main task to exploit in a dynamic and far-sighted way the full capacity of the human brain.

限りなき発展

人間の頭脳は、限りなき発展をとげる源泉である
頭脳の源泉は限りなき未来を創造する
創造への努力は、限りなき挑戦にあり
湧き出る創造は、限りなき夢を成果に結びつける
ECCOは、人間の頭脳による限りなき未来を創造することを最も重視し
限りなき発展をめざしている

Display 7.1 Memorandum at the entrance of Achilles' headquarters, by Karl-Heinz Toosbuy, 1 February 1995 (the complete version of the Japanese quote on the cover-page)

ECCO Culture – An Entrepreneurial Spirit

ECCO is the fifth largest brown[3] shoe brand in the world. The main competitive strength of the company is that it controls the whole supply chain, largely through vertical integration. ECCO buys their own raw materials and has tanneries in the Netherlands, Indonesia and Thailand. They produce their own designs, manufacture their shoes and finally have close contact with the end consumer through retail outlets. This is a winning concept, according to Jens Christian Meier. He is one of three executive directors and is responsible for ECCO production and logistics worldwide.

The ECCO group has managed to exploit the whole production chain economically by taking the margins out of each level of the chain in order to consolidate profits in a single, integrated operation. ECCO is competitive at all levels, at least in part thanks to the development of advanced production technology.[4] This technological capability enables both flexible production as well as the production of technologically advanced products. Today, most of ECCO's designs cannot be copied because both the technology and the production processes are unique.

However, technological advance and lean production strategies have not been the only factors that have led to ECCO's success. ECCO's corporate spirit is also an asset. According to Jens Christian Meier, the ECCO culture is imbued with dynamism and entrepreneurial spirit. "In principle everything is possible", he says. Jens Christian Meier has worked for ECCO for almost twenty years. Although he was away from ECCO for seven years, the experience gave him a basis for comparison:

> *Being away from ECCO gave me time to look at the company and discover its spirit and dynamism. There is a special power in the way we do things which I think only exists in a few companies. There is a close feeling of togetherness in the company that comes from the ongoing challenges we take upon ourselves and expect of each other. Of course, ECCO's culture is still very influenced by Toosbuy's vision and way of doing things. The ECCO way is less formal, without limiting etiquette and ways of doing things. At ECCO the barriers and boxes that you find in many companies do not exist. We challenge our employees a lot more than other companies I have worked in. I have experienced a lot of thinking inside the box and discipline for the sake of discipline. It is difficult for such companies to change when the environment changes. ECCO is geared towards change. We have an open, dynamic and flexible way of running our company.*

Flexibility is an integral part of everyday work practices, and is a result of ECCO's management philosophy and method. Similarly, according to all of the managers interviewed at headquarters, the foundation for action at ECCO is entrepreneurship.

But how does ECCO maintain and promote its entrepreneurial spirit and associated corporate values? This is one of the biggest future challenges facing the company, and one that has only become greater with the passing away of the company's founder. In addition, ECCO's rapid growth naturally makes it more challenging to communicate throughout the organization.

A central challenge in communicating the company's values, spirit and identity is to first define what they are, and a great deal of internal research has been done to identify employee values. This is a process which is still underway, and seminars have been held to further define, and redefine, the core ECCO values.

ECCO Maxims

1. In word, thought and action, keep your promises. Concealment is also a lie. No theory is better than good practice.
2. Strive for simplicity and simplification to the ultimate degree. Simple calculation is useful in a large company as well.
3. Face your weaknesses and turn them into your strengths.
4. It is good to be different. People who are similar can never complement each other.
5. Our national handicaps can only be overcome and turned into strengths through shared objectives, cooperation and high levels of training.
6. The next 25 years will bring more change and development than the past 200 years.
7. We are often imitated, but imitators will always be followers.
8. Success depends on everyone taking responsibility for shared objectives.
9. The best results – and maximum fulfillment – are achieved by people who have managed to turn their job into their hobby.
10. No one will create something from nothing without being thrifty, almost cheeseparing.
11. Our aim goes beyond common sense. ECCO builds on idealism.
12. If you want to be the Champion you must know your aim and lap-times.
13. Responsibilities and opportunities are not just handed out; you take the initiative yourself.
14. Everyone has the right to a challenge and to be challenged to develop their own potential. Unused talents fade away.
15. ECCO has always lived in the future.
16. Play all the keys on your piano, from creativity, and innovation to implementation and achievement – close to brutally when necessary.

ECCO does not merely sell shoes – we sell our culture.

Display 7.2 ECCO Maxims (Toosbuy Vision, Strategy and Story, 2002)

ECCO's vision and mission statement enable employees to understand the company's goals. The ECCO Vision, according to Jens Christian Meier, is to be the most desired brand within innovation and comfort footwear. ECCO can only attain that position by constantly and courageously researching new paths – investing in employees and in their core competencies of product development and production technology. "Our Mission is that our business drive and the thinking behind ECCO are the result of continuously new ideas, dynamism, capability and forward movement – and about being part of our own movement". The clarity of these definitions, according to Jens Christian Meier, helps to disseminate a common message about future goals throughout the organization. ECCO employees are also educated, he says, not only in all aspects of shoe-making 'from cow to shoe' but also in ECCO values and ethics.

An ECCO book of company values was published in 1991 and given to new employees, as the older generation knows and lives by them already (Noer, 1991). Another ECCO book *Toosbuy: Visions, Strategy and Story* from 2002 lists the corporate values in twenty-five sentences. The sentences are based on Toosbuy's life and business philosophy. An abbreviated version of the sentences is included in display 7.2. According to Kirsten Moesgaard, the vice president of human resources, internal research has shown that the values are ingrained particularly well at headquarters where people have been close to the founder.

ECCO Does Not Stop – The Legacy of Toosbuy

But how are ECCO's corporate culture and values perceived in Japan? The Achilles Corporation has been ECCO's Japanese license partner since 1982. The president of Achilles, Shizuya Yamanaka, explains:

We understand that Mr. Toosbuy's philosophy constitutes the basis of ECCO culture. Everyone working for ECCO in Achilles respects ECCO's values, and we try to take them into consideration when dealing with ECCO products. However, whether we can adopt ECCO's corporate culture that is another issue. We try to take in most of the ECCO values, but there is a limit to how much we can incorporate them in a Japanese business setting. Even the change of ECCO's logo had [financial] implications. But as far as ECCO's philosophy goes, we have deep admiration for it.

President Shizuya Yamanaka has taken many things to heart during his twenty-three year relationship with ECCO. He clearly remembers Toosbuy's motto, which was "Do not say there is not or you cannot". He also recalls an episode with Toosbuy that made a lasting impression on him:

Toosbuy came to Japan for one of his visits and we were having dinner together. He asked us if there was any more wine left, pointing at the almost empty bottle, and we said 'no'. He then spread a newspaper on the table, shook the empty bottle and said 'See, there is some if you squeeze it. It is same with ideas – there are plenty if you squeeze all you can.

It seems from this story that Toosbuy was a tough negotiator. Nevertheless, President Shizuya Yamanaka remembers Toosbuy with great admiration. Toosbuy was the principal figure in Achilles' relationship with ECCO. Recently new people have appeared in the ECCO-Achilles relationship, and they often want to implement changes or to head in a new direction. While this is a necessary process, according to President Shizuya Yamanaka there is a great discrepancy between the relationship that was built up during the last twenty-three years and the changes that are being brought on by new forces within the partnership. In other words, he concludes, an inevitable generation gap has developed, a gap in which Toosbuy and he were always on the same side:

> *When Mr. Toosbuy came with samples, he used to demonstrate the products and describe the required advertising all by himself. In this way, he taught us his philosophy directly, so that we absorbed ECCO culture through our skin, so to speak. 'Shoes have to be made to respect your feet. And to respect your feet means to respect your body and your health'. That is the principle. 'Our challenge is to create shoes that people feel comfortable in and that are fun to wear'. Mr. Toosbuy had other philosophical thoughts, but the principle of quality shoe-making was very clear. ECCO does not compromise – and that is good.*

One of the implications of this uncompromising attitude was that Achilles was not allowed to change the ECCO concept, for example by mass producing and selling low-quality, low-priced shoes.

According to President Yamanaka, Achilles also has strong principles as an established company with fifty-eight years of history. Throughout this history, while the principle of 'making shoes of value to costumers' has largely been maintained, once in a while Achilles has come across a situation where they have had to compromise, or even forget this principle for a moment, in order to sell. Toosbuy, however, was unyielding in his stand: he did not compromise on his basic principles. He therefore reminded Achilles from time to time of the importance of 'sticking to the principles'.

Market Entry – The Japanese Discover Danish Shoes

An agreement between Achilles and ECCO was concluded in 1982. The arrangement was actually a coincidence as ECCO was not actively looking for a sales partner in Japan. In fact, it was Achilles that approached ECCO. Achilles had had a joint venture for a long time with a Canadian shoe maker, Bata, one of the best shoes manufacturers in the world at the time. One day an employee brought home a pair of shoes from a company located in Denmark. An executive from Achilles saw the pair of ECCO shoes, and thought they were made in an interesting and unusual way. He became interested and immediately set out to contact the Danish manufacturer of this pair of shoes. Later, this vice president from Achilles visited ECCO with the intention of negotiating a cooperative agreement between the two companies. Eventually, these efforts led to the license agreement.

> *After all, we have a very short history of Western shoe culture in Japan. Japanese shoe culture stems from the long history of traditional Japanese shoes, such as Geta (wooden shoes) and Zori (flipflops), and we still have a different attitude towards shoes compared to that of the Western society. Reflecting on this background, our motivation for working with ECCO products was to utilize their special features to develop a new shoe culture in Japan. That was how we started working with ECCO,* said President Yamanaka.

The initial goal was to sell 300,000 pairs a year, which does not sound so ambitious now. However, at the time, the closest competitor for ECCO-type-shoes, Hush Puppies, was selling about 600,000 pairs a year. Thus, the goal was to sell half the volume of the top-ranking competitor already established in the market.

Importation of Western Shoe Culture

Through meetings between Toosbuy and Achilles, President Yamanaka continues, it became apparent that they needed to change ECCO's shoes to fit the Japanese foot. Compared to Western feet, the Japanese have feet that are flat and wide and European shoes would not fit them correctly. This issue of size was repeatedly stressed in negotiations with ECCO so that their existing products could be tailored to the Japanese market. However, the quality of the ECCO products was never an issue:

From the start of the collaboration, ECCO shared their strict and unwavering principle of quality shoe-making, which included leather quality, manufacturing method and product handling, said President Yamanaka.

An anecdote about quality is well known among managers at ECCO, and it also came up in the interview with President Yamanaka:[5]

When Mr. Toosbuy showed us a sample pair of shoes, he would not just take the product out of the box. He would first wipe the pair on his jacket before he showed it to us. This shows his respect for the quality of his shoes. This attitude is what I mean by 'shoe culture' – which was entirely missing in Japan and is something that ECCO has taught us.

At the time, just as today, the Japanese market was considered full of opportunities. However, there was also intense competition. Once a new product appeared in the market, competitors immediately followed with copies. Achilles was thus challenged to differentiate ECCO as a special brand somehow unique among all the other similar products. This task was not always easy. Japanese consumers were, and still are, generally concerned with the perceived value of a brand. Is the brand well known? Is it respected? While by the start of the 1980s ECCO was well-known in Denmark and its neighboring countries, such as Germany, the brand was not at all known in Japan, or even in the US. Therefore Achilles had to undertake sizeable marketing campaigns to both establish the brand and to emphasize that ECCO was different.

A key feature of these campaigns was the fact that ECCO's products in Japan were made to fit the shape of the Japanese foot. In fact, ECCO's ability to provide the technology to do this was the reason that Achilles had approached ECCO in the first place, and this feature was emphasized in the campaigns as a strongly differentiating characteristic of the brand.

The first exhibition of ECCO shoes was held in the famous La Foret building in Harajuku, a popular shopping area in Tokyo. This location was, at the beginning of the 1980s, one of few that offered enough space for big events. For the exhibition, music from the popular movie Flash Dance was used and a multimedia video was shown. Overall, Achilles' launch of the product was considered to be both quite innovative and effective.

However, it was not only in their marketing strategy that Achilles had to come up with something unusual – they also took a novel approach in their sales strategy. Achilles decided to educate the staff of the major retail stores about the advantages and differences of ECCO shoes. At the time, this amounted to educating a number of employees from roughly one hundred companies who knew absolutely nothing about ECCO the company, the brand, or the shoe. Nevertheless, Achilles kept its eye on the goal and tackled each company one by one. As President Shizuya Yamanaka recalls, the sales campaign was considered rather flashy:

> *I remember this episode very well. There was a product line called 911, which had eight different variations in color. The shoe market then consisted of only black and brown shoes, so ECCO was quite unusual. I myself visited one of the retailers to sell this product line, and the president of the retail chain said to me 'Nobody in Japan will buy such colorful shoes. They have to be more conservative.' I begged the president to just display the product as a test in his stores, and I promised him that I would come and take them back if nobody bought them. That night, the president called me and said: 'You win!'*

As has been mentioned, the annual sales of Hush Puppies at that time were about 600,000 pairs, and their sales have not increased much since then. Over the same period, by comparison, ECCO sales in Japan went from zero to 1.2 million pairs annually today.

The License Agreement

The first contract between the two companies was signed in 1982 and was a five year license agreement. For a period thereafter, staff from Achilles would visit the factory in Jutland fairly regularly. They typically arrived in a large group and would stay for an extended period of time. They observed closely, took pictures and returned to Japan with the know-how necessary to implement the production of ECCO shoes.

However, Toosbuy was well aware of the Japanese ability and reputation related to product imitation and he foresaw that infringement was one possible outcome of the collaboration. Although he always maintained his enthusiasm for the partnership, Toosbuy established one very clear goal for his employees: ECCO simply had to be quicker and better. Every time Achilles representatives came to

Denmark, ECCO employees had to be able to present them with both new technology and new products.

This strategy of open information sharing in turn enabled the Danish negotiators to place fairly high demands on their Japanese partners, and overall this was the foundation for the successful cooperation that continues to this day.

The 1982 license agreement stated that Achilles was to produce and market ECCO shoes in Japan. Achilles would receive instruction from the production headquarters in Bredebro and the design headquarters in Tønder, both situated in the Southern part of Jutland. They would then change the sizes, colors and materials to fit the Japanese market.

During the 1980s, Japanese shoe styles, colors and sizes were different from Western standards, so Achilles adapted the products they received from Denmark. Only the designs were identical. Essentially, Achilles bought technology and know-how to produce shoes adapted for the Japanese market, and the Danish company provided training and support.

For their part, Achilles had the knowledge of how to market shoes in Japan. During the early 1980s, leather shoes were quite rare, and textiles and artificial materials were the basis for the product. In this environment, ECCO quickly became the largest leather shoe brand in Japan. Currently, the use of traditional materials is changing even more rapidly because the Japanese are importing larger quantities of finished, often leather shoes. It has become easier to enter the market, and there is also greater demand, as Japanese consumers are actively seeking foreign brands. They are moving away from more traditional products and there is an increasing tendency to buy name-brand imported shoes.

At ECCO headquarters, thirty designers led by the head designer and now president of ECCO, Dieter Kasprzak, create brand designs and prototypes for use worldwide. They create six new collections every year. Achilles buys all its designs from ECCO Denmark. Again, they adapt the forms and shapes to the Japanese market.

In 2003, Toosbuy and the top managers from both companies signed a new ten year agreement. The contract's extended duration and its terms reflect an exceptional level of partnership between the two companies. Before 2013, ECCO expects annual sales in Japan to double to between 2.5 - 2.8 million pairs, with half of these being imported.

Negotiating Goals – 50 ECCO Stores

High goals have been set with the renewal of the contract, and ECCO Denmark wants Achilles to increase direct sales by establishing a greater retail presence and opening more ECCO stores in Japan. Achilles has agreed to this in principle, but must tackle the problem of the very high cost of direct retail outlets. For example, the ECCO store in Hong Kong was established by Achilles for an investment of JPY 700-800 million, and later handed over to ECCO when ECCO decided to take direct control of operations in Asia outside Japan.

In Japan, setting up a retail store is also an investment of several hundred million yen. Since not all stores are a guaranteed success, the risks can be substantial, says President Yamanaka:

> *At the time of the contract renewal, the creation of fifty ECCO stores by 2007 was planned. The original plan has been amended. The plan is now thirty-five stores by 2007, which is still high, I believe. I am not sure how many years it will take, but there will be fifty stores in the end. Recently the strength of specialized stores has weakened, so we have to increase the number of shop-in-shops too. In the beginning, we had a plan of 130 shop-in-shops. Now, realistically, we are aiming at around a hundred stores by 2007. I personally think expectations are high.*

As indicated, ECCO is encouraging shop-in-shops, namely designated areas for ECCO products in other larger, general retail outlets such as department stores. Presently there are ten ECCO Stores and forty shop-in-shops in prominent shopping areas of Tokyo. Besides these franchise and specialty stores with shop-in-shops, ECCO is also represented in general shoe stores across Japan.

ECCO's global efforts to expand business affect operations in Japan, and headquarters is pushing Japan to perform. However, according to the managing director of Asia, Michael Hauge Sørensen, despite ECCO's aggressive strategic and operational goals, it takes time to put these plans into action in different parts of the world, and there are occasionally limits to what can be achieved. This then leaves some negotiating room for Achilles with respect to operations in Japan.

Display 7.3 The signing of a new ten-year license agreement: from left Karsten Borch, vice president of ECCO board of directors; Achilles president, Shizuya Yamanaka; ECCO owner, Karl-Heinz Toosbuy; Achilles general manager, Mr. Tonooka.

The Achilles Corporation – ECCO Sales Japan

Achilles' business[6] is controlled from their headquarters in Tokyo. During the initial phase of their cooperation, ECCO made it clear that their partnership should be a joint effort in the production and sale of real *leather* shoes. Achilles' production and marketing of textile shoes and leather shoes therefore had to be separated. Achilles subsequently created a separate division for sales and marketing of ECCO shoes called ECCO Sales. They also produced ECCO shoes in a separate factory, the know-how for which, as discussed above, was acquired from ECCO headquarters in Denmark.

These organizational changes were of great importance for the success of the partnership. By establishing an ECCO Sales unit, Achilles sent a clear signal that the ECCO part of their business was to be handled completely independently of their other activities.

For Achilles, it was very important that ECCO had approached the partnership as one of equals, and had also acknowledged elements of Achilles organizational history and culture.

Differences in organizational forms, cultural values and business practices, not to mention the language, have affected the cooperation between these two companies. However, each side has taken initiatives and made organizational changes in order to enhance cooperation across organizational and national borders. The next section provides some concrete examples.

Importance of Hierarchy for the Japanese

The ECCO Sales Japan department has twenty-six employees. On several occasions over the years, ECCO headquarters has asked for a more 'effective' organization, including the assignment of specific responsibilities to certain people in certain positions.

In the vertical system of a traditional Japanese organization, it is important to follow the hierarchical order when making decisions. Decisions require consent from several people and no one takes individual responsibility. This has been an ongoing issue of discussion between the two companies. President Shizuya Yamanaka explains:

> *ECCO asked us in a meeting to rearrange our organization to match that of ECCO's headquarters, and to decide who would be in charge of ECCO activities. There are many Achilles people, including myself, involved in ECCO operations. So we agreed that the managing director, K. Tonooka and the general manager, Teruaki Nagashima, plus the team under their supervision, would deal with ECCO. ECCO finds it easier to deal with a limited number of people and we agreed to that. Even if we [people in upper management, including himself] attend certain meetings or are involved in special management issues, we are not always able to follow up afterwards. So, in this way, it makes sense to have a fixed department and people who are in charge. So we agreed with ECCO to make this distinction and indicate who is really in charge.*

When asked whether individual responsibility is becoming more common in Japanese management, President Shizuya Yamanaka answered:

We are moving toward this management style in Japan too, but old traditions linger. When top people from ECCO visit us for instance, we [the executive management] *always appear. Our attendance at such meetings is symbolic, and it does not mean that we are involved with ECCO operations in Japan.*

The organizational chart (see display 7.5 below) of the ECCO Japanese sales organization, at first glance, looks like a Danish organization at the formal level. The organizational chart is explained by Chiyaki Yoshii, who has worked for Achilles for seven years as a legal advisor and translator: the managing director is at the top of the hierarchy, and under him is the general manager. The managers of marketing, product, stores/retail and sales are next in the hierarchy, with sales broken down by Japanese region. The sales subsidiaries again have area managers who engage with and report to the general manager who is ultimately responsible for all of them. The people in charge of the sales subsidiaries take care of the stores and the wholesalers in their designated area. The staff in charge of women's and men's shoes, as well as the staff in charge of collection development for women and men, travel with the general manager Teruaki Nagashima to the international ECCO conferences. Teruaki Nagashima is the person who has the closest cooperation with ECCO in Jutland and in Hong Kong.

In the traditional Japanese vertical organizational system, ideas and projects have to go through many people to get approved before they are actually implemented:

It is very typical in conservative Japanese companies to have to get permission from many different layers of the hierarchy. Many people are involved, so it takes time until the product is actually launched and implemented, says Chiyaki Yoshii.

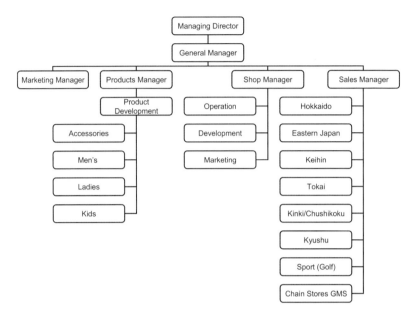

Display 7.4 Achilles' organizational chart

This process seems time consuming to foreign companies. While many international companies treasure effectiveness and want to save time through direct negotiation and decision-making, Japanese companies want to make sure that a project will work perfectly, even if it takes extra time to double check and build consensus. The reduction of risk through detailed planning is a virtue for Japanese employees, she says.

The negative side of the vertical organization, in Chiaki Yoshii's view, is that it ruins the ability to work freely and to 'see new horizons'. In the Japanese vertical structure, the people who are on the front lines of actual daily operations are not able to exert themselves fully. They cannot freely generate new ideas and promote them. Flexibility, creativity and a sense of individual responsibility are not enhanced in the vertical organization. According to Chiaki Yoshii, change is under way at ECCO Sales in Japan, as well as at Japanese companies in general:

Responsibility at the individual level is increasing, and the demand for it is increasing. I think we will see a change in the future leading to increased challenges for the individual.

According to Michael Hauge Sørensen, this idea of giving responsibility to individual managers cannot be implemented quickly enough. In his opinion, the people in charge of ECCO Sales in Japan could take business much further, much more quickly, if they were given personal responsibility and the freedom to act independently.

It has taken time to get Achilles to implement Toosbuy's ideas, and ECCO has demanded that the organization of ECCO Sales in Japan be restructured even further to resemble the organization in Denmark. ECCO still wants each ECCO sales section or functional manager in Japan to have more responsibility in their own field with more direct control of marketing, product development and sales. These more direct, simplified communication lines, ECCO believes, would a) encourage direct negotiations between managers at headquarters and managers at ECCO Sales in Japan, and b) keep managers accountable for their goals. ECCO Sales is now a separate unit from the rest of Achilles, and according to President Yamanaka, the section members are evolving towards a more effective and self-sufficient team.

In conclusion, the formal structure and organizational chart of the ECCO sales team in Japan do not differ significantly from those of ECCO headquarters. However, the strict hierarchical structure that the Japanese read into them, and the fact that individual positions in Japan do not have corresponding responsibilities assigned to them, mean that functionally the two organizations operate and behave quite differently.

Differences in Meeting Styles and Relationship Building

As we have seen in the previous chapters, the Japanese place more importance on the formality and symbolic importance of meetings than do their Danish partners. As with the case of organizational decision making, ECCO managers simply want to be 'efficient' and 'get on with business'. They evaluate the results of meetings based on the number of important business decisions made. The Japanese, in contrast, value the status of the people present and see meetings as a formal ritual to reinforce business relationships. Being present is what counts for the Japanese.

Chiaki Yoshii explains that whenever someone comes from ECCO headquarters, President Shizuya Yamanaka and a number of staff will participate in a meeting to formally greet them, just as they will gather for a ceremonial greeting when they depart. This is customary in Japan and serves to show respect for ECCO as an important partner. The president's formal greetings, *aisatsu*, last twenty minutes and serve to generate a general understanding of the present business situation and to reinforce social relationships. Afterwards, the president leaves the rest of the meeting to the operational managers.

Normally, the meetings in Japan start with the presence of President Yamanaka, Teruaki Nagashima and a few others. Even when the managing director from Hong Kong visits, which is on a monthly basis, he is greeted by the president. While many other Japanese employees may attend the meetings, most of the time they just listen, although they may comment on the rare occasions when asked to do so. This differs greatly from the Danish meeting style where managers contribute actively, often even interrupting their colleagues. Participation is much less formal in Denmark, where the argument being expressed is considered much more important than the hierarchical position of the person expressing it.

According to most ECCO staff who deal with Japan, being silent at meetings and the more somber atmosphere are difficult to get used to. When the Japanese have completed their ritual greetings, they have essentially fulfilled their role. If they are not called upon to talk, it would be rude to do so voluntarily. Danes, on the other hand, find silence threatening and uncomfortable at first, and it takes time for them to get used to it.

As these examples highlight, the Japanese value and place a great deal of importance on relationship building. It is therefore critical for top executives from ECCO to make formal visits to Japan when they take a new position. Although these meetings may not be business related, and therefore not seen as efficient or important from a Western perspective, they are social encounters that serve to foster mutual trust and understanding – two key elements of Japanese business culture.

People in New Positions

The procedures (or non procedures) connected with the change of staff in key positions marks another difference between Japan and Denmark, according to President Yamanaka:

> *ECCO is continuously filling positions with better qualified employees. When a new person fills a position, s/he may even undermine their predecessor's work in order to show that s/he is better qualified. These changes may even become company policy, but the new approaches can be difficult for us to understand unless they are well communicated.*

In Denmark, people change positions and companies regularly, whereas in Japan people are much less mobile both within and between companies including the Japanese tradition of lifetime employment within a single firm. Even if there are changes in staff over time, there are also carefully kept records which allow someone new to a position to carry on the work of their predecessor, says President Yamanaka.

Language – The Biggest Communication Bottleneck
Another ongoing challenge in the communication between the two companies is language. At joint meetings, everything is translated into Danish and Japanese respectively; thus all discussions go through a translator.

This translation process is time consuming, particularly if the points being made are not clear. However, this has always been the procedure, so both parties know what to expect, says Teruaki Nagashima.

According to Managing Director Michael Hauge Sørensen, the fact that he cannot communicate with his Japanese business colleagues without an interpreter is a great hindrance to establishing close personal relationships. The necessity of a translator makes even the smallest issues a formality, and this is a great problem, he says.

According to Teruaki Nagashima, most Danish people speak English, but in Japan only a limited number of people master foreign languages. When ECCO visits Japan, Achilles uses a translator who has been briefed on the background for the meeting. Similarly, ECCO has used the same two translators for meetings over the last twenty-three years. It is an advantage to work with the same translators as they understand the purpose of meetings and the background for negotiations, and this knowledge helps ensure that meetings run as smoothly as possible. Nevertheless, according to Teruaki Nagashima, language is still the biggest hindrance to proper communication. He has been dealing with ECCO for twenty-three years and is familiar with the negotiation processes that have taken place during this time:

Even the Japanese misunderstand each other as there are many ambiguous words in Japanese. First, the Japanese translator must understand what I say and then translate into English or Danish. During this process, there are many occasions where I feel that what I meant to say is not communicated to the other side. So I feel a strong need to develop bilingual staff who can communicate

> *what they mean directly in order to improve communication. But this is not something we can do in the near future. Even if we exchange a staff person with someone who can speak English, the new person will have no knowledge about ECCO. Conversely, among the current staff people who deal with ECCO, few speak English. Balancing areas of staff competence is a time consuming process. Unfortunately, fewer than one out of ten university graduates in Japan can speak English – and I myself was one of those other nine.*

English education has been a political issue for decades in Japan. Although speaking and comprehension are emphasized in more recent English language education, Japan is still far behind other developed countries in English communication skills. Only the Japanese and Taiwanese teams bring translators to ECCO's international conferences and meetings as other subsidiaries or agents send English speaking employees.

Consequently, there is a communication gap between the two companies, and even though this gap has decreased over the years, there is still a need for improvement among the ECCO Sales employees. Translation not only takes time and effort, it is also costly. Chiaki Yoshii currently translates all incoming correspondence for ECCO Sales into Japanese. Similarly, she translates outgoing messages into English. While catalogs and marketing materials are translated by third parties, Chiaki Yoshii recently tackled such large projects as the translation of the tool box and manuals for the franchise system.

As one step to bridge this communication gap, ECCO recently initiated a program to educate younger employees from both cultures to be 'cultural mediators', and this program is described in the next section.

Human Resource Development – An Intercultural Strategy

Previously, from the perspective of ECCO headquarters, cultural issues were solved by recruiting locally for foreign markets. However, in a globalizing environment, ECCO managers now must make an effort to adjust to and understand various local cultures. According to Kristen Moesgaard, vice president of HR, 'Jutland ways' do not always work globally, and more attention needs to be paid to the cultural education and preparation of ECCO employees who work and live abroad. The same applies to the employees who deal with foreign subsidiaries or markets.

While the ECCO code of conduct outlines ECCO's expectations for employee behavior around the world, a simple code of conduct is not enough. Managers also need tools to help them successfully adapt to local cultures, and Kirsten Moesgaard is working towards developing these cultural tools using Japan as an ongoing example.

With respect to the cultural ambassador initiative, Jens Aarup Mikkelsen was identified as a promising candidate for the ECCO global training program that was initiated by Toosbuy. As part of a three-year program, Jens Aarup Mikkelsen first completed a year of in-house training at ECCO, subsequently spent a year at the tanning factory in Indonesia, and is now working at Achilles in Japan. Before being assigned to Achilles, he also completed one year of intensive language studies at the Executive Trainee Program[7] (ETP) in Tokyo. The main reasons for creating a position for Jens Aarup Mikkelsen and educating him as a project manager were to establish closer links between ECCO headquarters and Achilles on the one hand, and to get first-hand knowledge about the Japanese market from a Danish perspective on the other.

From Achilles, a young man who is fluent in English, Shingo Imai, spent half a year in Denmark in order to learn the 'ECCO way' of doing things. He then returned to Achilles with this knowledge and understanding and the goal of sharing it with his coworkers.

It is important that ECCO's values are implemented globally in order to tie managers and employees together through shared values, says Kirsten Moesgaard. The implementation of ECCO values is remarkably successful in the United States, where the Danish director has spent a substantial amount of time and effort working to integrate, with certain adaptations, ECCO culture with that of American organizational and national culture. In particular, the pioneering and entrepreneurial spirit of ECCO fits well with the American way of thinking. While the process in the United States has been much admired by other managers of the ECCO group, the approach and resulting culture are not directly applicable to Asia, says Kirsten Moesgaard. In Hong Kong, the managing director, Michael Hauge Sørensen, takes a different approach with respect to Asian values. While this approach is no less successful, knowledge about Asia is less widespread within the ECCO group (as opposed to that of the United States, for instance), so his success in Japan and Hong Kong are not necessarily the first examples that come to mind when group executives are asked about cultural integration.

These initiatives exemplify how ECCO is working to integrate culture and communication on a worldwide basis, and at the same time also show how the implementation of company values depends on the local context.

Having discussed issues related to cultural difference and language, the following sections will describe how ECCO has been challenged by other local factors in Japan.

The ECCO Brand Meets Government Restrictions

The Japanese leather shoe market is largely protected by the Japanese government. Achilles president, Shizuya Yamanaka, talked about this at length during the interview because he found that he is not able to properly convey the complexity of the problem to his ECCO business partners. This action by the government to protect the market is connected to issues from Japanese history which are still taboo within Japanese society today.

> *This policy is a bit nationalistic and I am hesitant to mention this, but the Japanese government implements high tariffs and other restrictive measures in order to protect the domestic shoe manufacturers. This is something that ECCO Denmark has problems understanding. When ECCO wants to import into Japan shoes that have been cheaply manufactured in Thailand, it is not just a question of high tariffs, but also of import limitations.*

Currently, Achilles pays an additional JPY 800-1,000 (DKK 50) for every pair of ECCO shoes imported from Thailand. According to President Yamanaka, ECCO puts pressure on Achilles to sell more and apparently views the quota system as an opaque set of import restrictions that Achilles may be tempted to use as an excuse for not doing more. Sometimes Achilles is able to pay the above mentioned price to obtain an extra allotment from other importers so they can enlarge their import quota. The issue is a continuous point of discussion between ECCO and Achilles.

The reality from Achilles' point of view is that the company is stuck in a protectionist system imposed by the Japanese government. Japan is in the process of signing, and is expected to sign, FTAs (free trade agreement) with several countries, such as Cambodia, Vietnam and Thailand. The existing restrictions on imports from these countries would then be removed. However, the products from these countries are of rather low quality and target the low end of the market. If these products are allowed to flood the Japanese market, Achilles is concerned that it will upset the existing market structure.

Meanwhile, the leather industry in Japan is protected by the government because it is dominated by a group of people, *Buraku*[8], who have been severely discriminated against throughout much of Japanese history. The issue is still taboo in Japan, particularly among the older generation, and it was not mentioned directly by President Shizuya Yamanaka, who rather referred to it as 'that problem'.

The Japanese government is preparing to remove the restrictive measures completely by 2007. While Achilles is expecting this to eventually happen, it is doubtful that it will happen according to this schedule, says President Yamanaka, because the specific political climate in Japan makes it difficult for the Japanese government to introduce changes.

If the changes are introduced, we will be happy to import shoes made abroad instead of manufacturing them under expensive conditions in Japan. As you know, ECCO Denmark has constructed a manufacturing factory in China. If ECCO can produce quality shoes in China that meet the needs of the Japanese market, we are happy to receive shoes from China and market them in Japan. We don't have any intention of insisting on manufacturing in Japan forever. There are possibilities for us to work in new ways. But, first and foremost, the problem of tariff and emergency measures has to be solved before we can do anything. It is a real problem for us in Japan, says President Yamanaka.

For ECCO, the partnership with Achilles was a means to get around the many restrictions on the importation of leather goods into Japan, restrictions which have kept many foreign companies at arms length. The only possibility to avoid the restrictions was to produce inside Japan, and more than ninety percent of the ECCO leather shoes sold in Japan to date have been produced in Japan for just this reason.

The Japanese Distribution System – Another Bottleneck

Another complexity of the Japanese market is the distribution system, where consumer goods pass through a number of intermediaries. ECCO wants their shoes to be sold in greater quantity directly though retailers, such as large department stores. However, even if Achilles agreed to this strategy, they would not be able implement it. The presence and power of wholesalers is overwhelming in the Japanese market, and many department stores are dependent on them.

Even if we want to skip wholesalers and sell directly to department stores, we cannot due to the tradition in the industry. This is one aspect of the Japanese market which is incomprehensible to foreigners, according to President Yamanaka.

Three functions make intermediaries important, according to President Yamanaka. First, department stores in Japan do not buy ten pairs of the same shoes at a time like they do in Europe and the United States, so they depend on the wholesalers to keep inventory for them. Due to the lack of space in Japan, retailers, including specialized stores and department stores, try to avoid maintaining their own inventory. The wholesalers provide a supply of goods and ensure deliveries when needed. This enables department stores to continuously have their displays filled with the latest products. A second function of the wholesaler is 'screening'. Retailers are dependent on the wholesalers for purchasing the proper products. Wholesalers will also take back goods that are not sold, which means that the retailers do not have to sell them at reduced prices. This in turn helps the retailers maintain their exclusive image. A third function of the wholesalers is a financing one where they sell products to retailers in exchange of bills of credit with generous repayment terms.

For these reasons, wholesalers have been indispensable for the retailing industry in Japan. This level of complexity, according to President Shizuya Yamanaka, is simply incomprehensible to foreigners whose market systems do not have the same local constraints or heritage.

Relationships Rather Than Business
Due to the recession and deflation in Japan starting in the late 1990s, the number of wholesalers has been decreasing. However, wholesalers still play an important role for department stores, not least because of the value the Japanese place on business relationships.

Over the years, reciprocal favors in Japan strengthen a relationship and create loyalty. According to President Shizuya Yamanaka, Japanese business obligations (*giri*) are strongly connected to personal relationships (*ninjo*). Of course in severe crises, some wholesalers have no choice but to end the relationship.

From a Danish perspective, the wholesaler system is built on favoritism that makes it difficult to bypass old connections. Networking and personal relationships supersede arguments in favor of efficiency, says Michael Hauge Sørensen.

However, one benefit of Japanese relationship building that ECCO has enjoyed is the dedication and loyalty of their partners, with Achilles leading the way. In fact, one of the things that Toosbuy appreciated about Japan was their involvement in and the passion for the ECCO brand. Under Achilles ownership, the growth in sales has been one of the key elements in telling the ECCO brand story in Japan and behind all of this is a lot of commitment. For instance, to upgrade ECCO's image, Achilles has managed to decrease the number of retailers from 2600 to 800.

Cultural hurdles and market specific problems remain, but as detailed in the next section, the presence of an ECCO office in Hong Kong has stabilized and improved communication between the two companies and this bodes well for the future.

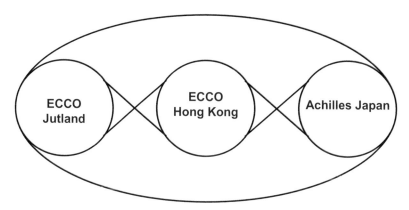

Display 7.5 ECCO, communication diagram: Bredebro in Jutland, Hong Kong, and Tokyo

Hong Kong Brings Proximity and Consistency

In 2002, a subsidiary was opened in Hong Kong to oversee ECCO's activities in the Asia Pacific region, including Japan, and the office now employs twenty-five people. The managing director of the Asia Pacific office, Michael Hauge Sørensen, is responsible for the Japanese market and he visits Tokyo on a monthly basis. Additionally, the Hong Kong office is also in charge of the business plans and strategies for other countries in the Asia Pacific region, as well as for the region as a whole.

Once a year, ECCO headquarters holds a conference for all the market directors and partners which consists of several days of workshops and new design shows. At these annual events, Michael Hauge Sørensen and the Achilles representatives work together to decide on new shoe collections and strategies, and the Achilles team chooses the products they wish to distribute.

The representatives of the ECCO Sales division in Japan are continuously in contact with the development department in Denmark in order to get the latest specifications for new products. They also get samples of prototypes and the specifications for the production of these. The acquisition of forms and tools for the production are also coordinated directly through the development department in Denmark.

Many of ECCO's suppliers are situated in Europe, so headquarters coordinates the deliveries to Japan to make sure they are correct. Finally, the Japanese team is in Denmark three to five times a year. Michael Hauge Sørensen always joins these meetings.

The fact that ECCO has established a strong position in Japan is the first step towards strengthening their position in Asia, and the establishment of the office in Hong Kong is building on this for the long-term.

Japan from a Hong Kong Perspective

The mission of the Hong Kong office is to develop a platform and a model for ECCO in Asia which can then be used as a benchmark for the development of markets throughout the region.[9]

Concerning Japan, Michael Hauge Sørensen strategic goal is to get more feeling for and control of the market. ECCO originally licensed Achilles its manufacturing, sales and distribution in Japan, but with a new strategy of a single global brand ECCO would like to have more influence in the Japanese market.

Michael Hauge Sørensen has been working with the Japanese market for the last ten years. He meets with the Achilles team once a month and all strategic business decisions concerning Japan pass through him at the Hong Kong office. When asked about the Japanese work culture, he said that he finds the Japanese extremely well prepared. They are very detail oriented, which is good to get things right, but is also a weakness in discussions about strategy when broader business decisions have to be made. Since Michael Hauge Sørensen spends much of his time traveling, he wants to use his time efficiently and get a lot of business done when he is in Japan.

He finds the Japanese to be excellent hosts, but the formal meetings and the relationship-building activities, in his view, are generally perceived as being much less important to Westerners than their Japanese counterparts. He goes out for dinners at night and occasionally for drinks afterwards, but he has politely refused the second and third rounds of after work get-togethers throughout his years of doing business in Japan. Although it is important to be social after work in a Japanese business setting, he has adopted his own professional strategies in Asia, where he deals with many different cultures even within the same country. Above all, he has kept his Danish values: business is business and free time is free time. When he explains this to his Japanese colleagues, or says to them that they have been working so hard that they should go home and spend time with their families, they do not even understand what he means. The Danish separation between work and free time does not make sense in a traditional Japanese business setting.

Silence is Golden

Michael Hauge Sørensen's communication style is appreciated by his Japanese colleagues. Although he is young to be a managing director from a Japanese viewpoint, his many years of working with Japan create trust. As expressed by his Japanese colleagues, including Chiaki Yoshii:

> *Michael is first of all a very good listener and that is why he is important for us.*

Being patient and good at listening were mentioned by all ECCO interviewees as important skills when dealing with the Japanese.

According to Chiaki Yoshii, there is an expression in Japanese: the Japanese listen nine times and talk once, whereas Westerners talk nine times and listen once. Michael is seen as a good listener and a helpful mediator for both sides. The general manager Teruaki Nagashima agrees:

> *One thing I see as a change on the ECCO Denmark side is that they have also begun to show an appreciation for the complexity of the Japanese market. Michael Hauge Sørensen, in Hong Kong, demonstrates a real understanding, and we feel that he is backing*

us. At the beginning of his assignment, it may have been difficult for him to understand the conditions and overall functioning of the market in Japan. However, since he was given responsibility for Asia, we feel that mutual understanding between ECCO Denmark and Achilles has improved, so we are grateful for him.

Teruaki Nagashima continues:

In the past, ECCO did not visit often. On top of that, the people who did come were representatives from ECCO headquarters and therefore did not have an understanding of the Japanese market, or they did not understand Achilles' concepts and ideas fully. Communication, it seems, is finally coming to a half way point now. Both sides are making an effort to cooperate as a team. It is not just one way interaction.

An ongoing point of contention is still the fact that Japan, from an outsider's point of view, is a highly attractive market given its high income consumers who are willing to spend money. However, the truth is, according to President Shizuya Yamanaka, that although the market is enormous, there are constantly new entrants who are aiming at the same consumers, and as a result, the playing field becomes highly competitive and overcrowded. The problem then becomes one of how to fight in such an environment.

Michael Hauge Sørensen understands the competitive conditions, says President Yamanaka. In this sense, the staff at Achilles feels that it has become easier to work with ECCO since he has taken the lead in Hong Kong.

Display 7.6 'Shoes designed to move you' promotion in Japan, 2005

Global Communication Strategies

One of the main philosophies from the Danish headquarters is that as many decisions as possible should be made by the local subsidiaries and factories around the world. Most companies in the ECCO group work with independent strategies, and Toosbuy encouraged this. The main connection to headquarters is through budgets and business plans that are decided upon once a year. The ECCO group works in five regions, and in the case of Japan, the business plan is supervised by the managing director at the Hong Kong office.

However, headquarter-subsidiary and alliance partner communication is something that still needs to be worked on from both sides. Autonomous decision-making means that the organization as a whole is not homogeneous in its business practices. It does not need to be entirely uniform, according to Vice President Axel Carlsen, but communication and 'cultural togetherness' are still important for the coherence of the ECCO group. This is even truer now that the corporate strategy of 'one global brand' is seen to be an important part of ECCO's future.

From Global to Local – Cultural Differences

When asked about how the ECCO global strategy is perceived from a Japanese perspective, President Shizuya Yamanaka says:

> *Well, if ECCO says 'global strategy', then there is not much room for negotiation, is there? Of course we are always suggesting what would be more appropriate for the Japanese market. The desire to create a global image is probably the result of globalization, but many images are perceived differently in Japan because the language is different, and the way we think is different.*

As an example, an ECCO shoe and boot in Europe called 'The Shark' has sold in record numbers. The advertisement posters sent from headquarters said 'Shark Attack'. This was translated into Japanese as *'Same no toorai'* which did not make sense to the Japanese. The original 'Shark Attack' in English did not make sense, either, according to Teruaki Nagashima. Perhaps not surprisingly, 'The Shark' did not sell in Japan:

> *It is not only the language, the culture is different too. That is the way it should be. But I think ECCO itself is probably in search of direction. After instructing us to follow the global policy, they have recently started to say that in some cases each regional area can decide.*

If ECCO had started in markets all over the world at the same time, he said, then the single global strategy might work. However, as each market has a different history and positioning, it can be problematic when ECCO tries to group them into one and apply a single strategy to all. These days, however, ECCO pays more attention to the cultural and historical differences between regions. Even though they want to promote a set of core of ideas globally, regional differences need to be taken into account. In this sense, Teruaki Nagashima believes that there will be changes. Applying a single policy across markets may work in the future, but at this stage, given the above-mentioned differences, there will be markets, including Japan, where the global strategy will not fit well. According to Teruaki Nagashima, he is not able to advise on the global strategy, he merely knows what suits the Japanese market.

According to Michael Hauge Sørensen, annual meetings in the region are gradually allowing regional representatives to find common ground among their perceptions of ECCO's global strategy. Importantly, he says, the Japanese representatives are starting to realize that they have things in common with the other countries in the region. They are discovering that "They are not that different", he says. With the regions coming together, the process of influence is becoming multidirectional, he says. Decentralization makes the regions become stronger and more aware of their cultural needs. This in time will have implications on global strategy. In the future, he expects headquarters to become more in tune with the different regions. The regions then will have more input on the global strategy, including product development and marketing plans. In this scenario, the influences on strategy will be global, with contributions not only from Europe, as is the case presently, but also from Russia, Eastern Europe, Asia and the United States.

'ECCOes of the World' – Global Images in Japan

The 2005 global brand strategy 'Shoes designed to move you!' was also implemented by ECCO Sales, or rather it was partly implemented, according to Michael Hauge Sørensen.

Several years of disagreement on brand strategies have continued into the new millennium. Achilles has had difficulties understanding ECCO's ideas for both language and cultural reasons. Achilles wants to promote ECCO as being 'Danish' and to promote 'foot comfort'. If ECCO could come up with a slogan that conjures up the 'slow and comfortable life' it would be great, according to Teruyaki Nagashima. The slow and comfortable life is an attractive image that the Japanese have of Scandinavia, all the more so because they feel that their lives reflect just the opposite. In 2002, the slogan 'ECCO is so comfortable that you feel like jumping' was a hit in Japan. In 2003, a Zen Buddhist atmosphere was promoted. It was an idea inspired by Japan, but with no involvement from Achilles, and it was understood only vaguely by the Japanese, says Teruyaki Nagashima. The 2004 Movement Campaign was good because it emphasized movement and comfort. So far, ECCO has shown no interest in promoting Danishness despite the attractiveness of this idea for ECCO Sales in Japan.

In the end, ECCO Sales in Japan accepted the 2005 global campaign, but they wanted to use costly local actors for their promotion. Michael Hauge Sørensen has agreed to this strategy as long as they use the

ECCO logo and promote an image that is inline with ECCO's global brand.

The implementation of ECCO's global brand strategy in Japan is currently fifty-fifty, according to Michael Hauge Sørensen. He is content with this degree of implementation for the moment, as long as everyone is moving towards a hundred percent global brand image by 2013.

Two Factions of Image Creators – A Generation Gap

A 2004 image survey in Japan showed that ECCO's image is 'obasankusai', which means mid-aged lady-like (not trendy). Until recently, the largest percentage of loyal costumers was at least fifty years old. However, a new generation at ECCO headquarters is working to replace the 'good for your feet' image with one that has the potential to become trendy worldwide. In Japan, it will take a huge effort to change this image because the focus on comfort and foot anatomy was the reason why Achilles chose to work with ECCO in the first place. 'Concern for your feet' is the soul of the brand and the right image, according to the ECCO Sales viewpoint. The 'soft', 'light', 'flexible' and 'anatomical' concepts linger, not at least with the wholesalers, who have been the most difficult to convince that a new image is necessary.

According to Teruaki Nagashima, there are also competing image factions at ECCO headquarters. The new ECCO gencration is trying to change its target market towards younger, cool and trendy customers. Previously, ECCO catered to an older generation of loyal customers. The discrepancy between these two views from ECCO headquarters has been a problem in Japan. ECCO hires many young people who do not know the product history – which of course has its advantages. History in this sense is both a strong point in brand building and a hindrance for change, says Teruaki Nagashima.

At the same time, there is also a group of employees who understand what he sees as the true strength of the ECCO brand. These employees believe that attracting a broader range of customers that includes the younger generations can be accomplished without abandoning ECCO's traditional, loyal core of older consumers.

'Japan is Japan' – Lessons Learned

From a Japanese point of view, ECCO has changed their image and their marketing dramatically. Their slogans have been changed, and in the new millennium there has not been a consistent theme to link the various campaigns. However, in 2005, with the 'Shoes designed to move you' campaign there was a core message in the image promotion that even ECCO Sales in Japan agreed with.

Over a long period of time a lot of different people have been involved with Achilles, and this has created a lot of confusion in Japan, according to Jens Aarup Mikkelsen, who is now the 'owner's representative' working inside Achilles at ECCO Sales. Consequently, it has been difficult for ECCO Sales in Japan to know who they are dealing with. The creation of the new marketing position that Jens Aarup Mikkelsen fills aims to ensure that there is both consistent communication of ECCO's messages to the market and its partners, and that market knowledge flows back to ECCO headquarters.

The biggest lesson learned so far by ECCO is that it is challenging to change the direction of a Japanese company. On some occasions, ECCO Sales has been at fault because of the lack of consistency in communication from headquarters. Consistency in messages and strategies from headquarters will naturally benefit both parties, but according to Jens Aarup Mikkelsen, "everyone at ECCO knows that". Unfortunately, there has been a tendency for people entering a new position to change the strategies promoted by their predecessor. For a while, it was difficult for Japan to keep track because the managers involved had different solutions and there was not a single corporate line or message.

It has also been difficult for ECCO Sales Japan to change their strategies within the Japanese market. Many of their customers are wholesalers that have been in the business for a long time, and they still promote the old image of ECCO. The machinery that needs to be changed is heavy, according to Jens Aarup Mikkelsen.

So, patience is important. The Japanese will use their silent moments to think, but they need clear messages about what ECCO wants, as well as time to 'translate' this into action, he says.

From a Global Perspective – Japan Is Not That Different
ECCO headquarters is pushing franchising and global branding strategies. ECCO Sales in Japan – from their end – will always say that they are different, and that strategies need to be adapted to the Japanese market and way of doing business.

Japan is different, no doubt about it, says Jens Aarup Mikkelsen, but it is also dangerous to engage in this kind of argumentation because there is a tendency to make Japan seem a lot more different than it actually is. There are so many examples of global brands in Japan, where companies are following the same strategy in Japan that they follow in other countries. There might be a few market specific adjustments required, but it is not *that* different.

Bibliography

Berlingske Tidendes Nyhedsmagasin (2004) "ECCO vil fordoble salget på ti år", year 3, no. 7, pp. 26-30 [ECCO Will Double Sales in 10 years]

Noer, H. (1991) *"ECCO-Kulturen"*, ECCO [The ECCO Culture]

Noer, H. (red.), Lauridsen, P.F & Toosbuy, K. (1988) *"Fremtidens store visioner: ECCO Jubilæumsbog 1988"*, Eccolet Sko [The Big Visions for the Future: ECCO Jubilee Book 1988]

Pyndt, J. & Pedersen, T. (2006) "ECCO A/S – Optimizing Global Value Chain Economics" in *"Managing Global Offshoring Strategies. A Case Approach"*, Copenhagen, Copenhagen Business School Press

Tid og Tendenser (2003) "Et globalt rungende ECCO", volume 8, no. 4, pp. 15-17 [A Global ECCO]

Toosbuy, K. & Noer, H. (2002) *"Visions, Strategy and Story, ECCO Sko A/S"*

Chapter Seven: Endnotes

[1] After the death of the founder Karl-Heinz Werner Toosbuy in 2004, his daughter Hanni Toosbuy Kasprzak has become the owner and chairperson of the supervisory board. His son-in-law - Dieter Kasprzak - is now the president of ECCO. Mikael Thinghuus is the COO and Jens Christian Meier is the executive vice president.

[2] ECCO's turnover in 2004 was DKK 3.2 billion, employees counted 9400 worldwide, they produced 12 million pairs of shoes and they were present in over 55 markets with 3000 locations worldwide.

[3] 'Brown' shoe is a trade classification for work/casual shoes. 'White' shoes are sport brands such as NIKE.

[4] In 1980, the DESMA machine, a high-tech production method that allowed soles to be directly injected, was introduced in Bredebro. By 1985, ECCO was leaving its footprints around the world thanks to the printing of the ECCO logo in the soles, a technical feature for which it was awarded the IG prize. In 1990, ECCO opened up a fully owned sales subsidiary in the United States. The 1992 inauguration of the ECCO Design Centre in Tønder placed all product development under one roof, and one year later Futura was established allowing development from design to prototype in just hours.

[5] Toosbuy had close and strong connections with Mr. Yagi (who retired in 2004) and the chairman at the time, Mr. Tonooka (the father of the present general manager K. Tonooka).

[6] Achilles has different branch offices in the Southern part of Japan, Osaka and a big office in the Northern part of Japan, in Hokkaido. The different divisions produce and market several products including rubber boats, PVC film and shoes. Achilles' shoe factories are located in different areas of Japan, with a production base situated in Ashikaga, north of Tokyo. Achilles also makes their own brand of inexpensive rubber boots and indoor shoes for kindergarten children from inexpensive PVC textiles.

[7] The European Trainee Program (ETP) program offers a one year intensive language training course and six months of company practice. It is arranged and largely financed by the European Union. The language at Achilles is Japanese, and the plan is that Jens Aarup Mikkelsen will spend one month with each of Achilles' three biggest customers: the largest men's wholesaler, the largest women's wholesaler and the largest retail chain. The main focus of this experience will be to

get to know the Japanese market, ECCO's customers and Japanese consumers in order to build a knowledge base relevant to ECCO in Japan. The last three months will consist of a traineeship at Achilles in order to become acquainted with the organization. Jens Aarup Mikkelsen's primary responsibility during this time will be to be involved with formulation the annual business plan. More than 50 Danish companies have benefited from the participated in ETP including Aarhus Oil, Ramboll, Radiometer, Fritz Hansen, Danish Serum Institute, Løvens Chemicals. Maersk, Novo, Danisco, Louis Poulsen.

[8] Buraku people are a caste-like minority. When the social status system was established in the seventeenth century (early Edo era) with three classes (warrior, peasant, townsfolk), the Buraku people, were placed as outcasts at the bottom of the society. They were assigned work, such as slaughtering animals, which was perceived as 'polluting' under Buddhist and Shintoist beliefs. They also worked with the skins of these animals. Because of the severe discrimination of the Buraku in Japanese society even today, the government protects the industry which they largely dominate – namely, the production of leather goods.

[9] The priorities for ECCO are to: focus on the continued development of the key markets of Hong Kong, Japan, China, Australia, and New Zealand; change current partners and either establish their own operations or appoint new distributors in: Taiwan, Korea, Singapore, Malaysia, Indonesia, Brunei; and finally to launch ECCO in India.

Chapter Eight

CONCLUSION: FIVE CORPORATE CASES IN JAPAN

Complexity and Dynamics of Communication

This chapter presents conclusions based on the lessons learned by fifty managers from five Danish companies and their Japanese alliances. The conclusions are organized systematically following the multi-level communication model developed in Chapter Two. The *global* level relates to global strategies and brand images and their reception in Japan by alliances, intermediaries and consumers. The *national* level analyzes the cultural issues that have influenced the considerations and strategies concerning the entry mode and organizational structure of the operations of five companies within Japan. The *organizational* level demonstrates the importance of the organization of communication processes. It shows how Danish and Japanese national values, as well as corporate cultural values, affect communication. The *professional* level presents the communication of professional (functional) knowledge including product specific information. Finally, the *individual* level highlights how intercultural competence influences business communication and relationship building in the bi-cultural context of Denmark and Japan. In conclusion, I argue that cultural co-creation rather than transmission of information provides maximum benefit in intercultural communication. Studies of micro-processes through interviews, such as the present one, can help explain the complexity of intercultural environments and the various influences on global managers in their decision-making processes. They also provide insights into the implementation of headquarters driven strategies from a global to a local context. In short, multiple-level analysis provides insight into business encounters in their full complexity.

Global Strategy and Image Development in Japan

This level concerns the reception of brand images in Japan. The company headquarters in Denmark work to apply their brand-image messages worldwide. Yet, how are these images received in Japan? The challenge is to make a unique claim and to find the right frame for presenting products and concepts in relation to the Japanese market. It is a matter of zeroing in on the perceptions and mind-set of the target Japanese consumer. The closer brand images and concepts get to commonly held perceptions, the easier it is to communicate the message and to gain the 'mental market share' of both business alliance partners and consumers. In other words, the challenge is to motivate business alliance partners to agree on strategies and encourage consumers to purchase products.

In Denmark, Bo Bendixen is an icon of 'Danish-ness', given his use of Danish scenery and national symbols in his graphic design. In Japan, he has struck a cultural nerve for a different reason, where he has been fortunate to capitalize on the Japanese culture of 'cute' (although he does have limits on how far he is willing to go in this direction). In Japan, Bo Bendixen's Danish designs are used to create an image of the Netherlands. A few tulips and some windmills are all he has to add to make the Scandinavian images Dutch. Danish cows, dogs and cats are seemingly likeable universally. His Danish nationality does not surface for visitors to the Dutch theme park who care more about the exclusivity of his brand. In fact, his animal designs have become icons for the park.

	Bo Bendixen	Rosendahl	Scandinavian Tourist Board	Bang & Olufsen	ECCO
Global image strategy/ reception in Japan	Cute culture Danish 'authenticity' promotes Dutch theme park	H.C. Andersen fairy tales	Cute culture (the Viking Mascot and the Green Santa Claus)	Danish simplicity in lifestyle and design accommodates Zen Buddhism aesthetics	Global image concepts are localized
National issues in entry modes	Opportunity through discovery	From importer/ agent to headquarter control	Tourism industry Long-term investment (in Japan)	Transition from wholesaler to subsidiary, uphill battle	Leather shoe market quota - politics
Organization, communication and corporate culture	Direct confrontation	Japanese cultural knowledge in headquarters	Mixed Scandinavian – Japanese values within Tokyo office	Assimilation efforts promoted by headquarters to share 'soul' and corporate values	Reinforcing headquarters' (Danish) values in ECCO Sales Japan
Professional/ functional knowledge	Inspired by Japan – organizational learning	Co-creation of market opportunities Sales and co-marketing	Differentiation Regional promotion and branding	Standardization Regional coordination: Sales, Marketing, Retail, Merchandising	Standardization Regional coordination
Individual intercultural competence	Jutland meets Japan	Bi-lingual and bi-cultural knowledge	Bi-lingual and bi-cultural knowledge	Jutland integrates Japan Internationalization through hiring and training	Jutland meets Japan International career development

Display 8.1 The multi-level communication model and the five cases in Japan

The events surrounding the H.C. Andersen bicentennial became an opportunity for Rosendahl to produce a special fairy tale series of porcelain. The Andersen project drew on general Japanese cultural knowledge of H.C. Andersen. Although the general population does not know that he is Danish (many think he is German), most Japanese know of his fairy tales. This access to cultural knowledge embedded in the Japanese mind was a goldmine, and the event and image creation surrounding the H.C. Andersen bicentennial was a marketing coup. The H.C. Andersen events were easy to relate to for Rosendahl's Japanese partners and a year before the bicentennial they committed to the project without hesitation. The H.C. Andersen porcelain was a unique opportunity to upgrade the brand and to create business alliances through events and commitments connected to the H.C. Andersen bicentennial celebration. Rosendahl skillfully took advantage of this opportunity to eventually leverage many other product lines beyond the porcelain.

The Viking image has been revived – albeit only in Japan. Scandinavian Tourist Board in Tokyo invested in the professional development of an image for the Scandinavian countries. By using the Viking image, Scandinavian Tourist Board took advantage of favorable, if somewhat ambiguous and misplaced, Japanese cultural knowledge in order to create and promote an iconic connection with Scandinavia. That the chosen mascot resonates particularly well with the Japanese mentality and culture of 'cute' is certainly no coincidence. At the same time, given the Danes' national ambivalence towards the Viking symbol and all it represents, it is similarly no coincidence that it is not used anywhere else in the world to promote Danish tourism.

While Bang & Olufsen is an upscale lifestyle product in Denmark, it is promoted even more exclusively in Japan. Esteemed Japanese artists are engaged to arrange design exhibitions, and some give personal accounts to lifestyle magazines of the reasons why they use Bang & Olufsen in their own homes. The Danish Royal Family has similarly promoted the products by making pictures of various Royal interiors available in which one can clearly see Bang & Olufsen sound systems. The *White Book*, an exclusive marketing device designed to target and engage the social, economic, and political elite of Japan, has been a success in creating a shared brand community among the international luxury brands which are the book's founding partners. However, this idea is only pursued in Japan.

'Shoes designed to move you' is a brilliant tag line in the West. It connotes moving ahead – progressing emotionally and physically. It is based on Western conceptual thinking and play on words: however, this tag line does not translate well into Japanese. Because of perceived cultural as well as concrete language differences, ECCO's global standard concepts are continuously renegotiated in Japan. Several years of discussion on brand strategies have continued into the new millennium. The license partner wants to promote ECCO as being 'Danish' and synonymous with 'foot comfort'. Ideally, they would prefer a slogan that evokes the 'slow and comfortable life', an attractive image that the Japanese have of Scandinavia. However, ECCO does not want to promote Danish-ness. Currently, the implementation of ECCO's global brand strategy in Japan is a fifty-fifty compromise that is moving towards a one hundred percent streamlined global brand in 2013. The biggest challenge ahead for ECCO in Japan is to change their present image of 'foot comfort', geared towards the older generation, in a way that will appeal to a younger generation of Japanese while at the same time preserving their loyal customer base. As we have seen, it will take skillful communication and consistency of messages to change the perceptions held by their Japanese alliance partner and intermediary sales channels, let alone the Japanese consumer.

In sum, when Danish companies are successful in introducing cultural phenomena, such as the Green Santa Claus, the Viking Mascot, and H.C. Andersen, it is because they are able to capitalize on pre-existing cultural knowledge. When they associate products with Royalty, 'cuteness', simplicity or 'slow life', they reinforce cultural phenomena that are already well known and attractive to the Japanese. On the other hand, when companies use international (Western) concepts in their global branding efforts, they have to communicate even more effectively in order to bridge the 'gap' and have them accepted within the local Japanese context. One thing is certain in both cases: branding conditions in Japan are both more important and more advantageous than in other countries. Japanese enjoy brands – namely quality products combined with good stories – and this cultural trait has been leveraged in the strategies of all five companies participating in this study.

National Cultural Issues in Entry Modes

The Japanese setup for most companies differs not only because of different cultural perceptions, as described above, but also because of different structural factors that have developed over time due to elements of national cultural particular to Japan. For instance, it is well known that the number one prerequisite for success in Japan is the ability to draw on local connections and networks. While good connections are also important in other countries, the difference in Japan is that you cannot even take the first step without introductions. Even then access is not guaranteed. It may take a prolonged effort to arrange a single meeting with a department store in Japan. Meanwhile the traditional distribution system obliges you to go through several intermediaries before you reach the consumer.

The following presents the various company entry modes and the considerations relevant to each. The pro and cons are briefly discussed based on the experiences of the five companies. Considerations related to market entry are presented more in depth as part of the preceding case stories.

Distribution and Intermediaries

In ten years the intermediary system in Japan will have dissolved and companies will deal directly with one another. Many intermediary agents and wholesalers have already gone bankrupt and it is now better for us to set our minds on taking the risk ourselves (CEO, Mike Kurosaki, Royal Copenhagen Japan, interview, 17 November 2004).

A common challenge for all five companies is the complexity of the Japanese distribution system. From a Danish perspective, the wholesaler system is built on favoritism that makes it difficult to bypass old connections. Networking and human relationships take precedence over conducting business efficiently. From a Japanese perspective, however, it is only natural that business relationships should imply obligation and the exchange of favors. Nevertheless, it is important to emphasize that the Japanese distribution system is changing. Old connections are not honored in the same way, or at all, if they are simply financially unsustainable. As the examples in this book show, the Danish companies have had to deal with the challenges of the old distribution system while at the same time working to conduct business in new ways. Bang & Olufsen, for instance, have reduced their distribution network from several hundred retailers to 40 outlets for all of Japan. Bang & Olufsen now have direct contact with their dealers, and this enables the implementation of global standards and franchising concepts. ECCO similarly have been up-scaling their outlets by cutting down the number of retailers. In the 'old days', more intermediaries were involved, and there were several layers of communication within each company. This is now circumvented by direct dealership, franchising and brand stores.

Financial Risk and Brand Control

The key factors for success as seen by the participating companies are to get control of the brand and to build and attract the key competencies required for the brand and retail business in Japan. Thus, the primary considerations in deciding upon an entry mode have been:

- Balance between the desire for management/brand control and the risk of financial exposure.
- Evaluation of existing organizational competencies relative to the Japanese market.
- Legal options for terminating partnerships (since the process can be very costly).
- Estimation of the time required to successfully enter the market (which has often been underestimated).

Distribution method	Control	Financial commitment	Margin	Comments
License partner	Weak	Zero	Royalties	Risk of brand dilution
Agent/ importer	Weak	Zero/low	Wholesale	Risk of brand dilution
Multi brand retailers	Moderate	Very low	Wholesale	Lack of focus by retailer
Franchises, sales corners	High	Low	Wholesale	Higher dedication from partner
Own stores, subsidiary, or/and marketing office	Total	High	Wholesale + retail	Brand positioning/ building. Getting knowledge of customers

Display 8.2 Entry modes in Japan. Control, financial commitment and brand building opportunity

License Partner

The fact that Bo Bendixen was approached by a large Japanese company interested in licensing his products provided him with the opportunity to enter the Japanese market in a very low cost way. The positive aspects of the exclusive licensing contract have been: a) the opportunity to be represented in Japan, b) the mutual enthusiasm that has characterized the business partnership over the years, c) the presence of a strong partner capable of combating infringement, and d) the opportunity to sell to others given the approval of his license partner. However, Bo Bendixen now wants to extend his business even further (this is also possible with the agreement of his license partner). Extension of the product line has made him eager to sell in larger quantities. Ideally, he would like to have the opportunity to connect with wholesalers that service the prestigious department stores, as this would make his brand available all over Japan. Under the current agreement, Bo Bendixen has no financial exposure. Moreover, his close working relationship with his license partner and his contractual right to approve items before production have allowed him to preserve or even enhance his brand image.

ECCO has done business with their license partner in Japan for more than twenty years, and they have recently renewed their agreement for another ten years until 2013. Since the Japanese 'leather' shoe market is largely protected by the Japanese government, ECCO's cooperation with Achilles has been a means to circumvent these trade barriers. Although the Japanese license partner takes the financial risk of the brand stores, ECCO has wanted more and more control of the brand in order to implement their global brand strategy.

Agent/Importer

Both Bang & Olufsen and Rosendahl worked with importers and agents until they decided to reorganize their operations in Japan. The difference between an agent and an importer is that an *agent* does not deal with distribution and payment issues. Without handling any inventory, the agent's role is to carry out business development, collect data about the retailers, find new retailers and expand into new segments. An *importer*, on the other hand, handles payment and distribution. S/he buys a container of products and distributes them through existing channels. If business is good, importers can handle large turnovers. However, they do not spend much time on developing and expanding the business. Opportunities for market learning are low and the company has no control over the development of its brand name. Bang & Olufsen and Rosendahl both wanted more control and decided to make other arrangements.

Multiple Retail Networks

Rosendahl wanted control and was looking for opportunities to build the brand. They choose a retail network of specialized local companies and trading houses that each work with different segments of the market. This enabled market learning and the building of a strong brand name under headquarters' control. The merits were that reentry into the market was made with relatively low cost and was risk free. Perhaps most importantly, Rosendahl had the opportunity to develop a strong brand name, as it was possible to maintain a high degree of influence throughout the channels all the way to consumers. The company preserved its flexibility and gained access to segment specific information. However, there are limits to how big a turnover the small-scale sales force at headquarters can handle. For further growth, cooperation with an importer or a wholly owned subsidiary may still be favorable options. Although it is doubtful that Rosendahl would be interested in this option given the level of involvement they have demanded up until now.

Franchising

In this distribution mode, dealers run their own stores and the head company or franchisor offers marketing support together with product development and distribution. Within the franchising concept, dealers are able to tailor the content of their stores to their specific customers segments although all three companies wish their franchisees to carry close to the full product range. Bo Bendixen, Bang & Olufsen, and ECCO Shoes have franchises, and brand stores in Japan that follow their global marketing concepts. These stores are important for the development of a global image. The actual business model, contractual agreement, sharing of financial risk, and support through training and development differ between companies and individual dealers.

Subsidiary

Bang & Olufsen had the opportunity and the financial strength to create a subsidiary, and they have found this to be the best way to both learn about the market and maintain full management control of operations in Japan. The financial commitment required for this approach was justified by the fact that they see tremendous market potential in Japan. By maintaining full control over strategy and branding, as well a local execution, the intention is that they will be able to develop this market potential to its fullest.

It deserves mention that Scandinavian Tourist Board operates as an independent Danish company owned by Denmark's, Norway's and Sweden's national tourism offices and has its Asian regional office in Japan. An industry-government business model finances the operations in Japan. STB went for the subsidiary model to gain market knowledge and to build long-term relationships with the Japanese tourism industry.

As it has become apparent from this research, strategic choices that affect the company's status and operations in the market arise continually at every phase of engagement. Most of the companies have been represented in Japan from a few years to several decades. Importantly, strategic choices do not only involve insights into the Japanese market, but also depend on the successful communication of the knowledge gained in order to obtain acceptance from headquarters. For the manager working with Japan, learning and communication are two inextricably linked processes.

Organization, Communication and Culture

Another evident lesson learned while studying the five companies is that the organizational division of responsibility within the company is paramount for the enhancement of communication between individuals at headquarters and the subsidiary or alliance partner. The organization of communication greatly influences information flow, just as perceptions of how issues should be communicated shape the outcome. Shared practices and values are important as a common base for understanding. Representatives from the companies in the cases studies identify varying degrees of shared cultural values between headquarters and operations in Japan. In particular, the companies with subsidiaries have the closest ties and the greatest number of shared practices as a result of institutionalized communication with headquarters. The subsidiaries also have knowledge of corporate values, although they may not entirely share them due to different cultural interpretations. The license partners in the two cases are strongly embedded in their national and organizational cultures but work closely with their Danish partner to find a middle ground for cooperation. In all cases, individuals have national and organizational cultural perceptions that influence communication, yet new perceptual platforms slowly emerge as a result of their encounters.

Bo Bendixen is the sole person in charge of communication with his license partner. He handles all business matters by himself. As a consequence, he has been dealing with gate-keepers at the Japanese license partner on minor administrative issues such as orders and feedback on designs, rather than communicating with decision-makers at his own executive level. In this way, the organizational hierarchy between Denmark and Japan has been asymmetrical and it may have made his experience of decision-making processes more complex than it needed to be. On the other hand, if his administrative staff had dealt with everyday communication and he had dealt only with higher-level business decisions, he may not have experienced and come to understand all the cultural obstacles in their full complexity. As it is, Bo Bendixen has experienced cultural encounters up front and in person. A number of cultural issues have arisen between Bo Bendixen and his Japanese counterparts concerning organization, communication and cultural differences. From the historical account, it seems like both sides have changed their perceptions and gained more understanding of the other over time. However, neither side has changed their business practices to accommodate the other. Bo Bendixen has not done anything actively to improve his language skills, and the staff of his Japanese partner still struggle to read his handwritten faxes. The Japanese continue to make decisions through lengthy processes, while Bo Bendixen wants an immediate response. The Japanese tend to take a methodical and detailed approach to every issue, while Bo Bendixen prefers creative sparring. The Japanese license partner gathers a large committee of people for meetings, and Bo Bendixen continues to arrive alone. While traditional cultural values as they are embedded in business practices have been preserved, an understanding of product and people has emerged over time and mutual inspiration has moved business forward.

In the case of Rosendahl, organizational skills and cultural knowledge were important factors for success. The strategy was to bring native knowledge and understanding of the Japanese market in-house through the creation of a special autonomous unit within Rosendahl's headquarters. Japanese costumers are attended to immediately – in Japanese. One of the key components to success was that culture and language were dealt with properly. If someone in Japan has a problem, they know who to contact to get immediate service and this is greatly appreciated by the business partners. Also flying to Japan to do business made meetings urgent and many decisions were made in this momentum. Knowledge about cultural dos and don'ts was optimized and this provided Rosendahl with strategic power to make informed choices. Cultural knowledge enabled Rosendahl to both negotiate as equals with the Japanese and to capitalize on being a foreign company. Putting all of this together, the H.C. Andersen project was an opportunity and chance well taken.

At the VisitDenmark headquarters in Copenhagen and at Scandinavian Tourist Board office in Tokyo, the level of reflection on and awareness of both Danish and Japanese culture are high. The very core of tourism is cultural understanding and this came across in the interviews. At headquarters, all interviewees agreed that tourism promotion in Japan was different in many respects due to Japanese culture. Also, the corporate values and decision-making processes differed in Japan. While VisitDenmark had recently implemented their corporate values through top-down processes, the Tokyo office worked bottom-up to identify the most suitable commonly shared values. While most foreign subsidiaries in Japan are headed by an expatriate and staffed with locals, the STB office has several foreign staff. The Tokyo office management draws on the best from both cultures and has worked towards creating a bi-cultural environment that has been one of the ingredients of their success. Thus there has been a mix of Scandinavian individual responsibility with Japanese group decision making. In this way, Japanese employees are encouraged to express their opinions in meetings and even trained to do so. At the same time, the Scandinavians have the opportunity to learn first-hand the informal Japanese decision-making process of *nemawashi*. Nevertheless, it was acknowledge by most employees from both sides that real cultural understanding and personal change in thinking and behavior takes time.

At Bang & Olufsen the process of building a subsidiary team culture from the remnants of the previous partner's wholesale operation took three years of 'uphill work'. The employees who had thrived in the traditional Japanese vertical hierarchy could not fit into the new egalitarian and open organization. In particular, taking individual responsibility for business plans made them feel very insecure. Changing company culture involved the negotiation of both Danish and Japanese cultures in the Tokyo office. Meanwhile, management made an effort to 'infuse' the Struer culture and family feeling into employees at the Japanese subsidiary through training and visits to headquarters. As part of this process, an understanding of the brand, mission statement, core values and product identity were critical to maintaining a consistent and unique conception of the products

250

throughout the entire value chain from production to the end consumer. In addition, face to face encounters encouraged and enhanced intercultural communication by creating stronger personal links and understanding throughout the two organizations.

Although ECCO's license partner has created a separate division for ECCO Sales Japan, ECCO headquarters is still asking for a more 'effective' organization. This includes the assignment of responsibility to specific people in certain positions. Although one would think that this had been done by looking at the organizational chart, the expected behavior is usually not forthcoming. A culture of individual responsibility is not developed over night. In the vertical system of a traditional Japanese organization it is important to follow the hierarchical order when making decisions. It requires the consent of several people to make decisions and it is not considered proper to take individual responsibility. Decision making processes, the allocation of responsibility, the degree of formality, meeting structure and protocol, and the role and level of respect accorded to authority all differ between ECCO and their Japanese partner. Nevertheless, success has emerged from the meeting of ECCO's 'entrepreneurial' spirit and Achilles' traditional Japanese mentality through a mutual belief in the products, the brand, and the partnership.

The organization of communication and the allocation of responsibility have been challenging for all the companies. In particular, the contrast between Japanese formality and Danish informality has been a challenge. The interviews show that the larger the organization the more managers have knowledge of and are concerned with corporate values. Corporate values naturally are easier to institutionalize in subsidiaries than with partners. Cultural values, as they are presented in the interviews, include national, organizational and brand identity characteristics. They also include vision and company objectives. These are not neatly grouped or listed as on the company homepage or HR documents. Rather, in practice they are encountered as fragmented knowledge. However, at the end of the day, while some cultural values may be shared and others may not, professional will to move business forward in these five cases has superseded cultural conflicts and perceptual difference.

Professional Knowledge Factors

The professional level concerns the communication of functional (divisional or departmental) expertise about specific business and product related issues.

Bo Bendixen does not have functional divisions of labor in his design studio. He handles the business aspects of his company by himself, and is in particularly close contact with his license partner about product development. From the other side, his Japanese license partner and the manufacturers who deal with his products have studied his simple strokes and bright color combinations in almost scientific detail. Although it has demanded hard work on both sides, the Bo Bendixen brand has remained true to its origins and is in this sense 'authentic'. Over the course of the partnership, Bo Bendixen has advanced from making just t-shirts and postcards to making 700 different items of clothing and souvenirs. In this sense, Japanese consumerism and the excitement of producing and selling have inspired him to develop his business.

Rosendahl's networking and deliberate choice of partners in different segments has enabled the company to gain market knowledge and optimize sales. Joint marketing is one element of the cooperation. The fact that some segments overlap is considered interesting and a source of healthy competition. Perhaps most significantly, the professional criteria of greatest importance to the Japanese partners are in place, namely that orders are flawless and on time.

The emphasis of Scandinavian Tourist Board in Tokyo is to qualify its decision-making based on research facts rather than mere intuition about trends in the market. Danish tourism partners then get insight in this pool of knowledge about the market when they participate in the various programs. As a rule of thumb, the tourism business is driven by short-term thinking: if there is no return on investment within a certain number of months, new strategies are tried. In Japan, the strategy is to look at efforts as a long-term investment of resources. While the way VisitDenmark works in Japan is not that different from the way tourism is promoted in other markets, the people who work with Japan have a cultural knowledge 'monopoly'. The STB Tokyo office juggles with an abundance of knowledge about both Denmark and Japan. This cultural knowledge includes an understanding of the mentality and practices of people in both countries. This is STB's core competence and value-add to bring to the promotion of Scandinavian tourism. Their ability to circulate stories between the different knowledge areas including, for instance, branding, media and development is a best practices example.

In 2003, the Bang & Olufsen Asia Regional office was opened in Singapore. In this new setup, only one out of the four managers at the top level in Asia will physically be in Japan. The daily tasks related to retail and marketing are headed by the retail and marketing manager in the Tokyo office. The remaining functional areas in Tokyo such as training, after sales service, and finance and administration report directly to the respective regional managers in Singapore. Thus, the functional part of business works mainly through virtual communication.

The ECCO Sales Japan representatives are frequently in close contact with the development department in Denmark to get specifications for the products. They also get samples of prototypes and the specifications for their production. The acquisition of forms and tools for the production is also coordinated directly through the development department in Denmark. All departments at ECCO are involved with Japan, including: marketing, branding, sales, development, human resources and finance. However, all decisions between headquarters and Japan are communicated via the Asia Regional office in Hong Kong. Budgets and business plans are also controlled by Hong Kong.

Professional knowledge is closely connected to functional organizational charts. Interviews show that managers are challenged to communicate professional knowledge even with people in the same organization. For instance, communication bottlenecks may be found between designers and production, or between sales and marketing. Needless to say, when managers with specialized knowledge have difficulties communicating within a single company, crossing cultural barriers makes communication even more challenging. However, sometimes it works the opposite way: functional specialists are often able to communicate through their shared professional language and culture, despite the fact that they do not understand each other's national language or culture.

Individual Intercultural Competence

While the level above concerns professional knowledge and its effect on communication, the personal level is associated with the degree of mental internationalization. The internationalization level is based on the linguistic ability, cultural knowledge and training and, above all, field experience of the individual.

Bo Bendixen has experienced the 'foreignness' of Japan and communication with the Japanese in a profound and personal way. He has been treated like a 'Panda Bear' (a big, friendly, somewhat rare and cuddly foreigner) and has been subjected to the whole range of typical first-time experiences, such as eating fresh raw fish, the dilemma of what to bring as a present, the exchange of numerous business cards, long meetings with formal speeches, hierarchical order, and the overwhelming experience of big, busy Japanese cities. The Japanese, for their part, have enjoyed both Bo Bendixen's kind and genuine spirit and their direct contact with the designer and owner of the company. Bo Bendixen is his brand. In other words his designs are created to sell, and he sells himself through his product. These processes are interconnected. He has a message that he genuinely believes in and adheres to without budging an inch. His business concept is to be both artistic and business driven, which is a paradox in itself. Bo Bendixen wants to be in on every decision. While this allows him to maintain the soul of the brand, it unfortunately also sets natural limits to the kind of growth he can achieve. Nonetheless, both Bo Bendixen and the other people involved have become more international through many years of personal encounters.

The Rosendahl Japan team has been hired for their professional and business competencies. They are cultural experts, have good personal communication skills, and possess cultural knowledge about how to behave through direct experience with both Danish and Japanese culture. In addition, within the Japan unit, organizational learning has been institutionalized through collective experience and knowledge sharing. Communication with the Japanese market is setup to best cope with cultural differences by paying attention to language and cultural competencies during the hiring process. Everyone involved with Japan at Rosendahl is bi-cultural and bi-lingual at a minimum. Japanese nationals who speak their mother tongue fluently work with their respective clients. Most have been working and living in Denmark so that they are also, to differing degrees, fluent in Danish and knowledgeable about Danish culture. Cultural crossings – which are a challenge to most companies – are managed internally at Rosendahl and dealt with on a day to day basis.

The Scandinavian Tourist Board office has mixed foreign and Japanese staff to create different cultural alliances and opportunities for dynamic and innovative thinking. The expatriate director knows the

Japanese language and culture and thus has complete access to both cultures. He is well aware of what kind of decision-making works best for both groups. The Scandinavians are close to the director, while the vice director works with the Japanese staff to help them develop the communication skills that will enhance their situation at the office. In their experience, it takes 2-3 years to change staff from a mode of traditional thinking and education to one more receptive to and productive under Scandinavian management. Change takes place through the active and ongoing mediation and facilitation of understanding as it relates to both individual behavior and that of the 'other'.

For Bang & Olufsen, building a new office team took three years. It was not only a question of hiring new people, but also of hiring new people that would function well within the new setting. In particular, the president of Bang & Olufsen Japan targeted young Japanese 28 to 32 years-old who had been abroad and were fluent in English. Some of them were bi-cultural and tri-lingual. In this way, Bang & Olufsen hired people who were able to interact directly with their counterparts in Denmark – people with international mind sets. The international mind set was further encouraged through training in Denmark. A key goal was to hire people who were able to pick up the phone or write an e-mail in English. The new employees were sent to Struer for sales and marketing training and, perhaps more importantly, to learn about corporate values, brand strategies, and to meet their counterparts.

Previously, ECCO headquarters had solved cultural issues by hiring locally. However, as part of a globalizing environment it is now the corporate strategy for managers make an effort to adjust to the local culture. 'Jutland ways' do not always work globally, so more attention is paid to the cultural education and preparation of ECCO people who work and live abroad. ECCO identifies global talent through an internal ECCO educational system which often involves international exchanges and postings.

An ongoing challenge at ECCO in the communication between Denmark and Japan is language. At joint meetings everything is translated into Danish and Japanese respectively. All discussions go through a translator. The fact that negotiators cannot communicate with their Japanese business colleagues without an interpreter is a great hindrance to establishing closer personal relationships. The interference of a translator makes even the smallest issues a formality. Language is important. For Bo Bendixen language has also been a major obstacle both in everyday communication as well as in face to face business meetings which must be conducted through translators.

Conclusion

This chapter concludes the study of the intercultural and cross-organizational challenges faced by five Danish companies and their Japanese alliance partners. The study of communication processes between headquarters and the subsidiary/alliance partner shows that the transmission model of communication is less suited to intercultural business settings than a model that involves co-creation of meaning and market. In this study, levels are divided into the global, the national, the professional and the individual. Each level influences communication processes as described above. New understandings and cultural practices emerge, and these new ideas and approaches are ideally incorporated back into new corporate strategies. Only this feedback loop that overcomes communication gaps and cultural 'translation' difficulties to successfully incorporate the local into the global will provide for the triumph of truly global strategies and branding.

Related to this, and of particular importance to this study, is the ethnocentrism, or 'island' mentality, present as a *potential* factor in the cultural makeup of companies and managers from the two countries. Japanese culture has historically been characterized in these terms, and while Denmark is not technically an island, there is a similar heritage of cultural 'uniqueness'. In particular, some Danish managers still have a very Jutland-centric view of the world. However, while this type of mentality and outlook was held by some of the managers of this study, many more were internationally oriented. Nonetheless, although it was found that a deepening of intercultural business understanding comes with experience, ultimately only those managers with the education, motivation and ability to do so moved beyond the scripts defined for them by their own national (and organizational) cultures.

Perspective: Global Managers – Future Prospects

The increasing global integration of business activities continues to make effective communication and organizational processes across boarders more important in the new millennium. The globalization of the world economy and world industries put pressure on companies and their managers to adopt global strategies. Objectives such as standardization, homogenization, concentration and coordination on a world basis become central areas of focus that require effective communication. Areas that belong to the core of a business relate to principles that give the firm its identity and to issues that are important to costumers. This core should be integrated and standardized throughout worldwide operations (Riusala *et al.*, 2004). Thus, communication of related knowledge and strategic practices becomes the central prerequisite of success (Szulanski, 1996). Nevertheless, in spite of globalization processes, local cultural factors still have an influence on the adaptation of strategies and practices at the local level. In this setting, individuals concerned with global business are challenged to trim and skim information and to communicate in messages that can be understood across cultures. Alternatively, companies have to educate their international employees and partners to create a common ground for understanding. Even then, to get their messages across, managers have to be experts in their fields as well as understand the context and backgrounds of those who will be receiving the communication. The above analysis provides examples of how managers perceive and process information and how they best organize and communicate messages to people in a bi-cultural setting. It also shows how companies take different approaches to human resources. Although it was clear that professional business values move business forward, the cultural dimension is an important factor at every level of the analysis and in every business encounter. The companies who integrate human resource development into their strategies and focus on growing an international mindset among their employees will enjoy a competitive advantage in that they will be able to draw on the interculturally competent managers of the future.

Behind and Beyond Stereotypes

Some managers believe that organizational culture moderates or erases the influence of national culture. They assume that employees working for the same organization, even if they come from different countries, will behave more similarly than differently. But this is not necessarily the case according to Nancy J. Adler (2002: 67). Adler argues that managers who work for multicultural organizations become even more typical of their national culture. In other words, Danes become more Danish, Americans more American and Japanese become more Japanese. You may ask why organizational culture enhances national cultural differences. Neither managers nor researchers know the answer with certainty. Pressure to conform to the organizational culture of a foreign-owned company may foster employee resistance, causing them to cling more firmly to their own national identities. Another reason, Adler suggests, may be that ethnic culture is so deeply ingrained in people that by the time they reach adulthood the company's organizational culture cannot erase it (Adler, 2002: 69). Adding to these findings, the present study exemplifies how managers from two very distinct national and organizational cultures were able to meet in each of the cases, and yet evolve 'negotiated' cultures. In the bi-cultural relationships of Danish and Japanese managers as presented in the company case chapters, managers from both sides expressed a high awareness of their own national (and organizational) culture. It was found that reflection and the accumulation of new knowledge was enabled through the ability to change perceptions (mental scripts and models). It was also found that although managers, just like the rest of us, tend to be content to remain in their (mental) cultural comfort-zones, global managers who operate successfully are able to move their cultural knowledge into practice. They are able to venture behind *and* beyond cultural stereotypes.

Bibliography

Adler, N. J. (2002) Fourth Edition, *"The International Dimension of Organizational Behavior"*, Canada, North-Western

Riusala, K. & Suutari, V. (2004) "International Knowledge Transfers through Expatriates", *Thunderbird International Business Review*, volume 46 (6), pp. 743-770, November-December

Szulanski, G. (1996) "Exploring Internal Stickiness: Impediments to the Transfer of Best Practice within the Firm", *Strategic Management Journal*, 17, pp. 27-43, winter

Appendix

This project is based on an initiative by the Danish Social Science Research Council to further enhance cooperation between academia and business through research in management, organization and business competence (Ledelse, Organisation & Kompetence, LOK). Funding for this particular project concerning Japan has thus been provided by the Danish Social Science Research Council in cooperation with specific Danish companies and the Department of Intercultural Communication and Management at the Copenhagen Business School. From beginning to end, the project lasted two years, from April 2004 to April 2006. This book, which has evolved from the project, is based on interviews with managers from both Denmark and Japan, each of whom provided their perspectives on both business practices and cultural differences in relation to the two countries.

To begin the project, the key contact from each company was interviewed over the course of a business day, during which between 3-5 hours were recorded. The stories and lived experience of each of these key people from the five companies provided both the necessary background information and a story line for each company. After the initial interviews, I visited each company in Denmark to become acquainted with their products, communication flows and personnel. Afterwards, I conducted the same research in Japan, interviewing personnel from both partners and subsidiaries. One hour interviews were conducted with all employees in key positions related to communication between Denmark and Japan. In the book, I refer to the title and position of personnel at the time of the interview.

Characteristics of fifty managers from five companies			
Gender	Women 21	Men 29	
Nationality	Danish 20 (Incl. one Swedish manager)	Japanese 29	Japanese/ Norwegian 1
Interview Language	Danish 11	Japanese 9	English 30
Interview location	Denmark 13	Japan 36	Hong Kong 1 (By telephone)

Display A.1 Characteristics of interviews and managers

Out of the 50 people interviewed, 29 were male and 21 were female. This ratio of female managers is surprisingly high compared with previous management studies related to Japan. For instance, Peltokorpi (2004) interviewed 30 Nordic expatriates in Japan for a study of cultural differences between Nordic managers and their local staff. Among Peltokorpi's expatriates none were female. However, his study concerned the electronics industry, while the present study focuses on consumer goods companies. Peltokorpi's study was also based on interviews with top executives, while the present study includes interviews with employees at lower management levels where women are more common. Nevertheless, it is worth noting that all senior management positions in Denmark as well as in the Asian regional offices were occupied by men, except for human resource positions and coordinating functions. In Japan, women made up a stronger percentage of management among the Danish subsidiaries, reflecting a trend for foreign companies to hire Japanese women (Adler, 1987; Adler & Izraeli, 1994; 1998).

Among the interviewees, 19 were Danish, one was Swedish, 29 were Japanese and one was partly Japanese and partly Norwegian. Thus the majority of interviewed managers are Japanese. However, the main contact personnel interviewed at length were Danish. In this way, the weight of their interviews is balanced by the more numerous interviews of Japanese subsidiary or alliance employees. I conducted most interviews in English (30), some in Japanese (9) and some in Danish (11). The Japanese lack of personal pronouns made it difficult – even for the Japanese native who transcribed and translated the interviews – to assess gender, and indirect hints at previous issues made it difficult at times to translate exactly what was being referred to. However, I recalled most of each conversation and was able to fill in any gaps. In addition to the company managers, several experts were interviewed, including: diplomats from the Royal Danish Embassy in Tokyo, Japanese business advisors, alumni of the Copenhagen Business School who work for companies in Japan, a Danish headhunter and consultant and executives from the European Trainee Program (ETP).

In November 2004, I participated in the activities of the Danish business delegation visit to Japan and had a chance to meet again with some of the company managers. I also managed to talk to a number of officials who have not been cited in the book but nevertheless contributed to the overall description of events. During the research period I was frequently in touch with key company representatives to acquire additional information. This enabled triangulation and verification of interpretations that were necessary to help clarify and make sense of the statements and the evolution of events described in each company chapter. The quotes in the book are direct citations, but the language has been edited in places to make the statements more coherent. Repetitions, laughter and less coherent passages have been omitted. In total, more than 500 hours of tape-recordings have been transcribed and serve as basis for the book.

Bibliography

Adler, N. J. and Izraeli, D. N. (1994) *"Competitive Frontiers: Women Managers in a Global Economy"*, Cambridge, MA, Blackwell

Adler, N. J. and Izraeli, D. N. (1988) *"Women in Management Worldwide"*, Armonk, NY, M.E., Sharpe

Adler, N. J. (1987) "Pacific Basin Managers: A Gaijin, Not a Woman", *Human Resource Management*, volume 26, no. 2, pp. 21-33

Peltokorpi, V. (2004) "Culture, Communication, and Language in Subsidiary Management: Nordic Expatriates in Japan", paper presented at the From Jutland to Japan Seminar, Copenhagen Business School, 17 November 2004

Index